INFORMATION SYSTEMS DEVELOPMENT:
Methodologies, Techniques and Tools

INFORMATION SYSTEMS SERIES

Consulting Editors

D. E. AVISON
BA, MSc, FBCS
*Department of Computer Science and
Applied Mathematics, Aston University,
Birmingham, UK*

G. FITZGERALD
BA, MSc, MBCS
*School of Industrial and Business Studies,
University of Warwick, Coventry, UK*

This is a brand new series of student texts covering a wide variety of topics relating to information systems. It is designed to fulfil the needs of the growing number of courses on, and interest in, computing and information systems which do not focus purely on the technological aspects, but seek to relate these to business or organizational context.

INFORMATION SYSTEMS SERIES

INFORMATION SYSTEMS DEVELOPMENT:
Methodologies, Techniques and Tools

D.E. AVISON BA, MSc, FBCS
Department of Computer Science and Applied Mathematics,
Aston University

and

G. FITZGERALD BA, MSc, MBCS
School of Industrial and Business Studies,
University of Warwick

Blackwell Scientific Publications
OXFORD LONDON EDINBURGH
BOSTON MELBOURNE

© 1988 by
Blackwell Scientific Publications
Editorial offices:
Osney Mead, Oxford OX2 0EL
  (*Orders*: Tel: 0865 240201)
8 John Street, London WC1N 2ES
23 Ainslie Place, Edinburgh EH3 6AJ
3 Cambridge Center, Suite 208
  Cambridge, Massachusetts 02142, USA
107 Barry Street, Carlton
  Victoria 3053, Australia

First published 1988
Reprinted 1989

Printed and bound in Great Britain by
Billings & Sons Ltd.

DISTRIBUTORS

USA
  Publishers' Business Services
  PO Box 447
  Brookline Village
  Massachusetts 02147
  (*Orders*: Tel: (617) 524 7678)

Canada
  Oxford University Press
  70 Wynford Drive
  Don Mills
  Ontario M3C 1J9
  (*Orders*: Tel: (416) 441-2941)

Australia
  Blackwell Scientific Publications
  (Australia) Pty Ltd
  107 Barry Street
  Carlton, Victoria 3053
  (*Orders*: Tel: (03) 347 0300)

British Library
Cataloguing in Publication Data
Avison, D.E.
Information systems development:
methodologies, techniques and tools
1. Information systems
I. Title   II. Fitzgerald, Guy
001.5

ISBN 0-632-01645-0 Pbk

Library of Congress
Cataloging-in-Publication Data
Avison, D.E.
Information systems development:
methodologies, techniques and tools/
by D.E. Avison and G. Fitzgerald.
  p. cm.
Bibliography: p.
Includes index
ISBN 0-632-01645-0 (pbk.)
1. System design. 2. System analysis.
I. Fitzgerald, G. (Guy) II. Title.
QA76.9.S88A92 1988
003--dc19   88-10167

Contents

Preface

This book is designed for students of data processing, systems analysis and information systems at both undergraduate and masters levels. It is also aimed at practitioners and managers who wish to make sense of this currently highly confused field. The process of developing information systems has not always been successful and this book explains why this has happened. It examines some of the more recent methodologies, techniques and tools that aim to improve the record. Given this knowledge, the reader should be able to understand the principles involved, the benefits that are claimed, and to make a contribution to the practice of information systems development.

Early computer applications were implemented without the aid of an explicit information systems methodology. The emphasis was towards programming and this meant that the analysis work was rarely done well and that the design was frequently inappropriate for the application. This was at least partly due to poor communications between users and programmers. Soon the need for a more formal methodology was recognized, and the methodologies of the late 1960s and 1970s emphasized the importance of documentation standards and good training for systems analysts. This was certainly an improvement. However, there were still a number of problems associated with the methodologies of the 1970s. The systems that they produced were sometimes inflexible, unambitious, incomplete, had a high maintenance overhead, and frequently led to user dissatisfaction. The 1980s have witnessed a growth in the number and variety of information systems methodologies. Some are becoming widely used. Their designers claim that they will solve at least some of the problems associated with earlier methodologies and offer advantages over their competitors.

This increase in the number of methodologies has caused much confusion. Many are the same (or very similar) and yet they have different 'brand names'. They may use similar techniques and tools but give them different names. Some emphasize particular techniques and offer a 'scientific' approach, others emphasize the role of the computer, of documentation, and others, the role of the people using the system. Some methodologies emphasize the importance of data and the development of a computer database, whilst others concentrate on the processes that use the database. Some concentrate on analysis, others on design or implementation. Some methodologies have developed according to national traditions. Some are associated with particular consultancy houses or computer manufacturers. When looking at any approach in isolation, it is difficult not to be convinced by the advantages of that particular approach, but it may not be appropriate for all situations and its shortcomings may not be revealed without comparing it to other approaches.

The purpose of this text is to offer order out of the chaos. It looks at a number of information systems methodologies, and the techniques and tools that might be used in them. This book also attempts to classify methodologies, suggesting reasons why a type of methodology is important, perhaps suggesting situations where that type of methodology might be appropriate, and describing a particular example of each 'genre'.

Chapter 1 sets the scene, introducing information systems and methodologies as a way of developing information systems. It is argued that there is a need for a methodology. The track record of early computing is not a good one — schedules not followed, promises unfulfilled, and systems implemented but not used. Suggestions are made regarding what might be expected from a methodology.

Chapter 2 looks at the various approaches to information systems of the mid and late 1970s. It could be looked upon as a history of ideas and practice that led up to the present interest in information systems methodologies. This period was one where the need for a methodology to develop information systems was recognized but there were problems with the techniques and tools used. More importantly, they were limited in scope so that the methodologies tended to computerize the existing manual system without taking the opportunity to reassess the system itself.

Chapter 3 looks at the many themes in information systems methodologies which addressed the weaknesses described in Chapter 2. They include themes which could be described as process orientated, data orientated, software orientated and people orientated. Some can be described as formalized, others as being based on automation, and others on strategic planning. A section is also given to those themes which are at the moment research based, but may later bear fruits in new approaches to information systems development. Information systems is a fairly new discipline and a number of differences of opinion exist and are to be expected. This chapter also begins to categorize the approaches used by the 'brand-name' methodologies which are discussed in Chapter 6.

Chapter 4 describes the various techniques which are used in information systems methodologies. Many methodologies share techniques and a description of them at this point avoids unnecessary repetition. It also means that in Chapter 6, the general principles of a methodology are not obscured by a need to understand the particular techniques that it uses. Techniques described include data flow diagrams, decision trees, decision tables, structured English, action diagrams, entity modelling, normalization and entity life cycles. These techniques might be used to aid the analysis, design or implementation of the information system. They might be used to help communication between the technologists who are developing the system and users who will eventually use the information system.

Chapter 5 looks at the various tools that are available which support a number of methodologies and might be used to speed up the development of an information system or help to make the resulting system closer to the real needs of the users. These tools include fourth generation systems, database management systems, query languages, data dictionaries, analyst workbenches, project management packages and expert systems.

Chapter 6 looks at a number of information systems methodologies which are well used, respected, or typify the themes described in Chapter 3. These include: a structured approach, STRADIS, based on the work of Gane and Sarson; IE, based on the work of Martin and Finkelstein; SSADM, a methodology developed by Learmonth and Burchett; JSD, a systems development methodology by Jackson; ISAC, a methodology developed in Scandinavia by Lundberg; ETHICS, a methodology developed by Mumford; and SSM, a methodology developed by Checkland. We also look at Multiview, a hybrid methodology, which brings in aspects of other methodologies and adopts techniques and tools which might then be used in a contingency framework, applied as the application demands. In Chapter 6 the methodologies are described largely uncritically so that the readers can follow their principles and practice. We have not described similar methodologies, even if they are both equally well used, but have referenced this similarity where appropriate.

The main purpose of Chapter 7 is to step back and compare the background, philosophy, applicability, and concepts of the various methodologies. A framework is proposed for evaluating methodologies and we have illustrated the use of this framework by applying it to the methodologies described in the text. Its function is not to offer a 'best buy', as each methodology has different objectives as well as its strengths and weaknesses. Applying a methodology 'blindly' will not necessarily lead to success. The secret is to know when and where a particular methodology might be appropriate.

The book has been designed to be used in a number of ways. Students of information systems and business readers interested in an overview of the area might wish to read the text from beginning to end, but there are many situations where it is more appropriate to choose particular chapters or sections. For example, some readers may wish to assess methodologies in general and it might be best to start by reading Chapters 6 and 7. Others may wish to look at a particular methodology and read only the relevant section in Chapter 6. If readers come across particular techniques or tools which are new to them, then they can read the relevant sections in Chapters 4 and 5 for this information. Other readers may wish to have an overview of particular techniques (Chapter 4) or tools (Chapter 5). In order to provide this flexibility it has been necessary to incorporate some repetition in the text as well as cross-referencing.

The text will be of particular value to students of data processing and systems analysis in both computer science and business courses at polytechnics and universities. These readers could use the book to gain an overall appreciation of information systems development, and to understand the methodologies, techniques and tools used. We have assumed that readers have at least a basic knowledge of computer data processing which could have been provided by an introductory course or equivalent experience. The material in the text has been used as the basis of a final year undergraduate option in management studies and in various Masters programmes at the School of Industrial and Business Studies at the University of Warwick. It is also used in second year and final year options in the undergraduate courses in computer science and in the MSc courses in software engineering applications and information technology in the Department of Computer Science and Applied Mathematics at Aston University.

The text aims to be useful to students and courses following the IFIP/BCS curriculum for Information Systems Designers defined in Buckingham *et al.* (1987b). It is relevant for a number of modules in that curriculum, but especially the level 3 module, 3.1 'Information systems: the evolutionary process'.

The text should also be useful to professionals involved in the analysis, design and development of information systems. It would be useful to data processing managers before making a decision on 'what methodology to adopt?' or to re-assess the methodology used. Other professionals could be users or managers involved in an information systems project or the analysts and programmers developing that system. Systems analysts have often been trained to use a particular approach as if it were the only approach available but, armed with the knowledge gained from this text, they should be aware of its weaknesses and might compensate for them by incorporating certain relevant elements from other methodologies.

We are all too aware of the problems of writing such a text. Each methodology, technique and tool could merit a book in its own right. Sometimes such a book already exists. This present text provides an overview and appropriate references for further reading. Another problem is that the area of information systems development is a moving target. For example, since starting to write this book, the power and influence of 'fourth generation systems' has grown enormously. Efforts are now being made to develop expert systems which could hold the expertise of the systems analysts and researchers in information systems in their knowledge base. We have tried to reflect these aspects of this exciting area as well as reflect present practice.

We are also aware that we have attempted to be systems analysts, engineers, computer scientists, mathematicians, management scientists, sociologists, political scientists and psychologists in this work, because the world of information systems covers all these disciplines and more. We are not all of these things. Worse, we may have neglected and misinterpreted the views of many writers, researchers, and practitioners in the information systems field. The views expressed here are those of the authors of the text, not those of the methodology authors or vendors. You may also detect bias in our accounts. We have tried to avoid bias, but it almost certainly will be there, no-one is completely objective (even if some methodology vendors claim to be objective). We hope and expect that lecturers will question some of the arguments presented and use the text as the basis for discussion, rather than a factual account of the 'state-of-the-art'.

The authors are both academics who are presently teaching and researching into information systems. They have also had considerable experience in industry and commerce working in information systems development at, for example, CACI International, Conoco Europe, John Laing, British Telecom, Ranks Hovis Macdougall, Jones Lang Wootton, Rothschilds Intercontinental, and Abbott Laboratories.

We would like to thank Gilbert Mansell of Huddersfield Polytechnic and Bob Wood of Bristol Polytechnic who contributed much to the early planning and content of this text. We also express thanks to many of our friends and colleagues who have commented on the text at various stages in its production including Carol Byde of Aston University, Paul Catchpole of

Darlington Health Authority, Tom Gough of Leeds University, Rudy Hirschheim of Templeton College, Richard Veryard of James Martin Associates and Trevor Wood-Harper of University of East Anglia.

David Avison and Guy Fitzgerald
May 1988

Chapter 1
Introduction

1.1 INFORMATION SYSTEMS

This text is about information systems and discusses ways of developing information systems which will prove useful to organizations. The system is a grouping of people, objects and procedures. An information system provides information about the organization and its environment. This information, which is useful to members and clients of that organization, could concern its customers, suppliers, products, equipment, and so on. The organization could be a business, church, hospital, university, bank, library, and so on.

Most of the methodologies described in this text concern themselves with *formalized* information systems. By formalized, we do not mean 'mathematical', which is one interpretation of the term 'formal' (see section 3.6). We use the term to distinguish information systems discussed here from less formalized information systems such as the 'grapevine', consisting of rumour, gossip, ideas and preferences, which is also a valid information system. These informal information systems tend to be intuitive or qualitative. Organizations need also to develop formalized systems which will provide information on a regular basis and in a pre-defined manner.

We are mainly concerned with *computer-based* information systems, for the computer can process data (the basic facts) speedily and accurately and provide information when and where required and at the correct level of detail. This does not mean that it is 'purely' a computer system — there will be many manual (or *clerical*) aspects — it means that part of the system is likely to use a computer. The computer might be used to store data, produce reports or handle management enquiries.

Some examples of information systems might be helpful:
- A payroll system is an information system. All organizations have employees and they will normally be paid. The raw data of a payroll system includes the number of hours worked by the employees, their rates of pay, and deductions, such as tax and national insurance. The system might produce payslips, and reports for management about the payroll.

- A sales ledger system is an information system. It is a system relating to the accounts of customers. The raw data of a sales ledger system relates to sales to customers and remittances from them. The system will provide statements of any balances owing, and could produce analyses of debtors' balances according to area, sales representative and customer group.
- A project planning and control system is an information system. The raw data will include the various activities that make up the project and the range of resources that might be used to develop the project. The system schedules projects so that completion is at the earliest possible date, with the least drain on resources, and provides reports on progress during the life of the project. These reports enable management to act on projects that are behind schedule or where costs are above predictions.
- A decision-support system is an information system. The raw data includes the whole range of facts about the organization, or part of the organization, or sometimes relates to aspects external to the organization, (that is, its *environment*). The system is designed to enable managers to retrieve information which will help them make decisions about, for example, where to build a factory, whether to merge with competitors, which products to sell, the prices of products, and the salaries of employees.
- An airline ticket reservation system is an information system. It processes customers' requests for seats on aircraft. It may also be used to provide information regarding the take up of seats.

1.2 THE NEED FOR A METHODOLOGY

There have always been information systems, although it is only in the recent past that they have used computers. If firms have employees, there needs to be some sort of system to pay them. If firms manufacture products, then there will be a system to order the raw materials from the suppliers and another to plan the production of the goods from the raw materials. Companies need to have a system to deal with orders from customers, another to ensure that products are transported, and yet another to send invoices to the customers and to process payments.

In the time before computers, these systems were largely manual. The word 'largely' is appropriate, because the manual workers would use adding machines, typewriters, and other mechanical or electrical aids to help the system run as efficiently as possible. The use of computers represents only

an extension (though a significant extension) of this process. If a manual system proved inadequate in some way, for example:
- increasing workloads have overloaded the manual system;
- suitable staff are expensive and difficult to recruit;
- there is a change in the type of work; or
- there are frequent errors,

a solution which involves the use of computers may well be contemplated.

The early applications of computers — say, until the 1960s — were implemented without the aid of an *explicit* information systems methodology. In these early days, the emphasis of computer applications was towards *programming*, and the skills of programmers were particularly appreciated. The systems developers were therefore technically trained but were not necessarily good communicators. This often meant that the needs of the users in the application area were not well established, with the consequence that the information system design was frequently inappropriate for the application.

Few programmers would follow any formal methodology. Frequently they would use rule-of-thumb and rely on experience. Estimating the date on which the system would be operational was difficult, and applications were frequently behind schedule. Programmers were usually overworked, and frequently spent a very large proportion of their time on correcting and enhancing the applications which were operational.

Typically, a user would come to the programmers asking for a new report or a modification of one that was already supplied. Often these changes had undesirable effects on other parts of the system, which also had to be corrected. This vicious circle would continue, causing frustration to both programmers and users. This was not a methodology, it was only an attempt to survive the day.

As computers were used more and more and management was demanding more appropriate systems for their expensive outlay, this state of affairs could not go on. There were three main changes:
- The first was a growing appreciation of that part of the development of the system that concerns *analysis and design* and therefore of the role of the *systems analyst* as well as that of the programmer.
- The second was a realization that as organizations were growing in size and complexity, it was desirable to move away from one-off solutions to a particular problem and towards a more *integrated information system.*
- The third was an appreciation of the desirability of an accepted *methodology* for the development of information systems.

As Utterback and Abernathy (1975) argue, innovation has three elements: improved process, in this context better information systems development methodologies, improved product, in this context better information systems; and improved organization, in this context better decision support. We look next at the process of developing an information system.

1.3 REQUIREMENTS OF AN INFORMATION SYSTEMS METHODOLOGY

It was to answer the problems discussed in the previous section that methodologies were devised and adopted by many computer data processing installations. A *methodology* is a collection of *procedures, techniques, tools,* and *documentation aids* which will help the systems developers in their efforts to implement a new information system. A methodology will consist of *phases*, themselves consisting of *sub-phases*, which will guide the systems developers in their choice of the techniques that might be appropriate at each stage of the project and also help them plan, manage, control and evaluate information systems projects.

But a methodology is more than merely a collection of these things. It is usually based on some *philosophical* view, otherwise it is merely a *method*, like a recipe. Methodologies may differ in the techniques recommended or the contents of each phase, but sometimes their differences are more fundamental. They could differ according to the philosophy on which they are based. Some methodologies emphasize the humanistic aspects of developing an information system, others aim to be scientific in approach, others pragmatic, and others attempt to automate as much of the work of developing a project as possible. These differences may be best illustrated by their different assumptions, stemming from their philosophy which, when greatly simplified, might be that, for example:

* a system which makes most use of computers is a good solution;
* a system which produces the most documentation is a good solution;
* a system which is the cheapest to run is a good solution;
* a system which is implemented earliest is a good solution;
* a system which is the most adaptable is a good solution;
* a system which makes the best use of the techniques and tools available is a good solution;
* a system which is liked by the people who are going to use it is a good solution;

and so on.

This book is about methodologies, the differences between them, why these differences exist, and which methodology might be appropriate in any given circumstances. As we shall see, methodologies do differ greatly, often addressing different objectives. These objectives could be:

1 *To record accurately the requirements for an information system.* The users must be able to specify their requirements in a way which both they and the systems developers will understand, otherwise the resultant information system will not meet the needs of the users.

2 *To provide a systematic method of development in such a way that progress can be effectively monitored.* Controlling large scale projects is not easy, and a project which does not meet its deadlines can have serious cost implications for the organization. The provision of checkpoints and well defined stages in a methodology should ensure that project planning techniques can be effectively applied.

3 *To provide an information system within an appropriate time limit and at an acceptable cost.* Unless the time spent using some of the techniques included in some methodologies is limited, it is possible to devote an enormous amount of largely unproductive time attempting to achieve perfection. A methodology reflects pragmatic considerations.

4 *To produce a system which is well documented and easy to maintain.* The need for future modifications to the information system is inevitable as a result of changes taking place in the organization. These modifications should be made with the least effect on the rest of the system. This requires good documentation.

5 *To provide an indication of any changes which need to be made as early as possible in the development process.* As an information system progresses from analysis through design to implementation, the costs associated with making changes increases. Therefore the earlier changes are effected, the better.

6 *To provide a system which is liked by those people affected by that system.* The people affected by the information system, that is, the *stakeholders*, may include clients, managers, auditors, and users. If a system is liked by the stakeholders, it is more likely that the system will be used and be successful.

1.4 SOME DEFINITIONS

We have already introduced many of the topics in this text and we wish at
this point to provide some definitions. One problem in this area is that many
of the terms defined in this section are used inconsistently in the literature.
We will attempt to be consistent in our usage or explain where usage differs.
This is a fairly new discipline, and differences of opinion are to be expected,
but it does not make our task easy. Many concepts are complex and will be
developed later in the text. Some of the definitions provided here will be
further discussed in later chapters.

The first two terms have already been mentioned: *information* and *data*.
These represent different things. Data represent unstructured facts. When three
'strings' of data '250776', '78700199' and '19873' are associated, they could be
used to give the *information* that a person whose identity number is 19873
possesses a driving licence (number 78700199), even though that person is
under the minimum legal age for driving motor vehicles. The string of data
250776 is interpreted as the date of birth, 25 July 1976, showing that the
holder is only 12 years old in August 1988. The information comes from
selecting data and presenting it in such a way that it is useful to the recipient.
The essential difference between data and information, therefore, is that data
are not interpreted, whereas information has a meaning and use to a particular
recipient. Some writers equate knowledge with information. Buckingham *et
al.* (1987b) define information as 'explicit knowledge'. In other words,
information expresses what is meant clearly, with nothing left implied.

The distinction between data and information is context dependent. Let us
look at another example where a line manager analyses the departmental
figures and presents the results to the planning department. For the line
manager the results are an interpretation of events and are therefore
information rather than data. For the central planners, these figures are the
raw input for their own analyses, not yet interpreted, and are therefore *data*
rather than information.

Having given a preliminary definition of information, we need to define
what is meant by *system*. This is more difficult because it is a term which is
used widely in many different fields of activity. Thus the ecological system
includes the relationship between flora and fauna which we call the balance of
nature, and the educational system includes teachers, students, books, and
colleges and aims to pass on knowledge to others. Systems are related to each
other. Bills to pay for using the telephone service are produced by a billing
system, forwarded by a postal system, and paid for using a banking system.

The banking system will have a customer service system, a printing system, and a payroll system, amongst others. Smaller systems within larger systems are called *sub-systems*. An information system will also have sub-systems within it. An airline information system may have sub-systems to report on the status of passengers, report on flights, and to analyse costs and profits.

Systems also have a *purpose*. An information system aims to provide relevant information to users in the required fashion: that is, at the right time, at the appropriate level of detail, and accurate enough for the users who are presented with that information. This will help to ensure that the corporate information resource is utilized fully.

We have talked about users in the text. Who are these *users*? *Professional users* are the technologists: operations staff, systems analysts, systems designers and programmers. Sometimes the terms 'professional', 'data processing professional' or 'technologist' are used for this type of user. None of these terms is entirely suitable, because other users are, presumably, also professionals, although not computing or information systems professionals, and, further, the term technologist is also ambiguous as it is sometimes interpreted to mean someone technically trained in, for example, electronics.

The information provided by an information system is normally used by people who are not experts in computing. These users could be clerical staff, secretarial staff and often middle managers who may well be *regular users* who might input data, process text or interpret reports. *Casual users* are frequently middle managers or top managers whose use of the system might be very varied. Their enquiries may be related to different parts of the information system as they look for information as the basis on which to make decisions about the organization. Other users include external users such as auditors, for example, government tax inspectors, or customers or the general public, for example, people who are using the author database in a library.

We have introduced the term *information system* and used the term in its widest sense: any system that provides information about the organization and its environment, a definition that encompasses all the data processing systems of the organization. Sometimes the term information system is used more narrowly, as a system designed to help managers make better decisions. We prefer to use the term *decision-support systems* for these systems which are dedicated to management needs, which therefore represent a category of information system, sometimes referred to as '*management information systems*'.

Buckingham *et al.* (1987b) define an information system as a:

'system which assembles, stores, processes and delivers information relevant to an organization (or to society), in such a way that the information is accessible and useful to those who wish to use it, including managers, staff, clients and citizens. An information system is a human activity (social) system which may or may not involve the use of computer systems.'

One question that may already have occurred to many readers is 'what is the difference between *information systems* and *data processing systems*?'. Many texts seem to regard information systems as being a more fashionable term for data processing systems, indeed we have ourselves said that information systems encompass all the data processing systems in the organization. These terms are indeed similar, but they are not the same: information systems reflect management requirements for information, for example, information about sales (which can be obtained by processing of sales orders). Information systems also reflect the desire for integrated systems which are more than one-off solutions to immediate problems. This means that the methodologies that might have been adequate for data processing applications, may not be adequate for the development of information systems. We will return to this topic in Chapter 2 where we discuss conventional systems analysis and some of the problems associated with that approach.

We have also already introduced the term *methodology*, but readers may wish to distinguish this from a technique or tool. We defined a methodology as a collection of procedures, techniques, tools, and documentation aids which will help the systems developers in their efforts to implement a new information system. It will consist of phases, themselves consisting of sub-phases, which will guide the systems developers in their choice of the techniques that might be appropriate at each stage of the project and also help them plan, manage, control and evaluate information systems projects. A methodology represents a way to develop information systems systematically. A methodology should have a sound theoretical basis, though it will be based on the 'philosophy', 'interests', 'viewpoint' — 'bias' if you like — of the people who developed them, for no-one is completely objective.

Techniques and tools feature in each methodology. Particular techniques and tools may feature in a number of methodologies. A *technique* is a way of doing a particular activity in the systems development process and any particular methodology may recommend techniques to carry out many of these activities.

Each technique may involve using one or more tools which represent some of the artefacts that might be used. A non computer-orientated example may help. Two techniques used in the making of meringues are (1) separate the whites of eggs from the yokes and (2) beat the whites. The methodology may recommend the use of *tools* in these processes, for example an egg separator and a whisker. In this text, tools are usually automated, that is, computer tools, usually software to help the development of an information system. Indeed, some of these have been designed specifically to support activities in a particular methodology. Others are more general purpose and are used in a number of methodologies.

An information systems methodology, in attempting to make effective use of information technology, will also attempt to make effective use of the techniques and tools available. But information systems are about balancing these technical specialisms with *behavioural* (people-orientated) specialisms. As we shall see in the text, there are many views as to where this balance lies and how the balance is achieved in any methodology. At one extreme are the methodologies aiming at full automation of information systems development as well as the information system itself. However, even in these systems people need to interact with the system. At the other extreme, perhaps, are attempts at full user participation in the information systems development project. Even here, user solutions may make full use of the technology and there is a growing number of tools designed to aid the user in the development of information systems. The balance between technological aspects and people aspects is one which we will return to as it is a continual theme in information systems development.

Chapter 2
The Development of Information Systems Methodologies: An Historical Perspective

2.1 EARLY SYSTEMS DEVELOPMENT

This chapter describes the features of information systems methodologies which were prevalent in the 1960s and early 1970s and highlights problems associated with them. This provides the springboard for Chapter 3, which describes themes, be it humanistic, scientific or pragmatic, in the methodologies which aimed to take their place and thereby solve some of these problems. The specific methodologies discussed in Chapter 6 have their roots in one or more of these themes.

We look first at that period in the 1950s when there was no formalized methodology to develop data processing systems. Early computing was associated with scientific applications. In the 1950s some computers were installed in business environments but there were few practical guide-lines which gave help on their use for commercial applications. These business applications were orientated towards the basic operational level of the firm. They might include producing reports, keeping files and producing documents. A typical example of each would be reporting on the sales of the company, keeping customer records, and producing invoices. Another application might be producing the company payroll. These applications involve the basic *data processing* functions of copying, retrieving, filing, sorting, checking, calculating and communicating.

In these early days, the people who implemented these systems were programmers (see figure 2.1 (a)). As we described in section 1.2, programmers were not necessarily good communicators, making it difficult for users to communicate their needs to the technologists. Further, the development of applications frequently were more costly and arrived later than expected. Projects were seen more as short term exercises or one-off solutions to sort out problems than as long-term, well-planned implementation strategies for new applications.

The users were frequently dissatisfied with the operational systems because their needs had not been clearly identified in any analysis phase. Although some small systems may have worked well in this mode, particularly where the programmer knew the system inside-out and performed all roles, changes made to larger and more complex programs usually required many programmers to spend a day or two looking at the programs and making changes. Frequently these changes introduced new problems elsewhere. Therefore it might take a long time to make seemingly trivial changes.

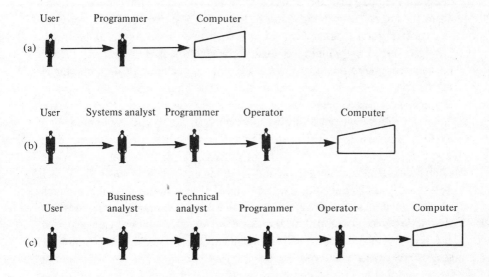

Fig. 2.1. The changing roles of the people in data processing.

Documentation, if it ever existed, was usually out of date, and the programmer did not have the time to update it. Documentation standards were resisted because they were said to restrict creativity, increase workloads and thus increase the overall development time. It is possibly true that documentation standards were resented by programmers, but a lengthening of the development schedule caused by documenting systems could well have reduced the problem of maintenance.

Most companies became over reliant on the few programmers who knew the systems inside-out. They were well paid by the company because they were very difficult to replace. New entrants could not take over because there was little documentation and no uniform practices and techniques. Sometimes it was necessary to rewrite programs from scratch to effect small changes in user requirements, because it was impossible to understand the original programs without documentation, particularly if the original programmers had left.

There were few courses giving the education and training necessary for the *analysis* and *design* work associated with developing data processing systems. Most courses that were available were designed to enable people to use and program the computer. Trainees entering the company would hope to learn from those presently doing the job. Even the best programmers were not necessarily good teachers and in any case they were likely to be much stronger in the programming, as against the analysis, part of their job.

As a reaction to this, there was a growing appreciation of the importance of that part of the development of the system that concerns analysis and design. There was a change of emphasis in many data processing departments. Some job titles changed to programmer-analysts, analyst-programmers, and systems analysts. There was a growing appreciation that there was more than one role in the systems development process. These were the roles of the computer operator, programmer and systems analyst. As seen in figure 2.1 (b), the operator controlled the running of the computer and the systems analyst acted in a role between the user and the programmer. Sometimes this distinction was developed further, as two types of analyst emerged: the business-orientated analyst and the technically-orientated analyst (figure 2.1 (c)). The former was concerned with finding out from the users about organizational needs and communicating these to the technical analyst who was concerned mainly with the design of the technical systems which would meet these needs. The technical analyst would communicate this design to the programmers. However, in this text we use the term 'systems analyst' to cover the role of business analyst and technical analyst, and 'systems analysis' to cover both analysis and design aspects.

Another reaction to these problems was the appearance of methodologies to develop computer applications and we look at this change in the next section.

2.2 CONVENTIONAL SYSTEMS ANALYSIS

It was to answer the problems discussed in the previous section that methodologies similar to that recommended by the National Computing

Centre (NCC) in the United Kingdom were adopted by many installations. This methodology, which was taught in a number of courses given by the NCC in a number of educational institutions, was designed in the late 1960s. It is fully described in Daniels and Yeats (1971) and its revised form is described in Lee (1979). We shall concentrate on the earlier version because it had a great impact on the data processing community and represented a model of a good methodology of the 1970s, although this term was not used at that time. This methodology has the following steps:

1 Feasibility study.
2 System investigation.
3 Systems analysis.
4 Systems design.
5 Implementation.
6 Review and maintenance.

These stages together are frequently referred to simply as 'conventional systems analysis', 'traditional systems analysis', 'the systems development life-cycle' or the 'waterfall model'. The term 'life-cycle' is well chosen as the process was iterative and, by the time the review stage came, the system was frequently found to be inadequate and the process started again with a new feasibility study.

1 Feasibility study

The feasibility study looks at the present (usually manual) system and its problems, and briefly investigates alternative solutions. These might include improved manual as well as computer solutions. For each of these, a description is given in terms of the technical, human, and economic costs and benefits of developing and operating the system. A 'recommended solution' is proposed. This information is given to management in a formal report and frequently through a verbal presentation of the proposal by the systems analysts. Management will then decide whether to accept the recommendations of the analysts.

2 Systems investigation

If management has given its approval to proceed, the next stage is a detailed fact finding or a systems investigation phase. This purports to be a thorough investigation of the application area. It will look at:

- The functional requirements of the present system and whether these requirements are being achieved,
- Any constraints imposed,
- The range of data types and volumes which have to be processed,
- Exception conditions, and
- Problems of the present working methods.

This information will be much more detailed than that recorded in the feasibility report.

These facts are gained by interviewing personnel (both management and operational staff), by questionnaires, by direct observation of the area of interest, by using techniques such as sampling, and by looking at records and other written material related to the application area:

- *Observation* can give a useful insight into the problems, work conditions, bottle-necks and methods of work.
- *Interviewing* is usually the most helpful technique for establishing and verifying information, and also provides an opportunity to meet the users and overcome possible resistance to change.
- *Questionnaires* are usually used where similar types of information needs to be obtained from a large number of respondents or from remote locations.
- *Searching* through previous records and documentation may highlight problems, but the analyst has to be aware that the documentation may be out-of-date.
- *Sampling* and other techniques often requires specialist help from statisticians or organization and methods (O & M) teams.

A great deal of skill is required to use any of these effectively, and results should be cross-checked by using a number of these approaches.

The NCC approach recommends a number of documentation aids to ensure that the investigation is thorough. These documentation aids include:

1 Various *flowcharts*, which help the analyst to trace the flow of documents, through a department. It is possible to include in the flowchart the processes that are applied to the document. These processes could include, for example, the checking and error correction procedures. Another flowchart could illustrate the system in outline as functions are carried out in a number of departments,

2 An *organization chart,* showing the reporting structure of people in a department,

3 *Manual document specifications*, giving details of documents used in the manual system,

4 *Grid charts*, showing how different components of a system, such as people and machines, interact with each other, and

5 *Discussion records* on which the notes taken at interviews could be recorded.

Typical charts which were used in this approach are outlined in figure 2.2.

3 Systems analysis

Armed with the facts, the systems analyst proceeds to the systems analysis phase and analyses the present system by asking such questions as:
- Why do the problems exist?
- Why were certain methods of work adopted?
- Are there alternative methods?
- What are the likely growth rates of data?

4 Systems design

This analysis phase leads to the design of the new system. Although usually modelled on the design suggested at the feasibility study stage, the new facts may lead to the analyst adopting a rather different design to that proposed at that time. Frequently, the new design would be similar to the previous manual system, but using the power of computing equipment, and (hopefully) avoiding the problems that occurred with the old system and without including any new ones.

This stage involves the design of both the computer and manual parts of the system. The design documentation set will contain details of:
- Input data and how the data are to be captured (entered in the system).
- Outputs of the system,
- Processes involved in converting the input to the output.
- Structure of the computer and manual files which might be referenced in the system.
- Security and back-up provisions to be made.
- Systems testing and implementation plans.

Again, there are documentation tools provided with which to detail the input, file and output formats, and to chart the procedures. An outline of some documents is shown in figure 2.3. The system outline provides a list of

DOCUMENT DESCRIPTION	SYSTEM	DOCUMENT	NAME	SHEET
Time sheet	5	1	Pay 1	1 of 1

STATIONERY REF	SIZE	NO OF PARTS	METHOD OF PREPARATION
Time sheet	A4	3	By hand

FILING SEQUENCE	MEDIUM	PREPARED/MAINTAINED BY
Payroll number	Paper	Wage clerk

FREQUENCY OF PREPARATION	RETENTION PERIOD	LOCATION
Weekly	1 month	Personnel

VOLUME	MIN	MAX	GROWTH RATE	
500	350	650	5% annually	

Manual document specification

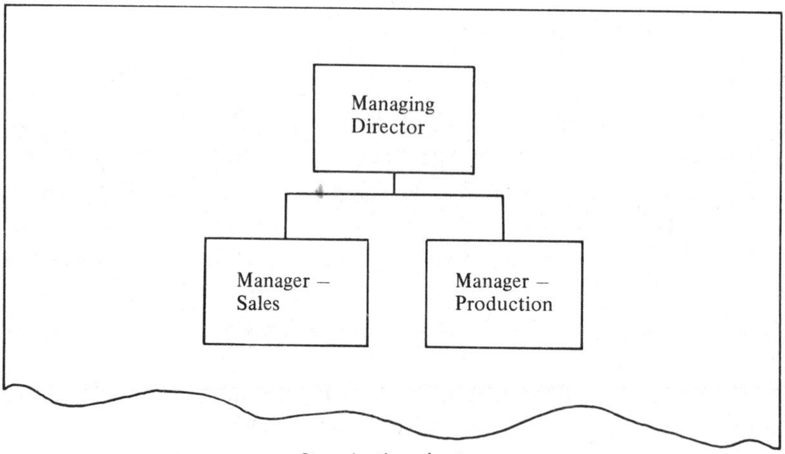

Organization chart

TITLE	SYSTEM	DOCUMENT	NAME	SHEET
Payroll system	5	1	Pay 1	1 of 7

PARTICIPANTS	DATE 25/7/75
Jim Smith, Payroll Manager	LOCATION
OBJECTIVE/AGENDA	Personnel
Overview of manual system	DURATION 1 hour

1 There are 17 staff involved, 5 part-time and ....

Discussion record

Fig.2.2. Various documents for systems investigation phase of conventional systems analysis.

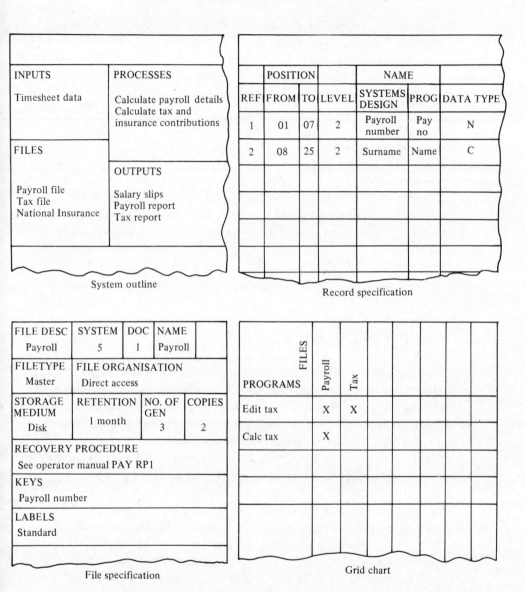

INPUTS	PROCESSES
Timesheet data	Calculate payroll details
	Calculate tax and insurance contributions
FILES	OUTPUTS
Payroll file	Salary slips
Tax file	Payroll report
National Insurance	Tax report

System outline

| REF | POSITION | | LEVEL | NAME | | DATA TYPE |
	FROM	TO		SYSTEMS DESIGN	PROG	
1	01	07	2	Payroll number	Pay no	N
2	08	25	2	Surname	Name	C

Record specification

FILE DESC	SYSTEM	DOC	NAME	
Payroll	5	1	Payroll	
FILETYPE	FILE ORGANISATION			
Master	Direct access			
STORAGE MEDIUM	RETENTION	NO. OF GEN	COPIES	
Disk	1 month	3	2	
RECOVERY PROCEDURE				
See operator manual PAY RP1				
KEYS				
Payroll number				
LABELS				
Standard				

File specification

| PROGRAMS | FILES | | | | | | |
	Payroll	Tax					
Edit tax	X	X					
Calc tax	X						

Grid chart

Fig.2.3. Documents used in systems design phase of conventional approach.

the inputs, outputs, processes and files to be used in the system. A file design specification includes details of:

- File medium (tape or disc).
- File organization, frequently sequential or random access.
- File size.
- Back-up procedures.

The record specification describes all the data items in a record, including

- Name and description.
- Size.
- Format.
- Possible range of values.

Grid charts could be used to show which programs use which files, either for updating or reading. The flow of procedures, either manual or computer, are illustrated by flowcharts. A computer run flowchart for a payroll system is shown in figure 2.4. More rarely, decision tables, described in section 4.5, might be used.

5 Implementation

Following systems design, come the various procedures which lead to the implementation of the new system. If the design includes computer programs, these have to be written and tested. It is important that all aspects of the system are proven, otherwise failure will cause a lack of confidence in this and, possibly, future computer applications. The design and coding of the programs will normally be carried out by computer programmers. In this approach, the analysis and programming functions are considered as separate tasks carried out by different people. This represented an improvement over earlier systems development when the two functions were combined.

The manual procedures have also to be tested. The departmental staff need to practise using the system and any difficulties experienced need to be ironed out. The education and training of user staff is an important element of this phase. Documentation such as the operations and user manuals will be produced and the live (real, rather than test) data will be collected and validated so that the master files can be set up. Once all this has been carried out, the system can be operated and the old one discontinued. If this is done 'overnight' then there could be problems associated with the new system. Frequently, therefore, there is a period of *parallel running* until there is complete confidence in the new system. Alternatively, parts of the new

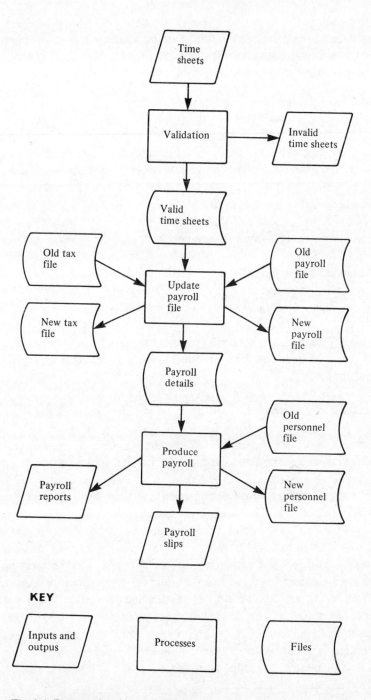

Fig. 2.4. Documenting the computer run.

system can be implemented in turn, forming a *phased run*. If one part of the system is implemented 'to test the water' before the rest of the system is implemented, this is referred to as a *pilot run*.

6 Review and maintenance

The final stage in the system development process occurs once the system is operational. There are bound to be some changes necessary and some data processing staff will be set aside for *maintenance* which aims to ensure the continued efficient running of the system.

At some stage there will also be a *review* of the system to ensure that it does conform to the requirements set out at the feasibility study stage, and the costs have not exceeded those predicted. A report should be produced. As commented earlier, because there is frequently a divergence between the operational system and the requirements laid out in the feasibility study, there is sometimes a decision made to look again at the application and enhance it or in the worst case develop yet another new system to replace that presently running. This could also occur for another reason. Changes in the application area could be such that the operational system is no longer appropriate and should be replaced.

This conventional systems analysis methodology has a number of features to commend it. It has been well tried and tested. The use of documentation standards helps to ensure that the specifications are complete, and that they are communicated to systems development staff, the users in the department, and the computer operations staff. It also ensures that these people are trained to use the system. The education of users on subjects such as the general usage of computers is also recommended, and helps to dispel fears about the effects of computers. Following this methodology also prevents — to some extent at least — missed cut-over dates (the date when the system is due to become operational) and unexpectedly high costs and lower than expected benefits. At the end of each phase the technologists and the users have an opportunity to review progress. By dividing the development of a system into phases, each sub-divided into more manageable tasks, along with the improved training and the techniques of communication offered, the conventional approach gave much greater control over the development of computer applications than before. Indeed, it makes possible, due to the establishment of development phases, the use of project management techniques and tools (see section 5.6).

In other words it *was* a *methodology* and this was a great improvement on previous practice. It had all the attributes that we expect of a methodology:
- A series of *phases* from the feasibility study to review and maintenance, and each of these has *sub-phases*.
- A series of *techniques*, such as ways to evaluate the costs and benefits of different solutions.
- A series of *tools*, which could be used, such as project management tools.
- A *training scheme*, so that all analysts could adopt the standards suggested.
- A *philosophy*, perhaps implied rather than stated, which might be that 'computer systems are usually good solutions to clerical problems'.

But there were also serious limitations to this approach. This text addresses itself to methodologies, techniques and tools, which the authors feel are improvements on this conventional approach or could be incorporated into this approach to make it more effective. It is therefore necessary to discuss criticisms of the conventional approach and how it is used before considering alternatives to it. We would like to stress that the methodologies typified by the NCC approach of the 1970s were adequate, indeed enlightened perhaps, for their day, but there have been a number of developments since then which make such methodologies less appropriate in the late 1980s and beyond.

2.3 CRITICISMS OF THE CONVENTIONAL APPROACH

The criticisms of the systems development approach to applications development, or to be more precise, to the way in which it was used, include:
- Failure to meet the needs of management.
- Unambitious systems design.
- Instability.
- Inflexibility.
- User dissatisfaction.
- Problems with documentation.
- Incomplete systems.
- Application backlog.
- Maintenance workload.

We will discuss each of these in turn.

Failure to meet the needs of management: As can be seen in figure 2.5, although systems developed by this approach often successfully deal with such operational processing as payroll and the various accounting routines, middle management and top management have been largely ignored by

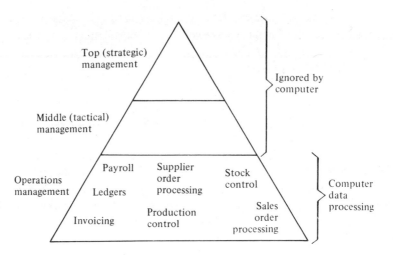

Fig. 2.5. Failure to meet all the needs of business.

computer data processing. Management information, such as that required when making decisions as to where to locate a new factory, which products to stop selling, what sales or production targets to aim for, and how can sales be increased by 10%, are neglected. The computer is being used only for routine, repetitive tasks. Instead of meeting corporate objectives, computers are being used to help solve low-level operational tasks. Top managers and computers are not mixing, apart from the lip-service required to sanction the expenditure necessary to buy and develop mainframe computer systems. There is now a growing awareness amongst management that computers ought to be helping them more directly in their tasks.

Unambitious systems design: Computer systems usually replace manual systems, which are proving inadequate in changing circumstances. But apart from using a new technology, the computer system designs are often similar to those of the existing systems. Systems analysts talk of 'computerizing' the manual system. It is therefore not surprising that the new designs are unambitious. More radical, and potentially more beneficial, computer systems are not being implemented.

Models of processes are unstable: The conventional methodology attempts to improve the way that the processes in businesses are carried out. However, businesses do change, and processes need to change frequently to adapt to new circumstances in the business environment. Because computer systems model processes, they have to be modified or rewritten frequently. It could be said therefore that computer systems, which are 'models' of processes, are unstable because the real world processes themselves are unstable.

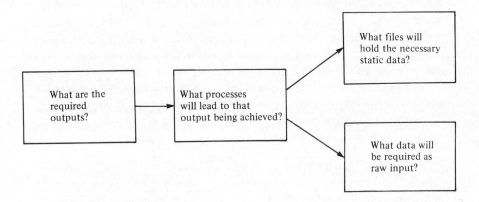

Fig. 2.6. Design is output driven.

Output driven design leads to inflexibility: The outputs that the system is meant to produce are usually decided very early in the systems development process. Design is 'output driven' (see figure 2.6) in that once the output is agreed, the inputs required, the file contents, and the processes involved to convert the inputs to the outputs can be designed. However, changes to required outputs are frequent and because the system has been designed from the outputs backwards, changes in requirements to outputs usually necessitate a very large change to the system design and therefore cause either a delay in the implementation schedule or an unsatisfactory system.

User dissatisfaction: This is often a feature of many computer systems. Sometimes systems are rejected as soon as they are implemented. It may well be only then that the users see the repercussions of their 'decisions'. These decisions have been assumed by the analysts to be firm ones and as computer systems prove inflexible, it is normally very difficult to incorporate changes in requirements once the systems development is under way. Many companies expect users to 'sign off' their requirements at an early stage when they do not have the information to agree the exact requirements of the system. The users sign documentation completed by computer-orientated people. The documents are not designed for the users. On the contrary, they are designed for the systems analysts, operations staff and programming staff who are involved in developing the system. Users cannot be expected to be familiar with the technology and its full potential, and therefore find it difficult to contribute to the debate to produce better systems. The period between 'sign-off' and implementation tends to be one where the users are very uncertain about the outcome. They are frequently disillusioned with computer systems and, as a consequence, fail to cooperate with the systems development staff. Systems people, as they see the situation, talk about user staff as being 'bloody minded' or unable to make a decision. This alienation between technologists and users has even been known to lead to users developing their own informal systems which can be used alongside the computer system, ultimately causing the latter to be superfluous.

Problems with documentation: In section 2.2, one of the benefits of the NCC approach discussed was the documentation that the methodology uses. Yet this is not ideal. The orientation of the documentation, towards the computer person and not the user, has already been mentioned as a source of problems. The main purpose of documentation is that of communication and a technically orientated document is not ideal. A further problem which occurs is that the forms tend to be completed reluctantly by the programmer or analyst as a requirement of the computer or data processing department. It is rarely done well. Worse, frequently it is not changed as modifications to the system are implemented during development or maintenance. This makes the documentation useless because it cannot be relied upon as an accurate reflection of the actual system.

Incomplete systems: Computers are particularly good at processing a large amount of data speedily. They excel where the processing is the same for all items: where the processing is structured, stable and routine. This often means that the unusual (exceptional conditions) are frequently ignored in the computer system. They are too expensive to cater for. If they are diagnosed in the system investigation stage, then manual staff are often assigned to deal with these exceptions. Frequently they are not diagnosed, the exceptions being ignored or forgotten, and the system is falsely believed to be complete. These exceptions cause problems fairly early on in the operational life of the system. These problems mark a particular technical failure, but it also indicates a systems failure, a failure to analyse and design the system properly.

Application backlog: A further problem is the application backlog found in data processing. There may well be a number of systems waiting to be developed. The users may have to wait some years before the development process can get under way for any proposed system. Many systems will take a number of years from feasibility study to implementation. Users may also postpone requests for systems because they know it is not worth doing because of the backlog. This phenomenon is referred to as the *invisible backlog*.

Maintenance workload: The temptation, then, is towards 'quick and dirty' solutions. The deadline for cut-over (when the systems 'goes live') may seem sacrosanct. It is politically expedient to patch over poor design rather than spend time on good design. This is one of the factors which has led to the great problem of keeping operational systems going. With many firms, the effort given to maintenance can be as high as 60-80% of the total data processing workload. With so many resources being devoted to maintenance, which often take priority, it is understandable that there is a long queue of applications in the pipeline. The users are discouraged by such delay in developing and implementing 'their' applications.

Before we consider approaches to systems analysis which represent advances on the conventional systems analysis approach, the reader ought to stop and consider that many systems developed today are still done using the rule of thumb methods discussed in section 2.1, in other words, using no real methodology at all. This is particularly true in organizations using microcomputers as their first taste of computing, particularly where there are no package solutions. Even when there is a package, it often needs adapting for the particular application. An alternative 'solution' to dealing with an inadequate package is to adapt the business application to the needs of the package.

It is often said that businesses developing their own systems for microcomputers are making the same mistakes as systems analysts made on the large computers of the 1960s. We therefore do not wish to assert that the methodologies we have chosen to call 'conventional' are of little value. However it is the purpose of this text to discuss methodologies which improve the craft of systems analysis and the effectiveness of information systems.

We also do not wish to assert that any of the alternative methodologies represents a panacea. A look at the *Information Technology Review for 1987/88* reveals that the major concerns in computing remain:

- Meeting project deadlines.
- Program maintenance.
- Staff recruitment and retention.

This review, see Grindley (1987), has been an annual feature since 1977 and reports on trends seen in information technology. The three major concerns mentioned above have been consistently highlighted in the reviews. We could also add 'general user dissatisfaction' to this list (see Eosys 1986).

Notwithstanding these continuing pessimistic trends, the next chapter looks at the various themes in information systems development methodologies that are seen as alternatives to the conventional approach discussed in this chapter. These alternative methodologies usually address one or more of the criticisms of the conventional approach discussed in this section.

Chapter 3
Themes in Information
Systems Methodologies

In this chapter we explore some of the themes that have evolved in information systems methodologies as alternatives to the conventional approach to information systems development. There is no panacea: no approach solves all the problems discussed in the previous chapter. We look first at the systems approach which in its 'pure' form is rather impractical, but the issues raised and principles established have given rise to practical information systems methodologies. Next we look at planning approaches which concern mainly the information systems requirements of strategic management. Emphasis on the people using the information systems is further emphasized in the theme of participation which follows. We look then at prototyping which can help participation through the use of system development tools. Attempts have been made to automate all aspects of the systems development process and these are described in section 3.1. We then consider software engineering and formal methods, structured systems analysis and design, and data analysis. These types of theme concentrate on techniques, but whereas software engineering and structured systems analysis concentrate on understanding the processes of information systems, data analysis concentrates on understanding and classifying the data relationships. Software engineering and formal methods emphasize techniques for developing programs; structured analysis emphasizes systems analysis and design techniques; data analysis emphasizes the importance of the data model and the database. All the themes discussed in this chapter have their counterparts in Chapter 6, actual methodologies which are used in organizations. Finally we look at some research themes which have influenced these methodologies and are likely to influence methodologies in the future.

3.1 THE SYSTEMS APPROACH

General systems theory attempts to understand the nature of systems which are large and complex. It stems in modern times from the work of Bertalanffy (see for example Bertalanffy 1968). Although such works might not seem relevant to information systems methodologies at first reading, many of the principles have been taken up by the information systems community. Systemic activities, that is the activities which use systems ideas, are an integral feature of a number of information systems methodologies, in particular SSM, which is described in section 6.7.

In Chapter 1 we attempted to define the nature of systems. We saw how systems relate to each other and that they themselves consisted of sub-systems. This gives rise to the definition of a system as *a set of inter-related elements* (Ackoff 1971). A system will have a set of inputs going into it, a set of outputs going out of it, and a set of processes which convert the inputs to the outputs. Systems also have a *purpose*, and the inter-related elements interact in the attempt to achieve this purpose.

We define a *boundary* of a system when we describe it. This may not correspond to any physical or cultural division. A payroll system might include all the activities involved in the payment of staff in a business. These activities fall within the boundary of that system and those systems outside it, with which it relates, are referred to as the *environment*. The systems approach concerns itself with interactions between the system and its environment. The staff recruitment system and production systems within the firm will be part of the environment of the payroll system, as will the government's system to increase employment or the town's leisure system.

One of the bases of systems theory concerns Aristotle's dictum that the whole is greater than the sum of the parts. This would suggest that we must try to develop information systems for the widest possible context, at least organization as a whole rather than for functions in isolation. If we fail to follow this principle then a small part of the organization may be operating to the detriment of the organization as a whole. Further, if we do break up a complex problem into smaller manageable units, a step in many of the methodologies discussed, in particular the structured approach (described in section 3.7), we are assuming that this division will not distort the overall system being studied. This is referred to as being *reductionist*. This may be reasonable in a scientific discipline, but information systems concern people as well as technology, and such *human activity systems* are more complex. The human components in particular may react differently when examined singly as when they play a role in the whole system. Methodologies which analyse systems by breaking them up into their component parts have therefore to be used with care.

Organizational systems are not predictable as they concern human beings.

The outputs of computer programs may be predictable and capable of mathematical formalism. Human activity systems are less predictable because human beings may not follow instructions in the way a piece of software does, nor interpret instructions in the same way as other people do or in the way that they themselves might have done on previous occasions.

Another aspect of systems theory is that organizations are *open systems*. They are not closed and self-contained, and therefore the relationship between the organization and its environment is important. They will exchange information with the environment, both influencing the environment and being influenced by it. The system which we call the organization will be affected by, for example, policies of the government, competitors, suppliers and customers, and unless these are taken into account, predictions regarding the organization will be incorrect. As organizations are complex systems this would suggest that we require a wide range of expertise and experience to understand their nature and how they react with the outside world. Multi-disciplinary teams might be needed to attempt to understand organizations and analyse and develop information systems.

It has been suggested that systems must have a purpose. What then is the purpose of an information system? An information system may aim to provide information to help managers decide on where to build a new factory. The aim might be to provide information about customers so that decisions can be made on their credit rating. It might be to maximize the use of aircraft seats in an airline ticket reservation system. In this way it is possible to control the environment rather than passively react to it.

Information systems usually have human and computer elements and both aspects of the system are inter-related. However, the computer aspects are closed and predictable, the human aspects are open and non-deterministic. Although not easy, the technological aspects are less complex than the human aspects in an information system, because of their predictable nature. Many information systems methodologies only stress the technical aspects. This may lead to a solution which is not ideal because the methodologies underestimate the importance and complexity of the human element.

Systems theory has had widespread influence in information systems work. It would suggest, for example, that whatever methodology is adopted, the systems analyst ought to look at the organization as a whole and also be aware of *externalities* beyond the obvious boundaries of the system — its customers, competitors, governments, and so on (see Churchman 1979, pp. 151-2). Systems theory would also suggest that a multi-disciplinary team of analysts, not all computer-orientated, is much more likely to understand the organization and suggest better solutions to problems. After all, specialisms are artificial and arbitrary divisions. Such an approach should prevent the automatic assumption that computer solutions are always appropriate as well as preventing a study of problem situations from only one narrow point of view. With this approach comes the acknowledgement that there may be a variety of possible solutions, none of them obviously 'best' perhaps, but each having some advantages. These solutions may involve structural, procedural, attitudinal or environmental change.

Checkland (1981) has attempted to turn the tenets of systems theory into a practical methodology which is called *Soft Systems Methodology* (SSM). It is further developed, in the context of information systems, in Wilson (1984). Checkland argues that systems analysts apply their craft to problems which are not well defined. These *fuzzy* problems are common in organizations. His description of Human Activity Systems, also acknowledges the importance of people in organizations. It is relatively easy to model data and processes, but to understand organizations, it is essential to include people in the model. This is difficult because of the unpredictable nature of human activity systems. The claims of the proponents of this approach are that a better understanding of these complex problem situations is more likely to result using this approach than with the more simplistic structured or data orientated approaches.

There are other approaches which have used systems ideas in their design. Beer's *Viable Systems Model* for example (see Beer 1985) provides a tool to study organizations holistically, analysing their structure and their information systems from many viewpoints.

3.2 PLANNING APPROACHES

These approaches stress the planning involved in developing information systems. Rather than look at individual applications and sub-systems in detail, planning approaches involve the top (*strategic*) management (the managing director, financial services manager, and so on) of the organization in the analysis of the objectives of that organization. Management should assess the possible ways in which these objectives might be achieved utilizing the information resource. The approach therefore requires the involvement of strategic management and data processing management in planning information systems.

Because of the requirement to develop an overall plan for the organization, there are obvious links with the systems approach, described in the previous section. Further, because of the top management involvement, and the emphasis attached to fulfilling the needs of top management in controlling the organization, there are also links with the participative approach which is described in the next section.

Planning approaches are designed to counteract the possibility that information systems will be implemented in a piecemeal fashion, a criticism often made of the traditional approach. A narrow, function-by-function approach, could lead to the various sub-systems failing to integrate satisfactorily. Both top management and technologists need to look at organizational needs in the early stages and they need to develop a plan for information systems development as a whole. Individual information systems are then developed within the confines of this plan.

There is a need for information systems to address corporate objectives directly. Planning approaches aim to ensure that management needs are met by information systems. More radically, some information systems are designed around management needs, a sort of 'top-down' approach, perhaps ignoring operational needs. Managers may also set standards for information systems and one of these requirements will be choosing the methodology for developing information systems. Maddison (1984, pp. 17-50) describes these aspects.

Many general information systems approaches discuss strategic planning. It may be considered as a separate stage called business analysis which is carried out early in the development of information systems. In Avison (1985) business analysis is described as involving an assessment of the strategic goals of the organization which could be long term survival, increasing market share, increasing profits, or improving public image. The business analysis stage looks at the environment of the organization — customers, suppliers, government, trade unions and financial institutions — whose actions will affect business performance. It also looks at the key personnel in the organization. With this knowledge, it is possible to assess the type of information that an information system might provide. The first stage of Information Engineering (section 6.2) also concerns itself with planning aspects.

Other approaches look at critical success factors (see Rockart 1979). These are the factors in the business environment which are considered critical to the continued success of the business. In this way it is possible to establish business goals. A methodology firmly based on critical success factors is described in Bullen and Rockart (1984).

Methodologies that emphasize these planning and top management aspects fully are classified as planning approaches. There is a need for this emphasis. A recent survey (Galliers 1986) has revealed that although most respondents agreed that systems planning and business objectives should be aligned, only 10% of 130 organizations surveyed claimed that they had successfully married planning with business objectives and only 43% expressed the view that there were even tenuous links in these organizations. The survey also showed that top management was unambitious about systems planning, for example, giving a low priority to developing systems which attempted to seek out those opportunities that could give the business competitive advantage. Three approaches which address these issues are BIAIT, BSP and ends/means analysis (Wetherbe and Davis 1983 and Davis and Olsen 1984).

In Business Information Analysis and Integration Technique (BIAIT) (see Carlson 1979 and Burnstine 1986), fundamental questions are asked which relate to the objectives of the business. In the approach these are reduced to seven basic questions. Each question is constructed in such a way that either there can only be two possible answers, 'yes' or 'no', or a choice is made from options provided. A grid or matrix of possible responses is formed in the model generated by BIAIT. This profile is used to suggest reports which analyse whether the set of objectives have been met and the information handling necessary. Only at this point does the method begin to look at possible information systems, computer-based or otherwise, which might support these requirements.

IBM's Business Systems Planning (BSP) (see IBM 1975 and Martin 1980) also addresses the requirements of top management and the importance of ensuring that information systems development coincides with and supports the business plan. BSP follows three principles. The first stresses the need for an organization-wide perspective. This factor alone separates the BSP approach from the conventional approach discussed in Chapter 2. Rather than address the information needs of any single area of the organization, it takes the perspective of strategic management. The second principle suggests analysis from top management downwards (but implementation from the detailed level upwards). It is strategic management that defines organizational needs and priorities to help ensure that their perspective predominates in the initial system definition. The BSP approach takes on a bottom-up orientation during the design and implementation phases. This is when the database is created and the processing requirements defined which are necessary to fulfil the organizational objectives. The final principle establishes the need for independence of the business plan from the computer application systems, including data storage aspects. This means that desirable organization changes are not prevented from taking place because of restrictions of the computer systems. Similarly, the computer application systems can be modified, perhaps by using newer technology, without affecting the organization.

The phases of BSP are:

- Identification of requirements.
- Definition of requirements.
- General design.
- Detailed design.
- Development and test.
- Installation.
- Operation.

This is not too dissimilar to the conventional approach, except for its emphasis on strategic planning in the early stages and its iterative design process from the general to the specific.

The organization-wide perspective is obtained by interviewing key executives and is structured to provide information relating to the organizational environment, organizational plans, planning processes, organizational structure, products, markets, geographical distribution, financial statistics, industry position, industry trends, and major problem areas. Information is also gathered about the current information systems and how these support the organization. Following this analysis it is possible to show how information systems can better assist in improving management decision-making. These information systems should be part of an integrated plan for using the information systems resource most effectively to help top management both in the short and long terms.

3.3 PARTICIPATION

In the conventional systems analysis methodology, the importance of user involvement was frequently stressed. However, the computer professional was the person who was making the real decisions and driving the development process. Systems analysts were trained in, and knowledgeable of, the technological and economic aspects of computer applications but far more rarely on the human (or behavioural) aspects which are at least as important. The end user (the person who is going to use the system) frequently felt resentment, and top management did little more than pay lip-service to computing. The systems analyst may be happy with the system when it is implemented. However, this is of little significance if the users, who are the customers, are not satisfied with it.

The planning approaches discussed in the previous section highlighted the necessity for top management to play a role in information systems development. The approach discussed in this section highlights the role of *all* users who may control and take the lead in the development process. If the users are involved in the analysis, design and implementation of information systems relevant to their own work, particularly if this involvement has meant user decision-making, these users are more likely to be fully committed to the information system when operational. This will increase the likelihood of its success. Indeed, in some Scandinavian countries such a requirement may be embodied in law, technological change needing the approval of trade unions and those who are to work with the new system.

Some information systems may 'work' in that they are technically viable, but fail because of 'people problems'. For example, users may feel that the new system will make their job more demanding, less secure, will change their relationship with others, or will lead to a loss of the independence that they previously enjoyed. As a result of these feelings, users may do their best to ensure that the computer system does not succeed. This may show itself in attempts to 'beat the system', for example, by 'losing' documents. Frequently it manifests itself in people blaming the system for causing difficulties that may well be caused by other factors. Some people may just want to have 'nothing to do with the computer system'. In this kind of situation, information systems are unlikely to be successful, or at the very least, fail to achieve their potential.

These reactions against a new computer system may stem from a number of factors, largely historical, but the proponents of participation would argue that they will have to be corrected if future computer applications are going to succeed and that it is important that the following views are addressed:
- Users may regard the computer department as having too much power and controls over other departments through the use of technology.
- Users may regard computer people as having too great a status in the organization, and they may not seem to be governed by the same conditions of work as the rest of the organization.
- Users may consider the pay scales of computer staff to be higher than their own and that the poor track record of computer applications should have led to reduced salaries and status, not the opposite.

These are only three of these arguments. Some views are valid, others less so, but the poor communications between computer people and others in the organization, symptomized by the prevalence of computer jargon, have not helped. Training and education for both users and computer people can help address the cultural clash between them. Somehow these barriers have to be broken down if computer applications are really going to succeed.

One way to help both the process of breaking down barriers and to achieve more successful information systems is to involve all those affected by computer systems in the process of developing systems. As we saw in the previous section, this includes the top management of the organization as well as operational level staff. Until recently, top management have avoided much direct contact with computer systems. Managers have probably sanctioned the purchase of computer hardware and software but have not involved themselves with their use. They preferred to keep themselves at a 'safe' distance from computers. This lack of leadership by example is unlikely to lead to successful implementation of computer systems: managers need to participate in the change and this will motivate their subordinates.

Attitudes are changing partly because managers understand this argument and partly because they can see that computer systems will directly help them in their decision making. The widespread use of microcomputers and the information about computing available in newspapers and other sources has also diminished the 'mystique' that used to surround the computing technology. Earlier computing concerned itself with the operational level of the firm; modern information systems concern themselves with decision-support as well, and managers are demanding sophisticated computer applications and are wishing to play a leading role in their development and implementation.

Communications between computer specialists and others within the organization also needs to improve. This should establish a more mutually trusting and co-operative atmosphere. The training and educating of all staff affected by computers is therefore important. In turn, computer people should also be aware of the various operating areas of the business. This should bring down barriers caused by a lack of knowledge and technical jargon and encourage users to become involved in technological change.

Another useful way of encouraging user involvement is to improve the human—computer interface. There are a number of qualities that will help in this matter. These include visibility, simplicity, consistency and flexibility.

Visibility: This has two aspects. Firstly it means that the way that the system works is seen by the users. This aspect is related to participation, for, if users understand the system, they are more likely to be able to control it.

Secondly, visibility means providing information on the current activity through messages to the users so that they know what is happening when the system is being run. Visibility is discussed further in Veryard (1986).

Simplicity: This means that the presentation of information to the users should be well structured, that the range of options at each point are well presented and that it is easy to decide on which option to choose.

Consistency: This means that the human-computer interface follows a similar pattern throughout the system (indeed, wherever possible, all systems that are likely to be used by one set of users should follow this pattern).

Flexibility: This means that the users can adapt the interface to suit their own requirements.

User involvement should mean much more than agreeing to be interviewed by the analyst and working extra hours as the operational date for the new system nears. This is 'pseudo-participation' because users are still not playing a very active role. If users participated more, even being responsible for the design, they are far more likely to be satisfied with, and committed to, the system once it is implemented. It is 'their baby' as well as that of the computer people. There is therefore every reason to suppose that the interests of the users and technologists might coincide. Both will look for the success of the new system. Without a high level of participation, their job satisfaction might decrease, particularly if the new system reduces skilled work. The result may be absenteeism, low efficiency, a higher staff turnover, and failure of the information system.

The advocates of the participative approach (see, for example, Land and Hirschheim 1983) recommend a working environment where the users and analysts work as a team rather than as expert and non-expert. Although the technologist might be more expert in computing matters, the user has the expertise in the application area. It can be argued that the latter is the more important. An information system can make do with poor equipment, but not poor knowledge of the application. Where the users and technologist work hand in hand, there is less likely to be a misunderstanding by the analyst which might result in a badly designed system. The user will also know how the new system operates by the time it is implemented with the result that there are likely to be fewer 'teething troubles' with the new system.

The role of computer analysts in this scenario may be more of 'facilitators' than designers, advising on the possibilities from which the user chooses. This movement can be aided by the use of application packages which the users can try out and therefore choose what is best for them. Another possibility is the development of a 'prototype'. There are packages available which will set up screen layouts and bring in blocks of code for validating or presenting data. The users can compare all these possibilities before making up their minds on a final design. (Prototyping is discussed in the next section.)

Mumford (1983b) distinguishes between three levels of participation. *Consultative participation* is the lowest level of participation and leaves the main design tasks to the systems analysts, but tries to ensure that all staff in the user department are consulted about the change. The systems analysts are encouraged to provide opportunity for increasing job satisfaction when redesigning the system. It may be possible to organize the users into groups to discuss aspects of the new system and make suggestions to the analysts. Most advocates of the conventional approach to system development discussed in section 2.2 would probably accept that there is a need for this level of participation in the design process.

Representative participation requires a higher level of involvement of user department staff. Here, the 'design group' consists of user representatives and systems analysts. No longer is it expected that the technologist dictates to the users the design of their work system. Users have equal say in any decision. It is to be hoped that the representatives represent the interests of all the users affected by the design decisions.

Finally, *consensus participation* attempts to involve all user department staff throughout the design process, indeed this process is user-driven. It may be more difficult to make quick decisions, but it has the merit of making the design decisions those of the staff as a whole. Sometimes the sets of tasks in a system can be distinguished and those people involved in each task set make their own design decisions.

In Chapter 6 we discuss a methodology called ETHICS which has been designed around these principles. A further participative methodology is found in Blokdijk (1980) which uses participative methods to produce pictorial models for an information system.

Of course participation does have its problems. It might result in polarizing or fragmenting user groups and there is a possibility of manipulating the process by selecting only those participants that are considered 'right' or by suggesting that users participate 'this way ... or there will be unhappy consequences'. Further, participation may cause resentment, either from analysts, who resent their own job being taken over by unskilled people, or by users, who feel that their job is accountancy, managing or whatever, and this is being cramped by demands to participate in the development of computer systems.

The research evidenced in Grindley (1987) suggests that participation is a growing theme of information systems development. It suggests that whereas advising users on producing applications — facilitating in other words — consisted of about 10% of the data processing department's effort in about 1982, it is about 45% in 1987, and in 1992 it is expected that it will be nearer 90%. Further, the source of IT skills was almost 100% trained data processing staff (as opposed to end-user developers) in 1982, it is nearer 75% in 1987, and is expected to be 40% by 1992. End user development is a form of user participation and, as these figures suggest, it is becoming increasingly popular.

Grundén (1986) suggests that participation implies even more fundamental changes in the organization. Figure 3.1, adapted from that paper, gives some of the characteristics of this approach when compared to the traditional approach. The focus of the two approaches is very different. In conventional systems development, the emphasis is on the technology: computer systems, hardware and software. The technologist drives the system. Users are given rules to follow and departures from these norms are not tolerated. The human-orientated view focuses on the people in the organization. This may result in less complex, smaller systems which are not necessarily the most efficient from a technical point of view. Nevertheless, they are more manageable, less reliant on technology and less reliant on 'experts'. Microcomputers are more frequently used as the technological base than mainframes. The conventional view specializes in aspects of the technology, whereas the human-orientated view is more interested in the organization as a whole and the user as creator in that environment. The implication is that the conventional view is more common in traditional hierarchical, bureaucratic organizations; the human-orientated view is more common in democratic, growing and changing organizations.

3.4 PROTOTYPING

Prototyping is common in other areas such as engineering where mass production makes it imperative that the design has been tested thoroughly first. It is also found in areas where the final version is one-off, like a bridge or a building, and it would be very expensive if the designers got it wrong. Information systems tend to be one-off but the cost of building a prototype

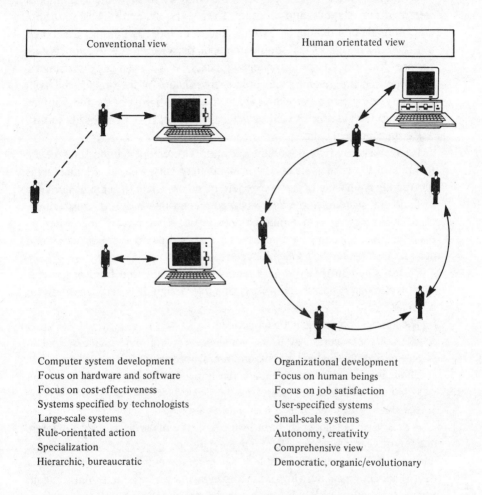

| Conventional view | Human orientated view |

Computer system development
Focus on hardware and software
Focus on cost-effectiveness
Systems specified by technologists
Large-scale systems
Rule-orientated action
Specialization
Hierarchic, bureaucratic

Organizational development
Focus on human beings
Focus on job satisfaction
User-specified systems
Small-scale systems
Autonomy, creativity
Comprehensive view
Democratic, organic/evolutionary

Fig. 3.1. Comparisons of conventional and human orientated views of information systems development (adapted from Grundén, 1986).

has in the past been a major proportion of final costs and therefore has been rarely a feature of information systems development. Prototyping was not common until the availability of software tools, in particular fourth generation systems, which greatly reduce the costs associated with prototyping.

By implementing a prototype first, the analyst can show the users inputs, intermediary stages, and outputs from this system. These are not diagrammatic approximations, which tend to be looked at as abstract things, but the actual figures on computer paper or on terminal or workstation screens. The formats can be changed quickly, as the users suggest changes, until the users are given a reasonable approximation of their requirements. It may only be by using this technique that the users discover exactly what they want from the system, as well as what is feasible. It is also possible to try out a run using real data.

Frequently it is only possible to develop a prototype having some of the features of the final system. The analysts may only wish to examine areas where they are unsure of the user requirements or where they are unsure how to build the system. Some analysts recommend that only the most critical aspects of a new system should be prototyped. Alternatively, the prototype may be built up using simple aspects and adding to them as users and analysts understand the application area more fully.

Prototyping can therefore be seen as a much improved form of systems investigation and analysis, as well as an aid to design. It is particularly useful where:
- The application area is not well defined.
- The cost of rejection by users would be very high and it is essential to ensure that the final version has got users' needs right.
- There is a requirement to assess the impact of prospective information systems.

It is also a way of encouraging user participation.

A prototype is frequently built using special tools such as screen painters and report generators which facilitate the quick design of workstation screens and reports. The user may be able to see what the outputs will look like in a day. Whereas a hand drawing of the screen layout will need to be drawn again for each iteration which leads to a satisfactory solution, the prototype is quickly drawn (or *painted*) again using the tools available. As with word processing systems, the savings come in making changes, as only these need to be drawn again. Thus the ease and speed with which prototypes can be modified are as important as the advantages gained from building the prototype in the first place, iteration becomes a practical possibility.

Some earlier prototyping tools included the programming language APL, although this required some programming skill to use. The operating environment PICK also has facilities which can be used to develop prototypes. There are now microcomputer versions of the popular mainframe operating environments. Sometimes a microcomputer will be used for prototyping using a database package such as dBaseIII. However, there are now a number of specially designed tools available which support prototyping and these *fourth generation systems* are discussed in section 5.4.

Frequently a prototype system can be developed in a few days, and it rarely takes more than 10% of the time and other resources necessary to develop the full operational system. This can be a good investment of time. Some systems teams use the prototype as the user sign-off. This is likely to be a much better basis for obtaining a user decision than the documentation of conventional systems analysis discussed in section 2.2.

One possible drawback of prototyping is that the users may question the time taken to develop an operational system when that taken to develop a prototype was so quick. There is also the risk that the system requirements may change in the meantime. Some users may also argue that the time, effort and money used to develop a prototype is 'wasted'. It is sometimes difficult to persuade busy people that this effort does lead to improved information systems.

Prototyping may be more than just another tool available to the analyst. It could be used as a basis for a methodology of systems development in the organization. This may have:
- An analysis phase, designed to understand the present system and suggest the functional requirements of an alternative system.
- A prototyping phase to construct a prototype for evaluation by users.
- A set of evaluation and prototype modification stages.
- A phase to design and develop the target system using the prototype as part of the specification.

Prototyping as part of the systems development cycle is discussed in Dearnley and Mayhew (1983).

Many prototypes are intended to be discarded. They have not been designed to be used as operational systems as they are likely to be:
- Inefficient.
- Incomplete, performing only some of the required tasks.
- Poorly documented.
- Unsuitable for integration with other operational systems.
- Incomplete, for example, lacking security features.
- Incapable of holding the number of records necessary.
- Inadequate, being designed for one type of user only.

They are used only as a development tool, as a learning vehicle. Prototypes lack features which are essential in an operational system but inappropriate in a prototype, and this needs to be stressed to users who may expect the target system to be developed in the same time as the prototype. A review of prototyping can be found in Hekmatpour and Ince (1986) and Mayhew and Dearnley (1987).

An alternative approach is to use the final prototype as the basis for the operational system. In this scenario, the system has 'evolved' by an iterative process. Once the users are satisfied with the prototype, it can be converted to become an operational system. It is now no longer a prototype.

The information system may be implemented in stages. At each stage, the missing components are those which give the poorest ratio of benefits over costs. The analysts in this case will have to be aware of robust design and good documentation when the prototype is being developed. The prototype must be able to handle the quantities of live data that are unlikely to be incorporated when giving end users examples of the prototype's capabilities. Otherwise prototyping will not improve the quality of systems development. Therefore, although prototyping is frequently regarded as a 'quick and dirty' method, it need not be 'dirty'. If the prototype is well designed, the prototype can feature as part of a successful operational information system.

Evolutionary information systems development is similar to the prototyping approach except that there is never a 'final version', there is always the possibility of iterative revision even when the system is live. In this approach the prototype may always develop in an evolutionary systems development process and may never 'die'. The prototype is changed to reflect new conditions. Here, maintenance is regarded as positive rather than negative (see McCracken and Jackson 1982), the likelihood of change is catered for, rather than being seen as a problem. This evolutionary approach therefore addresses the problem of dealing with change, an aspect which many other approaches do not address.

3.5 AUTOMATED TOOLS FOR INFORMATION SYSTEMS DEVELOPMENT

The theme of automating some aspects of the information systems development process is an abiding one, and has intrigued developers for many years. It has often been recognized that certain aspects of the process are repetitive or rule based and therefore susceptible to automation. Early examples include decision table software which could generate accurate code directly from a decision table (see section 4.5), project control packages (see section 5.6) to help organize and control the development process, and report generators to help speed up some programming tasks. On the analysis side, software has existed for many years to help in the construction of traditional programming flowcharts.

A variety of more ambitious projects are well documented and these include ADS (Accurately Defined System), which was a system definition and specification technique developed by NCR in the 1960s. Five forms were provided which were used to specify outputs, inputs, computations, files and process logic in the form of decision tables. Efforts were made to automate some aspects of ADS by using programs which interpreted the data on the forms to produce information and for cross-referencing.

Systematics (see Grindley 1966 and 1968) was a more ambitious project which attempted to incorporate, amongst other tools, automated decision table interpretation into an automated methodology of information systems design

TAG (Time Automated Grid) (see IBM 1971) was another attempt to automate some aspects of the systems analysis process. This was produced by IBM in 1966. Details of the required outputs of a system were fed into TAG and the package would work backwards to determine the inputs necessary to produce those outputs and in what sequence. Reports were produced which helped the analyst in the design process.

Perhaps the most important attempts in the 1960s and early 1970s were carried out at the University of Michigan which led to the ISDOS (Information System Design and Optimization System) project. The basis of ISDOS was PSL and PSA. Problem Statement Language (PSL) enables the analyst to state the requirements in formal terms (indeed in machine-readable form) which are then entered into a kind of database. The PSL statements are then analysed by the Problem Statement Analyzer (PSA) which has similarities with a data dictionary system and which interprets these statements, validates the data, stores it and analyses it, and then produces the output required. The PSL and PSA together produced a set of documents for the project including the systems analysts' formal specification and the users' requirements. These languages are described in Teichroew and Hershey (1977), Teichroew *et al.* (1979) and Welke (1987). The emphasis of the approach is on the documentation aspects, for they help the manual tasks of systems analysis rather than genuinely automating the processes of analysis and design.

ISDOS attempts to link all aspects of systems development, from a computerized problem statement into programming language statements. System requirements are input using PSL and PSA but ISDOS also incorporates an Optimizer, so that the code generated is as efficient as possible, and a file generation sub-system. ISDOS had as an aim the incorporation of all aspects of systems work in a complete automated package, but this proved over-ambitious at the time. Indeed, the ideal of converting a user specification in natural language automatically into verified software is still a long way off.

Whilst many of these attempts at automating various aspects of systems development were far sighted and valiant, they were not overly successful in terms of application. It has often been noted by users that data processing professionals have been very keen to automate everybody else but have shown a certain reticence to 'take their own medicine'. Apart from innate conservatism, there appear to have been a variety of reasons for this: some of the software was not very good or easy to use; it was often found that the benefits were outweighed by the effort and costs involved; and the technology was also a limiting factor.

Recently, some of these factors have changed. The technology is clearly more powerful, cheaper and widely available. Improved graphics facilities have also had an impact. The quality of the software has improved, and in general there is a growing climate of opinion that believes that automated tools are beneficial.

There are currently two categories of automated systems development tools, although in the near future they may well be merged into one:
• Analysis and design tools.
• Implementation tools.

The first category includes the tools that support the analysis and design process as it exists today. These are tools that support the techniques described in Chapter 4 such as data flow diagramming, entity modelling, process logic, and so on. They are sometimes described as documentation support tools, being designed to take the drudgery out of revising documents, because they make the implementation of changes very easy. They are in effect the diagrammatic equivalents of word processors. In addition, they can contribute to the accuracy and consistency of diagrams. The diagrammer can, for example, cross-check that levels of data flow diagrams are accurate and that terminology is consistent. They can ensure that certain documentation standards are adhered to. Probably the greatest benefit is that analysts and designers are not reluctant to change diagrams, because the change process is simple. Manual re-drawing is not satisfactory, not just because of the effort involved but the potential of introducing errors in re-drawing. Many a small change required by a user was never incorporated into the system due to the effort required to re-draw all the documentation. These kinds of documentation tools have proved both practical and useful.

They have, however, also proved limited in the sense that much of the information required for a data flow diagram, for example, would also be required, in a slightly different form, for the process logic software, and so on. It was realized that it would make more sense to have a central repository of all the information required for the development project. In fact, this is the *data dictionary*, or perhaps as it is more correctly known, because it contains information about processes as well as data, the *systems dictionary* or *systems encyclopaedia*.

Once most of the information concerning a development project is on a data dictionary it is only a short step to the automation, or at least the automated support, of many of the stages of the development project. Further, one of the goals of a number of methodologies is to provide automated support for all of their stages. Some have the automatic generation of code as the end result of the automation of the information systems development process. Chapter 5 discusses some of these tools in more detail.

Implementation tools, the second category of tools, are ones which address the construction end of the spectrum rather than the analysis and design end. In this category are included programming languages themselves, which we do not think of as automated tools any more, prototyping tools, fourth generation systems, and code generators.

Before we leave the topic of automated analysis, many information systems are developed 'automatically' by purchasing and implementing a ready-made *application package*. This can be an information system that is bought off-the-shelf from a supplier. This still needs a full requirements definition, and an application package needs to be assessed on the basis of answers to the following questions:

- Does it fit in with the information systems strategy?
- Does it meet functional requirements?
- Does it meet resource limits (for purchasing and running)?
- Does it meet documentation standards?

and so on. These aspects are discussed fully in Avison (1987). However, because normally not all the requirements are met by any single package, the use of application packages is limited, unless the information systems application is particularly discrete, well defined, common to many organizations, and stable. Further, it is unlikely to integrate with existing information systems.

3.6 SOFTWARE ENGINEERING AND FORMAL METHODS

'Software Engineering' stemmed from the work of Dijkstra and others (see Yourdon 1979), which suggested improved techniques of computer programming. These improvements were thought necessary because of the maintenance problem and the growing demand for larger and more complex programs. The principles established in software engineering have now generally been accepted as a genuine advance and an improvement to programming practice, primarily by achieving better designed programs and hence making them easier to maintain and more reliable. This has led to improved software quality.

In the period before the advent of software engineering, the conventional way of developing computer programs was to pick up a pencil or to sit at a computer terminal and code the program without a thorough design phase. This *ad hoc* process was also frequently used for larger programs, but a better method for these large programs was to develop a flowchart and code from this. However, even this method is not very satisfactory.

The time taken to develop a fully tested program will be far greater in the long run if effort is not spent on a thorough design process. Without this design, it is difficult to incorporate all the necessary features of the program. However, these omissions will only be brought to light at the program testing stage, and it will be difficult to incorporate the changes required at such a late stage. Problem-solving carried out by haphazard, trial-and-error, methods is far less successful than good analysis and design.

As we have mentioned, one solution to better program design was the use of flowcharting methods, but although program flowcharting does discipline the programmer to design his program, the resultant design can prove inflexible, particularly for large programs. Flowcharting usually leads to programs which have a number of branches, effected in programming languages by GOTO commands. With this method, it is difficult to incorporate even the smallest amendments to the program in a way which does not have repercussions elsewhere. These repercussions are usually very difficult to predict and programmers find that after making a change to correct a program, some other part of the program begins to fail.

This problem does not stop at the testing phase, because once the system is operational, the amendments necessary in general maintenance will be difficult to incorporate. When they are made, the flowcharts, which represent the main form of program documentation, are frequently not updated. This means that the programs do not have good documentation. In turn, this makes future maintenance even more difficult.

Software engineering offers a more disciplined approach to programming which is likely to increase the time devoted to program design, but will greatly increase productivity through savings in testing and maintenance. A good design is one achievement of the 'software engineering school' and a second is good documentation, which greatly enhances the program's 'maintainability'.

One of the key elements of software engineering is *functional decomposition*. Here a complex process is broken down into increasingly smaller subsets. This is illustrated in figure 3.2. 'Calculate weekly payroll' at the top level can be broken down into first level boxes named 'validate weekly return', 'calculate gross wage', 'calculate deductions' and 'print wages slip'. Each of these boxes is a separate task and can be altered without affecting other boxes (provided output remains unchanged). Each of these can then be further broken down. For example, 'calculate deductions', can be broken down into its constituent parts, 'calculate tax', 'calculate national insurance', and 'calculate loan payments'. Eventually this *top-down* approach can lead to the level where each module can be represented as a few simple English statements or a small amount of programming code, the *target base level*. This hierarchy is sometimes described as a *tree* with the root at the top and the smallest leaves at the bottom. This is similar to the process referred to as *step-wise* (or successive) *refinement* (Wirth 1971).

Figure 3.2 showed the way a process could be broken down into its constituent parts. Many programs can be broken down into the general structure shown as figure 3.3. The top level module controls the overall processing of the program. Separate modules at the lower level control the input and output routines (reading data and updating the files), validation routines (checking that the data is correct), the processing routines (such as those shown in figure 3.2), and the setting up of reports. Sometimes these structure charts include details of the data (called *parameters)* which are passed between modules. This information is written on the connecting lines in the diagram.

The alternative to a top-down approach is a *bottom-up* approach where the detail is specified first. Unfortunately, it is often difficult to make the 'chunks of detail' fit together at a later stage. Sometimes, particularly in a large software project, these chunks are designed and developed by different people and it is therefore likely that poor communication or vague specification will lead to problems when attempting to interface parts of the system. This may be discovered very late in the project, when delays will be particularly

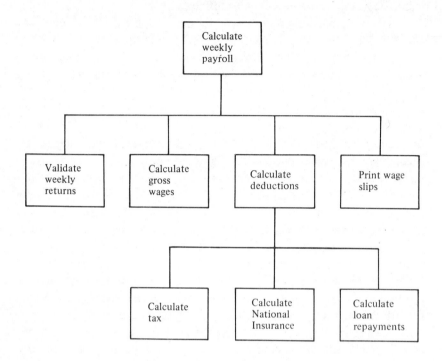

Fig. 3.2. Functional decomposition.

problematical and cause a loss of confidence in the system. With top-down development, these interfaces are designed first. At the eleventh hour it is far easier to correct a detail in an individual program than to correct a problem of fitting together programs or sub-systems.

Bottom-up design can sometimes be helpful when used alongside top-down. In some situations it may be difficult to identify the main elements in a problem area, a process which is necessary when designing a control module. A detailed level analysis might stimulate their identification.

So far, we have equated software engineering with good practice in programming design. But this is a narrow interpretation. The term is frequently used to cover the areas of requirements definition, testing, maintenance, and control of software projects, as well as the design of software.

The requirements definition must be clear and unambiguous so that the

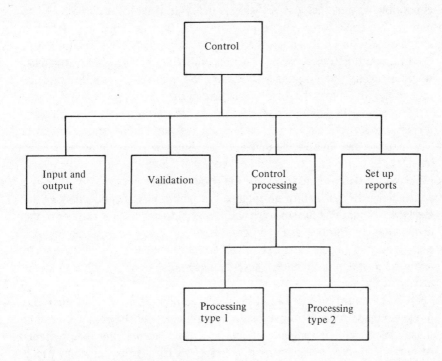

Fig. 3.3. Program design.

software designer knows what the piece of software should do. The designer can then devise the way that these requirements will be achieved. Even the best design will not lead to a successful implementation if the requirements are not clear. The problem with natural language is that it is frequently ambiguous, though there is a series of techniques which can be used to clarify the requirements. We may here be going beyond the boundary of software engineering into information systems development. We take the view that the requirements of the software designer will be made clear by the systems analyst, and we leave further discussion of this issue until the next section, which looks at structured systems analysis and design.

Supporters of software engineering practice claim that the reliability of software designed in this way is improved. These improvements do not only derive directly from better design. There is an indirect benefit. If the software is better designed, it makes adequate testing of that software much easier. By designing the program so that it is split into smaller and separate elements, it is possible to construct a series of tests for each of these 'black boxes'. The number of tests for a larger program will be much greater. Perhaps simplistically (but it illustrates the point), a program split into four modules each containing five processing paths, will require 5+5+5+5 (20) tests, whereas testing one program will require 5x5x5x5 (625) tests, because for each of the first five paths there will be five of the second, and so on.

Maintenance is also important because, as we saw in the previous chapter, it is an activity which takes up much of the analysts' and programmers' time. Maintenance can involve the update of programs whose requirements have changed, as well as the correction of programs which do not work properly. Maintenance will be made easier by the good documentation and good design which comes from the software engineering approach. The person making the changes will find that the software will be easier to understand because of the documentation. Further, as the program has been split into separate modules each performing a particular task, it will be easy to locate the relevant module and change it as appropriate. These changes will not affect other modules unexpectedly.

It is essential to use good control techniques to ensure that the implementation schedule for software is reasonable. Otherwise, the users and management will be unhappy about the system even if the requirements definition and software design work is first class, because expectations, which proved to be unrealistic, are dashed. A good methodology for the construction of software will be amenable to project control techniques. Breaking a system down into its parts does make estimating easier and more accurate.

The term software engineering, therefore, is often used to cover much more than simply the design of computer programs. This is the view of many of the writers of texts on software engineering, including those of Ratcliff (1988) and Sommerville (1985). However, the term is used by these authors to refer to the development of quality *software*. The wider 'environmental' issues, they argue, are the concern of *information systems*. We agree with this view.

In this text we are interested in producing quality information systems. We regard software engineering as a skill which improves program design and thereby makes software, an important element of *computer* information systems, more effective once implemented, and easier to maintain.

A software engineering phase is usually part (though sometimes not explicitly stated) of an information system development methodology, and is explicitly part of structured approaches, which are discussed in the next section. Areas such as:

- Understanding the problem area.
- Understanding the needs of the user.
- Looking at alternatives.
- Deciding whether a computer system is needed

lie outside the scope of software engineering. If a computer system is recommended, then there will be a software engineering phase. However, the skills of software engineering should be separated from those of information systems analysis and design. This is important as it was the lack of separation of the skills of the technologist from those of the analyst that was considered a major problem of the conventional approach to systems analysis. Further, it is important that the requirements of the analyst are expressed to the technologists in a way that the technologist can appreciate, and this provides one impetus in the movement towards the techniques of structured systems analysis and design which parallel, to some extent at least, those in software engineering.

Formal Methods

Before looking at formal methods, we should first clear up some confusion that may exist over the use of the term formal. The term is frequently used in the information systems community to mean 'clear structure', 'rule based' and 'technique orientated'. We prefer to use the term 'formalized' for this. In the context of this section the term 'formal' means *expressed mathematically*.

A methodology which incorporates formal methods uses mathematical precision in specification and design. For example, a formal specification will express in mathematically precise terms the user requirements which might originally have been expressed in natural language. Natural language can be criticized in that it is verbose and ambiguous. A formal design attempts to express these requirements (the *what*) concisely, unambiguously and completely and convert them into a design (the *how*). The requirements statement drives the design.

One major advantage of this approach, its protagonists argue, is that the result can be *proved* to be correct. In other words, if the requirements are correct, and they can be expressed mathematically, then a solution can be derived which will work. The process of proving both the syntax and the semantics of a solution can be automated:

Syntax — the logic of the requirements are expressed in the grammar of the system.

Semantics —the set of expressions used will achieve the results predicted.

Formal methods are particularly appropriate to producing quality software and can be usefully incorporated into a software engineering methodology. This, in turn, can be a subset of an information systems methodology. For example, Jackson Structured Programming (JSP) is incorporated into Jackson Systems Development (JSD), discussed in section 6.4. Methodologies in formal methods proper include Vienna Development Method (VDM) (see McGettrick 1980), Higher-Order Software (see Connor 1985), and Rigorous Method (see Bjorner and Jones 1982).

It can be argued that many aspects of user requirements in information systems, for example, the design of the human—computer interface which needs to be suitable for many types of user, are outside the realm of 'being able to be expressed mathematically'. Therefore formal methods might be used to express some aspects of information systems requirements but not all.

There are other problems associated with formal methods. Only some technologists have the skills necessary to use the language, and the symbolism of mathematics alienates many people. These techniques are unlikely to encourage user participation. Further, formal methods do not easily lend themselves to modularity, which is desirable for larger programs. Finally, striving for provably correct programs can be an expensive way to develop software.

Where formal methods are particularly applicable is in process control applications, such as missile systems or factory production systems. They are less applicable in the information systems arena, because of its people-orientation. We have chosen, therefore, not to discuss formal methods further. Chang and Lee (1973) and Ratcliff (1988) look at the subject in more depth.

3.7 STRUCTURED METHODOLOGIES

Structured methodologies are based on functional decomposition, that is the breaking down of a complex problem into manageable units in a disciplined way. We looked at an example of functional decomposition in figure 3.2.

The development of structured methodologies in systems analysis and design stemmed from the perceived benefits of software engineering (discussed in the previous section). Structured programming has been successful in increasing programmer productivity and ensuring that the programming code produced is easier to maintain. But programs, however well produced, may be useless if the analysis and design that preceded it was poorly carried out. Further, even good analysis and design, if poorly documented, may lead to incorrect interpretation by programmers and even the best programming techniques cannot overcome such problems.

Structured systems analysis and design has been associated with a number of authors and consultancy houses. These include Weinberg (1978), Yourdon and Constantine (1978), Gane and Sarson (1979) and DeMarco (1978). In section 6.1, we look specifically at the Gane and Sarson methodology (STRADIS).

Some of the techniques associated with structured systems analysis and design, specifically functional decomposition, decision trees, decision tables, data flow diagrams, data structure diagrams, and structured English, are looked at in Chapter 4, and data dictionaries, which are tools used in structured methodologies (and other methodologies), are discussed in section 5.3.

The techniques and tools to represent processes used in structured systems analysis and design prove to be a considerable improvement on the conventional techniques such as flowcharting discussed in section 3.2, both from the point of view of understanding the real-world processes and in communicating the knowledge acquired.

Structured analysis documentation includes documents describing the logical (real-world) analysis of the processes and not just their physical (implementation) level designs. In other words, there is usually a clear distinction between any application logic and the computer representation of that logic.

There will also be a separation of any data or information that the system is likely to input, output, process or store and the physical record — a computer file or part of a database. This separation of logical and physical designs is an important element of a number of methodologies discussed in Chapter 6. It gives a level of 'data independence', in other words the processes can change without necessarily changing the computer files. Similarly, the files can change without necessarily altering the user views of the data.

Two techniques that the analyst might use are data flow diagramming and structured English. Data flow diagrams are a particularly useful aid in communicating the analyst's understanding of the system. Users, whether the operator of the system when it is operational or the manager of the department it is aimed to help, can see that the data flow diagram accurately represents the system and, once there is agreement, the results are readily converted to computer procedures. Structured English, which is another technique used in structured systems analysis and design, is very like a 'readable' computer program. It is not a programming language though it can be readily converted to a computer program, because it is a strict and logical form of English and the constructs reflect structured programming.

There are other variations on the 'English-like' languages used in these methodologies. Though 'English like', they are not natural languages which tend to be ambiguous and frequently long-winded. These languages are designed to be simple, clear and unambiguous. This is particularly important. In the past, systems analysts were first and foremost computer people. Now they are using terminology and techniques that are easier for the users to understand. This is important in getting the willing participation of users. Most of the documentation aids are graphic representations of the subject matter. This is much easier to follow than text or computer-orientated documentation.

As well as improved communication tools, structured methodologies usually incorporate 'structured walkthroughs'. These are team meetings where the analysis and design specifications and other documentation (which should have been previously circulated) are exposed to review by the members of the team. Usually the group explores problems rather than looks for solutions (although some work this way) and the author of the documentation does not usually make comments (to avoid arguments), although again this depends on the organization. All comments are noted on 'action lists' so that they can be digested by the author and acted upon.

There are dangers however, even in this scenario, as unnecessarily long discussions and side-tracking must be avoided. It is essential that they represent meetings of peers and that 'management' are not involved. This will avoid the type of criticism which may have repercussions later on the team member's status or salary. A peer review is likely to reveal errors, omissions, ambiguities, inconsistencies and weaknesses in style, and also ensure a process of continuous training of the staff involved. Questions that the peer group might ask are:

- Can bespoke programs use routines already in the library?
- Is the user interface simple, understandable, and consistent?
- Does the design fulfil the specification fully?
- Will it work?

By having walkthrough sessions at each stage, requirements definition before analysis, analysis before design, and design before implementation, this should avoid the late detection of errors and flaws in logic, and hence greatly reduce the risk of failure when the system is implemented.

Some installations have frequent informal walkthroughs and more formal inspection meetings which take place after every major stage — about four or five during the lifetime of the project.

Structured systems analysis and design can be considered as an alternative to the conventional approach. In fact this is a simplification. The authorities on structured analysis do not view it in the same way. The techniques can be regarded as a useful alternative to many techniques used in the conventional approach, and therefore should be incorporated in that approach rather than replace it. A structured methodology may also replace the conventional approach. Some writers emphasize the analysis aspect, such as DeMarco, whilst others also stress design aspects, for example, Gane and Sarson. Writers also emphasize different techniques, although some techniques are common to all structured methodologies. A number of useful cases are described in Davis (1983).

3.8 DATA ANALYSIS

Whereas structured analysis and design emphasizes processes, data analysis concentrates on understanding and documenting data which, it is argued, represents the 'fundamental building blocks of systems'. Even if applications change, the data already collected may still be relevant to the new or revised systems and therefore need not be collected and validated again. The data model, the result of data analysis, is orientated towards that part of the real world it represents (organization, department, or whatever) and should be implementation independent. This means that data analysis is suitable whether the physical model is a database, file or card index.

The interest in data analysis stems partly from the problem of 'graduating' from computer files to databases. What may be called 'informal data analysis', an *ad hoc* approach to understanding the data structures in an organization, adequate for file processing systems, is not adequate for database applications where the data is shared between applications and therefore the data and its structure must be well defined. Early database experience did not always bring about the expected flexibility of computer applications, usually because the database was not a good reflection of the organization it was supposed to represent. Modelling the organization on a computer database is not easy. It is argued that data analysis has proved successful in creating a model which is independent of any database, accurate, unambiguous and complete enough for most applications and users. Its success comes in the

PART

PART NO.	COST	NAME	SUPPLIER
344	£10.00	Widgets	Smith
346	£12.00	Widgets	Jones
540	£10.00	Widget tops	Smith

Fig. 3.4. The part relation

systematic way by which it identifies the data in organizations and, more particularly, the relationships between these data elements, the 'data structure'.

Data analysis techniques (see Howe 1983) attempt to identify the data elements and analyse the structure and meaning of data in the organization. This is achieved by interviewing people in the organization, studying documents, observation, and so on, and then formalizing the results. A number of documentation aids, many of which are pictorial, also help in the process of data analysis. This becomes the first step in extrapolating the complexities of the real world into a model that can be held on computer. The documentation produced in data analysis is more easily understood by users than the documentation for data representation used in the conventional approach, such as the file and record specification forms.

Data analysis does not necessarily precede the implementation of a database or computer system of any sort. It can be an end in itself, to help in understanding a complex organization. Good models will be a *fair* representation of the 'real world' and can be used as a discussion document for improving the effectiveness of the role of data in an organization.

Avison (1981) describes a number of alternative approaches to data analysis. In the data collection approach, frequently referred to as document-driven analysis, the documents used in a department are analysed. Such documents include reports, forms and enquiry formats. The analysis of each document in turn will lead to the formation, and then improvement, of a data model showing the data and the relationships between these data. The particular structures arrived at are relations (special kinds of tables), an example of which is shown in figure 3.4, and rules are applied to the set of relations to ensure that the model is flexible for future use, such as its mapping on to a database. These rules, which are described in section 4.2, are known as the rules of normalization. The result of this type of data analysis is therefore a data model represented as a set of normalized relations.

The document-driven approach is a useful contribution, as documents in organizations are usually easy to analyse. But organizations are not always fully represented by the documents used in that organization. Frequently the number of documents is such that they would take too long to analyse. An alternative approach to data analysis, entity modelling, gains its information by interviewing people in the organization, such as department managers and manual staff. Entities such as customers, suppliers, parts and finished goods, are identified and the relationships between these entities are also ascertained. The entities and their relationships can be expressed as a graphical model. This is a more common approach to data analysis and we look at this approach in detail in section 4.1.

Data analysis is stressed in many methodologies for a number of reasons, particularly as data, it is argued, is more stable than processes and it is the 'lifeblood' of organizations. These arguments were made in section 2.3, but additional arguments for this approach are outlined below.

The data model is *not computer orientated*. It is not biased by any particular physical storage structure that may be used. The model stays the same whether the storage structures are held on magnetic tape, disc, or main storage. It is not biased towards the way that the data may be accessed from storage media. If the target system is a computer system, it could be mainframe, minicomputer or microcomputer. Further, it is not biased towards using any particular DBMS type.

It is a model which is *readily understandable* by the technologists, and also by managers and users. They can far more readily appreciate the meaning of the data relationships illustrated in a graphical form than they could in the file and record specification forms of conventional systems analysis which are computer-orientated. It is not necessary to know anything of computers or computer file structures to understand the model and to use it.

It does *not show bias towards particular users or departmental view*. The data model can reflect a variety of different views of the data.

Although the model can represent the organization as a whole, it can be *adapted* so that a particular part of the model can appear in a different form to different users. There will be one overall model but various user views can be represented. Such flexibility allows users to see that part of the data model that interests them and avoid an otherwise over-complicated view of the model. It can also support other requirements such as privacy and security.

The data model is *readily transformable* into other models, such as relations, hierarchies or networks, which are often but not exclusively the ways in which data base management systems require the data structures to be presented.

The *different data analysis techniques* available allows a choice in situations where alternative methods are appropriate. The results of one technique can be cross-checked with another. There is therefore some expectancy that the process does fairly represent that part of the real world modelled.

The modelling processes are *rule-based* which means that the results of other analysts' work can be followed and assessed, *proven,* at least to a certain extent. Further, the processes lend themselves to computerization and many aspects of data analysis have been automated.

The approach does have critics. Some argue that although the documents and the techniques used are easier to understand by users when compared to some traditional methods, data analysis does not lend itself fully to user participation. Others have argued that the emphasis on data may be misplaced. Further, the assumption in data analysis is that it is possible to model reality, is questionable, see Kent (1978). The data model can only be 'A' model and *not* 'THE' model of that part of the real-world being modelled. It cannot reflect reality completely and accurately for all purposes. Even if data analysis has 'gone according to plan', the resultant data model cannot objectively represent the organization. It is a subjective view distorted by the perception process. However, the data model derived from data analysis usually proves in practice to be suitable for the purpose.

For many, data analysis is one-sided and although it is beneficial to develop a data model which can be mapped on to a database, there is still a parallel need to understand the functions that will be applied to the database when it is implemented. Indeed most data analysis-based methodologies now address process aspects as well.

3.9 RESEARCH THEMES

In this section we look at research which concerns wider issues of information systems, because these systems concern interactions with the technology, organizations, and society at large. Keen (1987) argues that the mission of information research is to study 'the effective design, delivery, use and impact of information technologies in organizations and society' and he goes on to spell out some of the implications of this. For example, he uses the term *effective* to imply that practice should be improved through research. This type of research is referred to as 'action research', and this topic is discussed later in this section. He regards systems *design*, described as a craft, as the core area of information systems and it concerns the possibilities and constraints of applying technology. The interest is not with the information technology itself, but with its application. One IFIP Working Group (8.2) is particularly concerned with these larger issues, and researchers in this group are concerned about the organizational and societal consequences of information systems. We will look at some of the work of this group.

A particularly interesting set of papers is contained in Mumford *et al.* (1985) which sprang from a Colloquium in 1984 called 'Information Systems Research — A Doubtful Science'. This was an interesting and provocative title because much research in information systems is not concerned with scientific method (although some is — particularly aspects in formal methods and software engineering, structured methods and data analysis) but is concerned with human activities, and may therefore be more in the realm of social science methods.

One basis of scientific method is that an experiment can be duplicated. A hypothesis is put forward and a series of practical experiments justifies or refutes the hypothesis. The environment of information systems is one where a situation cannot be duplicated. The environment is one where people, not inanimate objects, are important. Even so, some methods which are used in information systems research — such as a survey/questionnaire — are often used in the sciences. An analysis of case studies illustrating the success or failure of information systems can also be handled in a scientific manner. But these survey questionnaires might require interpretation by the researcher, and interview techniques certainly will. Here, it is more difficult to argue that the methods are objective and therefore 'scientific'.

Other approaches rely on political, ethical and philosophical argument, rather than scientific research, but are relevant to information systems. These do not represent attempts to be objective and rigorous in the sense that research in the natural sciences attempts to be objective.

Some information systems researchers regard attempts to be scientific or reductionist as leading to a loss in the richness of the problem domain. Only a small part of the area of interest may be suitable to scientific method. How can research in information systems, they argue, be narrow enough to avoid questions about objectivity, rigour, repeatability, and yet be broad enough to be useful? It might be argued that information systems research is not amenable to scientific research methods because it concerns human, social and organizational issues or even that it is an area which is unresearchable.

One specific area of concern discussed at the IFIP 8.2 Colloquium was that research funds world-wide are directed more to the 'scientific' end of this spectrum of research in information systems. Further, non-scientific papers and research work may not gain the respect of researchers in other areas within their academic institutions. This distorts information systems research and thereby limits the future usefulness of that research. Researchers are also handicapped by the lack of a dominant model or framework which has gained general acceptance and from which research efforts in the area can be evaluated.

An interesting review was carried out by Nissen (1986). This contains the result of a survey of members of IFIP who were interested in information systems research. The survey asked the question (amongst others): 'What are the boundaries of information systems research?' Many respondents did not wish to put any such boundaries on information systems research. Further, when asked whether information systems only referred to formal, fully predictable systems, about 90% responded that they disagreed whereas only about 5% agreed fully.

We find Nissen's conclusions significant:

'The variety in the answers and comments testifies to the variety of perspectives represented among the respondents',

and later

'Another striking feature has been the interest espoused by a number of respondents not to exclude parts of the information systems research field outside of their own current work'.

This view on research is paralleled by the themes found in the real world methodologies. Some of these are formal and mathematical, others social and humanistic, others organizational, others pragmatic and flexible, and yet others based on the bringing together of a number of these themes.

Although some research is carried out in departments within higher education institutions, other research is carried out in the outside world, partly by academics and partly by practitioners. Here, there is a close interaction between practice and theory, the researcher suggesting alternatives and evaluating the results of changes made in the problem situation so that there is a feedback process 'tuning' the theory. The practitioners can include all actors in the organization, not just management. This type of research is referred to as *action research*. In action research it is recognized that the researcher is not impartial. In scientific method there is an assumption that the researcher is impartial, but when the domain of concern is information systems which include human activities, viewpoints, and politics, then the notion of impartiality is less convincing.

Another very useful source of papers in information systems research is found in Boland and Hirschheim (1987). Lyytinen's paper in this text (Lyytinen 1987) argues that the development methodologies available have weaknesses which should be addressed:

They lack synergy with other information systems research areas — many information systems development methodologies have ignored research in related areas such as socio-technical design which, it is argued, have much to offer.

They have a limited scope — and Lyytinen uses the concentration on design, and the lack of regard to social impact, changes in work processes, goal-setting and analysis of assumptions, as support for his argument.

They have an inadequate conceptual base — such as a clear definition of an information system, its parts and purpose, and a conceptual base which could be derived from systems thinking.

They lack or have limited theoretical foundations — such as that considered necessary in other disciplines.

They are unaware of the philosophical underpinnings of systems development — Every methodology is underpinned by assumptions about the development of an information system, but these are frequently not stated nor analysed, and therefore their impact on the development practices are neither evaluated nor anticipated.

These are issues with which many researchers in the area are attempting to grapple. We comment further on these issues in the final chapter, and the reader may regard it appropriate to consider them when evaluating the various methodologies discussed. Many of the methodologies in this present text attempt to address some of these important issues.

Another major issue in research is that related to semantics. We rather tentatively gave definitions of terms such as *data, information, information system, method, technique, tool,* and *methodology* in the first chapter. We were aware that we were entering a minefield. Disputes regarding terminology frequently arise because of the different assumptions and perspectives of the protagonists. Sometimes the problem is the use of sales hyperbole, such as 'our methodology is effective, formal, and standard'. What is meant by these terms? Further, much of the terminology, such as *set, entity,* and *system,* is used by the research community in different ways to that of general usage (as well as inconsistently in the research community). Some of these issues are discussed in Stamper (1987).

Another useful source of research ideas is the series of Scandinavian research seminars on systemeering (the practice of systems ideas). The paper in the 1986 meeting in Lund by Vainio-Larsson (1986) suggests how *metaphors* may be used in a library system to ease the learning process. Metaphors provide a way of helping communication between users and technologists to which both sets of people can relate. At the time of writing, this possibility has aroused a great deal of interest and Madsen (1987) has proposed a set of guide-lines for incorporating metaphors into information systems methodologies.

Dumdum and Klein (1986) discuss failures in the application of information systems methodologies. This is usually ascribed to technical complexity, volatility of the organizational environment and unrealistic user expectations. Dumdum and Klein attribute failure to five other reasons which are summarized below:

- Information systems methodologies may attempt and succeed in solving problems, but they may create other problems, many of which are unforeseen.
- Information systems methodologies may have good analysis and design principles, but the application may be wrongly or inappropriately applied.
- Information systems methodologies cannot solve all the problems which are naturally inherent in systems and these problems will not go away, however good the analysis and design.
- Information systems methodologies may be applied in situations which do not need changing at the time and most methodologies will lead to changes of some sort even in these situations.
- Information systems methodologies may be applied by people in ignorance and/or disregard of the social, psychological and organizational aspects of systems.

Much of the research work, and hopefully much of this text, attempts to address some of these problems. However, we are convinced that though the research will continue, these problems will not be completely solved.

3.10 CONCLUSION

Over this chapter we have looked at a number of general themes of information systems methodologies. Each of the actual methodologies discussed in Chapter 6 is likely to have as its base one of these positions, but is likely also to have elements of many of the others. Some, for example Multiview, have attempted to incorporate features of each of these views. The techniques and tools in different approaches are not mutually exclusive, and Multiview is also representative of those methodologies that are referred to as *contingency approaches,* where the techniques and tools available are chosen and adjusted according to the particular problem situation.

It is sometimes argued that professional systems analysts should not rely too heavily on one approach. These approaches can be suitable in some organizations and not in others. Each organization is unique and radical solutions may only work, for example, if the political climate in the organization is conducive to change. There is, however, a contrary argument. This is that the use of one methodology imposes good standards for the organization and many of the advantages of using information systems methodologies will be sacrificed by too much flexibility.

Although some methodologies lean towards scientific method (the 'hard' systems movement), for example data analysis and structured analysis, it is impossible to prove that any solution is optimal. In fact analysts using the same method may well come up with very different solutions. This is not necessarily a criticism of the method, but it is a criticism of the view that there is only one appropriate solution. In any case, a sub-optimal technical solution may well be appropriate if this gains user acceptance. Alternative views ('soft' systems approaches) place emphasis on the human side of systems, but that is not to assert that there should be no 'method' and no techniques and tools applied.

In our survey of themes in information systems development, we have looked at generalized information systems methodologies. We have not addressed the question of special purpose methodologies such as those designed specifically for:

- office automation (see Hirschheim 1985b),
- real-time applications (see Yourdon 1975),
- microcomputer applications (see Avison 1986), nor
- knowledge-based systems (see Huuskonen *et al.* 1986).

Some methodologies emphasize techniques and tools. These can be very useful to understand and communicate, but methodologies are usually much more. They are also about people, tasks, skills, control and evaluation.

When each of the methodologies is discussed in Chapter 6, it might be useful to see how the methodology answers some of the criticisms aimed at the conventional approach to systems analysis which were described in section 3.3 and consider criticisms that have been levelled against some of the types of methodologies described such as:

'Alternatives to conventional systems analysis do not stress at least one of two important aspects stressed in the conventional approach: (1) an analysis of costs and benefits (in the feasibility study) enabling the proposed system to be judged on sound cost-effective principles, and (2) thorough and detailed documentation standards for communication, training, and so on'.

'Data analysis may not solve underlying problems that the organization might have. Indeed it may have captured the existing problems into the data model, and made them even more difficult to solve in the future.'

'In breaking down a system into manageable units and then even more manageable units, structured analysis offers a simplistic view of a complex system and fails to identify fully the importance of the links between systems.'

'Participation leads to inefficient systems designed by those who are good managers, clerks, or salesmen, but poor, and unwilling, systems analysts, and further, it is demotivating to people trained and experienced as 'true' systems analysts.'

'Systems theory represents an idealistic academics' position and is not relevant to the practitioner.'

'Prototyping is only concerned with the user interface and does not address the fundamental problems of systems *analysis*, it simply makes poor systems palatable to users'.

'All methodologies are designed to provide information systems, but do not solve the fundamental problems of management'.

We will return to this topic in the final chapter.

Chapter 4
Techniques

We have chosen to describe techniques in a separate chapter for two reasons: firstly, most are common to more than one methodology and therefore to leave them to the methodologies chapter would lead to repetition there, and secondly, so that the principles contained in the methodologies (Chapter 6) can be described without going into the techniques used in too much detail.

Although the techniques described are used in a number of methodologies, this does not mean that they are interchangeable, for they could address different parts of the development process, have different objectives, or are applicable to different objects. Broadly, the techniques can be divided into two categories, those that address data objects and those that address process objects.

Entity modelling and normalization are techniques for analysing data. Data flow diagrams, entity life cycles, decision trees, decision tables, structured English and action diagrams are all concerned with the analysis of processes. Of course these sometimes overlap. For example, when constructing data flow diagrams it is necessary to know what data is required to support a process, and this data is depicted in data stores. Nevertheless, the technique is primarily one for analysing processes, the data identified is simply a by-product. Similarly, entity modelling is primarily a data analysis technique despite the fact that it cannot be carried out without knowing something of the processes that exist.

Figure 4.1 shows the position or stage in the development process where the technique is utilized and whether it is primarily regarded as a data or process orientated technique. The asterisk indicates the stage or stages where it is most commonly utilized. For example, entity modelling is used at three stages but its use at the strategic stage is much less common than at the other stages.

The techniques sometimes differ considerably from methodology to methodology although in most cases the principle of the technique is common and it is the notations and conventions that differ. We describe each technique once only but note the variations that exist. Sometimes the use of different conventions, particularly in the diagrammatic techniques, can make the result look radically different. It is a good discipline to look beyond the conventions of a technique and try to identify the underlying principles involved.

Many of these techniques described, particularly the diagrammatic ones, relate to the documentation of the processes involved in developing an information system. These techniques of documentation can be used to

*   Major use
     Process logic (i.e. decision trees, decision tables, structured English and action diagrams)

STAGE	DATA	PROCESS
Strategy	Entity Modelling	
Analysis	Entity Modelling*	Data Flow Diagrams* Entity Life Cycle* Process Logic
Logical Design	Entity Modelling* Normalization	Data Flow Diagrams Entity Life Cycle Process Logic
Program/ Database Design	Normalization*	Process Logic*

Fig. 4.1. A classification of techniques

communicate the results achieved to other analysts, users and programmers. The techniques can also be used to help in the process of analysis and design and to verify that all the steps in the methodology have been carried out. One of the generally acknowledged advances in information systems development is the improvement that has resulted from the use of these techniques.

In addition, most of the techniques, in particular those operating at a high level, embody the principles of abstraction and generalization. This means that the issues or concepts of importance are brought out in the first level diagram and that the detail is ignored. For this to be effective, it is necessary that the right objects are depicted in the technique. In entity modelling, for example, the entities and their relationships are thought to be important and the attributes are regarded as a point of detail. Secondly, the emergence of the detail at the later stage must not invalidate the results of the earlier stage. This is not to say that iteration must not take place, iteration helps obtain the correct results, it means that the techniques must lead us to the things of importance amid the confusion of all the details. It is useful to consider techniques in this light when exploring them in this chapter.

4.1 ENTITY MODELLING

The theme of data analysis has been discussed in section 3.8. Data analysis concentrates on the analysis of data in organizations and entity modelling is a particular technique used to achieve this. Entity modelling originated as a technique of database design. However, it is now perceived as a more general analysis technique relevant to all types of information system.

Entity models are used in the methodologies SSADM, Information Engineering, and Multiview, and in many other methodologies not examined in this book such as D2S2 (Systems Development in a Shared Data Environment), described in Palmer and Rock-Evans (1981), which was a precursor of Information Engineering.

An entity model views the organization as sets of data elements, known as *entity types*, which are the 'things' of interest to the organization, and the relationships between these entity types (usually referred to as entities).

Each entity type is represented diagrammatically by *soft boxes* (rectangles with rounded corners). Soft boxes are used to indicate that the entity type is a logical concept rather than a physical one. Relationships between the entity types are shown by lines between the boxes. A first approach to an entity model for a university department is given in figure 4.2. The entity types are STUDENT, ACADEMIC STAFF, COURSE, and NON-ACADEMIC STAFF. The entity type STUDENT participates in a relationship with ACADEMIC STAFF and COURSE. These relationships are not named but it might be that STUDENT 'takes' COURSE and that STUDENT 'has as tutor' ACADEMIC STAFF. The reader will soon detect a number of important things of interest that have been omitted (room, examination, research, etc.). As the analysts find out more about the organization, entity types and relationships will be added to the model.

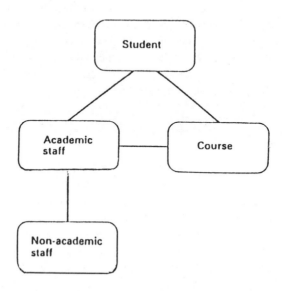

Fig. 4.2. Entity modelling — a first approach.

An entity type is a thing of interest and of importance to the organization, in other words it is almost anything that you want to define as such. It could include all the resources of the organization and it can be extended to cover such things as ORDER, INVOICE and PROFIT-CENTRE. It covers concepts as well as objects. It is not data itself, but something about which data could be kept. It is something that can have an independent existence. In creating an entity model, the aim should be to define entity types that enable one to realistically and effectively describe the organization. Such entity types as STOCK, ORDER and CUSTOMER are appropriate because they are quantifiable, whereas 'stock control', 'order processing' and 'credit control' are not appropriate, because they are functions, that is related to what the organization does, and not things of interest, which participate in functions. Entity types can be quantified — it is reasonable to ask 'how many customers?' or 'how many orders per day?', but *not* 'how many credit controls?' An *entity occurrence* is a particular instance of an entity type which can be uniquely identified. For example 'John Smith and Son' could be an occurrence of the entity type CUSTOMER. The term 'entity type' is often abbreviated to 'entity', but the term 'entity occurrence' should not be abbreviated. This convention is followed in this text.

An *attribute* is a descriptive value associated with an entity. It is a property of an entity. At a certain stage in the analysis it becomes necessary not only to define each entity, but also to record the relevant attributes for each entity. A CUSTOMER entity may be defined and it will have a number of attributes associated with it, such as 'number', 'name', 'address', and so on. The values of a set of attributes will distinguish one entity occurrence from another. Attributes are frequently identified during data analysis when entities are being identified, but most come later, particularly in detailed interviews with staff. Many are discovered when checking the entity model with users. An entity may be uniquely identified by one or more of its attributes, the *key attribute(s)*. A 'customer number' may identify an occurrence of the entity CUSTOMER. A 'customer number' and a 'product number' may together form the key of entity ORDER. Attributes are not usually recorded on the entity model itself, but they are listed separately as a supporting piece of documentation.

A relationship in an entity model normally represents an association between two entities. The entity SUPPLIER has a relationship with the PRODUCT entity through the relationship 'supplies', that is, SUPPLIER supplies PRODUCT. The next stage in the development of an entity model, having defined the entities and 'fleshed' out the entities with attributes, is to associate related entities by relationships. A relationship normally arises because of:

1 Association, for example CUSTOMER 'places' ORDER.
2 Structure, for example ORDER 'consists of' ORDER LINE.

The association between entities has to be meaningful, that is of importance and relevance to the business. The action 'places' describes the relationship between CUSTOMER and ORDER. The name given to the relationship also helps to make the model readable.

The degree of the relationship is usually defined in the model. This could be one-to-one, one-to-many, or many-to-many. A MEMBER OF PARLIAMENT can only represent one CONSTITUENCY, and one CONSTITUENCY can have only one MEMBER OF PARLIAMENT. This is an example of a one-to-one relationship. A one-to-one relationship is represented graphically by a line between the two entities (see figure 4.3(a)).

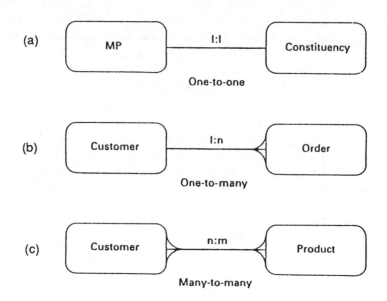

Fig. 4.3. Degrees of a relationship.

The relationship between an entity CUSTOMER and another entity ORDER is usually of a degree one-to-many (1:n). Each CUSTOMER can have a number of outstanding ORDERs, but an ORDER can refer to only one CUSTOMER. This is represented diagrammatically by having a line between the entities and a crow's foot at the 'many' end, that is to the ORDER in this example (figure 4.3(b)).

With a many-to-many (m:n) relationship, each entity can be related to one or more occurrences of the partner entity. A CUSTOMER can order many PRODUCTs; and one PRODUCT could be ordered by a number of CUSTOMERs. This will be represented diagrammatically by a line joining the CUSTOMER and PRODUCT entities with a crow's foot at both ends (figure 4.3(c)).

Sometimes a 1:m or an m:n relationship is a fixed degree relationship. The many-to-many relationship between the entity PARENT and the entity CHILD is 2:n and this may be written on the relationship line. Some relationships are optional relationships. An entity MALE and an entity FEMALE may be joined together by the optional relationship 'married to', this is usually represented by a dashed relationship line. A data relationship may be *involuted* where entity occurrences relate to other occurrences of the same entity. This can be shown diagrammatically by an involuted loop, as in figure 4.4. This can occur in the entity EMPLOYEE, where a 'manager' occurrence of the EMPLOYEE entity relates to a 'junior' occurrence of the employee entity by the relationship 'manages'.

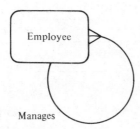

Fig. 4.4. An involuted relationship.

Figure 4.5 is an example of a more realistic entity model. It represents the chiropody service in a health centre. Although entity modelling is often said to be 'objective', the entity model that is built is a somewhat subjective model. It depends on the skills of the analysts and the views of the users and managers of what is important in that organization.

A good model is one that is a good representation of the organization or department or whatever is being depicted. The process of entity modelling is an iterative process and slowly the model will improve as a representation of the *perceived reality*. The entity model can be looked on as a discussion document and its coincidence with the real world is verified in discussions with the various users. However, the analyst should be aware that variances between the model and a particular user's view could be due to the narrow perception of that user. The model should be as far as possible, a global view. The size of that 'globe' could be a department, a number of departments, a company, or an organization. If a global entity model is built for a whole organization it is usual for entities to be grouped into important clusters, so that an overview can be obtained (see Feldman and Miller, 1986).

The process of entity modelling usually goes a stage further. The entity model is verified by looking at events and operations, for the entity model has to support the events that occur in the enterprise. Attributes are those elements which supply data to support the events. Consider the following example. 'Tom' is an occurrence of the entity EMPLOYEE. Tom's pay rise or

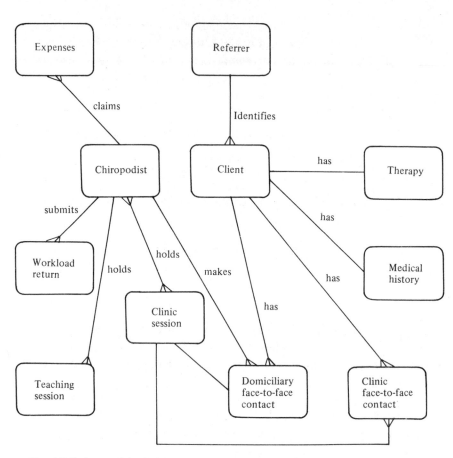

Fig. 4.5 Entity model of chiropody service.

his sacking are *events*, and attributes of the entity EMPLOYEE will be referred
to following these events. Attributes such as 'pay-to-date', 'tax-to-date',
'employment status', and 'salary' will be referred to. *Operations* on attributes
will be necessary following the event: an event triggers an operation or a
series of operations. An operation will change the state of the data. The
event 'Tom's salary increased by 10%' will require access to the entity
occurrence 'Tom' and augmenting the attribute, 'salary', by 10%. Figure 4.6
shows the entity EMPLOYEE expressed as a relation with attributes. It is
necessary to question whether the relation supports all the operations that
follow the event mentioned.

Employee

Employee

Empl. No.	Name	Status	Pay-to-date	Tax-to-date	Salary
756	Tom	Full	754.30	157.00	14000.00

Does the entity support the operations necessary following events?
  e.g. employee gets sacked
       employee gets a pay rise

Fig. 4.6. Event-driven (functional) analysis

It may at first seem confusing to discuss events, which are function-orientated concepts, when data analysis is supposed to be function-independent. The events and operations are of interest as a checking mechanism. They áre used to ensure that the entity model will support the functions (although events and operations are not depicted in the entity model diagram). This consideration of the events and operations may lead to a tuning of the model, an adjustment of the entities and the attributes.

Typically the phases in entity modelling are as follows:
- Define the area for analysis.
- Define the entities and relationships.
- Establish the key attribute(s) for each entity.
- Complete each entity with all the attributes, and
- Ensure all events and operations are supported by the model.

The first stage of entity analysis requires the definition of the area for analysis. Sometimes this will be the organization, but this is usually too large and ambitious for detailed study, and usually the organization will be divided into local areas for separate analysis.

For each local area, the entities are defined. The analyst will attempt to

name the fundamental things of interest to the organization. As the analyst is
gathering these entities, the relationships between the entities and their degree
can also be determined. The analyst will also give a name to the relationship
and begin to draw the entity model. The diagram will be like a doodle in the
beginning, but it will soon be useful as a communication tool. The key of
each entity will also be determined. The key attributes will uniquely identify
any entity occurrence.

It is often difficult to decide on what is an entity and what is an attribute.
If there is doubt over a particular item it is best to make it an entity at first
so that it does not get lost from the model and then if it ends up participating
in only one one-to-one relationship then it might better be defined as an
attribute. An example might be PRODUCT and PRICE. Should they be two
entities or should PRICE simply be an attribute of PRODUCT? An entity
should have attributes of its own. There may be occasions where PRICE is
defined as an entity, for example, where it is required to be defined in a
number of currencies. But this would be unusual, and in most organizations
'price' would be an attribute of PRODUCT.

A further example could be entity occurrences of persons who are female,
where they relate to (a) patients in a hospital (b) students at university and (c)
readers in a library. In the patient example, the fact that the person occurrence
is female is important, so important that the PATIENT entity may be split
into two separate entities — MALE PATIENT and FEMALE PATIENT. In the
student example, the fact that the person is female may not be of great
significance and therefore 'sex' could be an attribute of the entity PERSON. In
the reader example, the fact that the person is female may be of such
insignificance that it is not even included as an attribute. There is a danger
here, however, as the analyst must ensure that it will not be significant in
any current or future application in the library. This type of debate can only
be resolved when looking at the functions in some detail.

Sometimes there is useful information associated with many-to-many
relationships and it is better to split these into two one-to-many
relationships, with a third entity created to link these together. This should
only be done if the new entity has some meaning and relevance to the
organization in itself. The relationship between COURSE and LECTURER is
many-to-many, that is, one LECTURER lectures on many COURSEs and a
COURSE is given by many LECTURERs. But a new entity, MODULE, can be
described which may only be given by one LECTURER and is part of only one
COURSE. Thus a LECTURER gives a number of MODULEs and a COURSE
consists of a number of MODULEs. But one MODULE is given by only one

LECTURER and is part of only one COURSE. This is only a legitimate exercise if module is a concept that exists in the organization, otherwise it should be left as a many-to-many relationship. This example is shown in figure 4.7.

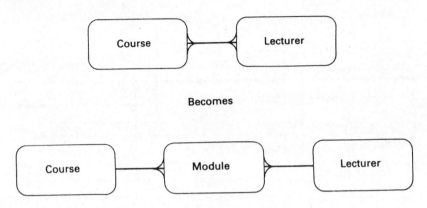

Fig. 4.7. Many-to-many relationship represented as two one-to-many relationships.

The analyst has now drawn the model in outline and is in a position to fill in the detail. This means establishing the attributes for each entity. Each attribute will say something about the entity. The analyst has to ensure that any synonyms and homonyms are detected. Synonyms are different words describing the same thing and homonyms are different things which are described by the same word. A product could be called a part, product or finished product depending on the department. These are all synonyms for 'product'. On the other hand, the term product may mean different things (homonyms), depending on the department. It could mean a final saleable item in the marketing department or a sub-assembly in the production department. These differences must be reconciled and recorded in the data dictionary. Ultimately any data element in the area of concern must be defined as an entity or an attribute.

The final stage of the approach will be to look at all the events within the area and the operations that need to be performed following an event, and ensure that the model supports these events and operations. We have already introduced this (see figure 4.6), and we will look into this aspect in more detail here. Events are frequently referred to as transactions. For this part of the technique, the analyst will identify the events associated with the organization and examine the operations necessary following each of the events.

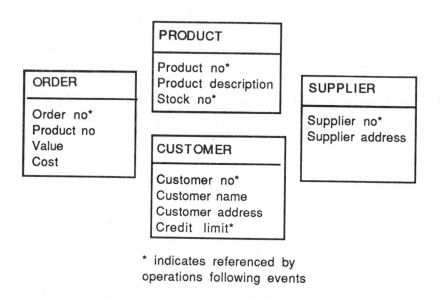

* indicates referenced by
operations following events

Fig. 4.8. Validating model through analysis of events.

Events in many organizations could include 'customer makes an order' and 'raw materials are purchased from supplier' and 'employee joins firm'. If, say, a customer makes an order, this event will be followed by a number of operations. The operations will be carried out in order to find out how much the order will cost, whether the product is in stock, and whether the customer's credit limit is satisfactory. The entities in the model such as PRODUCT (to look at the value of the attribute 'stock') and CUSTOMER (to look at the value of the attribute 'credit limit') must be examined (see figure 4.8). These attribute values will need to be adjusted following the event. It may be noticed that the 'product price' is not in either entity. To support the event, therefore, 'product price' should be included in the PRODUCT entity, or in another entity which is brought into the model.

The entity model is normally supported by documentation tools, to hold

ENTITY DOCUMENT

Form No. ··········	Entity name ·················	Date ········	Analyst ············
Aliases			

Description

Key		Size

Attributes

Relationships

Data dictionary name ·························	Privacy level ·················
Maximum No. of entries ··········	

Notes

Fig. 4.9. Entity documentation.

information on entities, attributes, and relationships. It is possible to obtain forms on which to specify all the elements of the data analysis process. It is also usual to document events and operations. Some sample forms are shown as figures 4.9, 4.10, 4.11, 4.12 and 4.13. It may be possible to use completed documents directly as input to a data dictionary system so that the data is held in a readily-accessible computer format as well as on paper forms. A description of data dictionaries is given in section 5.3.

Entity modelling is a communication tool as well as a modelling technique. The forms discussed help as an aid to memory, communication

ATTRIBUTE DOCUMENT

Form No.	Attribute name	Date	Analyst
··········	·····················	········	··········

Aliases

Description

Data dictionary name	No. of chars.	Type
·································	·········	························

Range	No. occurrences
·····························	·····························

Validation	Privacy level
	···································

Defined in entities

Notes

Fig. 4.10. Attribute documentation

with oneself, and the entity model is particularly useful, as a basis for communication with managers and users. They are usually readily understandable to non-computer people. They provide a pictorial description of the business in outline, showing what the business is, NOT what it does. Managers can give 'user feedback' to the data analysts and this will also help to tune the model and ensure its accuracy. A manager may point out that an attribute is missing from an entity, or that a relationship between entities is one-to-many and not one-to-one as implied by the entity diagram. Managers may not use this terminology, but the data analyst will be able to interpret

RELATIONSHIP DOCUMENT

Form No.	Relationship	Date	Analyst
....	....	....	....
Description			
Identifier			
Type			
Frequency			
Privacy level			
Notes			

Fig. 4.11. Relationship documentation.

their comments. Data analysis is an iterative process, the final model will not be obtained until after a number of tries and this should not be seen as slowness, but care for accuracy. If the entity model is inaccurate so will be the database and the applications that use it.

Each entity can be normalized to third normal form once the attributes have been added to the model. This process is described in section 4.2. The normalization process may well lead to an increase in the number of relations/entities in the model. At the end of the process, the entity model will show only the real data dependencies.

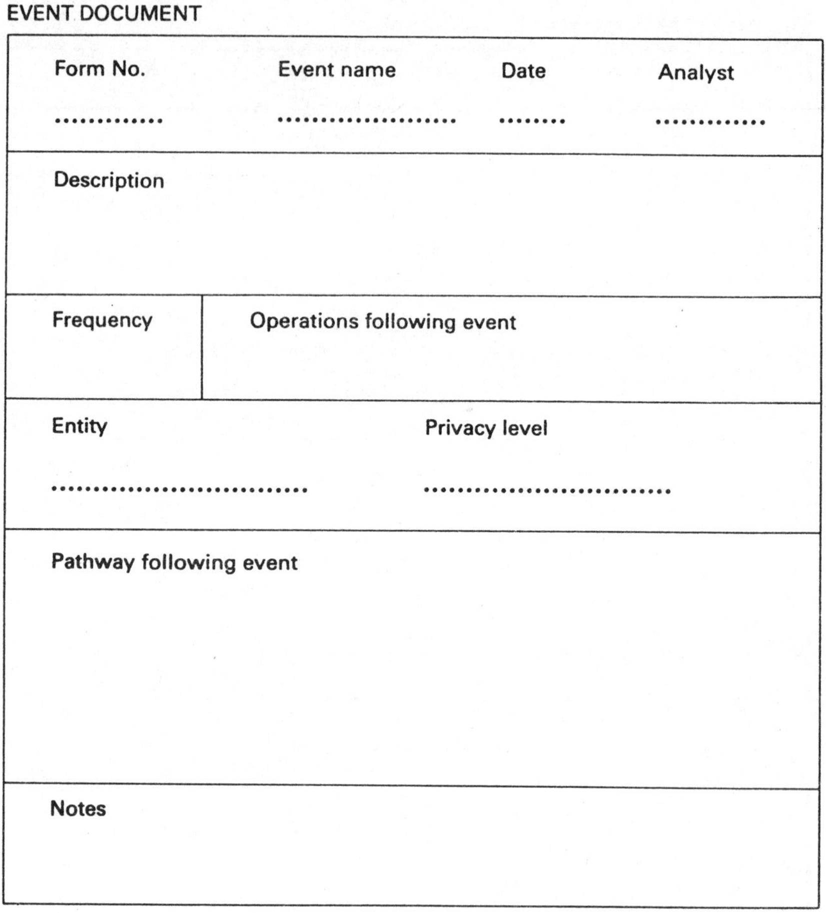

EVENT DOCUMENT

Form No.	Event name	Date	Analyst
....	....	....	....

Description

Frequency	Operations following event

Entity   Privacy level

....

Pathway following event

Notes

Fig. 4.12. Event documentation.

Entity modelling has proved very successful and is part of many systems development methodologies, as we shall see in Chapter 6, but it has been criticized. These criticisms have been highlighted by Rasmussen (1986) and include, for example, that entity modelling is not complete, in that there are some types of information which cannot be represented, particularly non-factual information, such as opinions. Further, entity modelling is not consistent, in that similar situations can be modelled in different ways. Different analysts may come to different conclusions on the 'entity or

OPERATION DOCUMENT

Form No.	Operation name	Date	Analyst
....	....	....	....

Description

Access key

Entities

Events

Response time

Frequency   Privacy level

Notes

Fig. 4.13. Operation documentation.

attribute' issue or on whether a concept is represented as one or two entity types. If decisions are arbitrary, it might lead to gross inefficiencies once the model is mapped onto a database.

There are different conventions used in entity modelling by different methodologies. Information Engineering (IE) uses square rather than round boxes to represent entities. The IE convention is that square boxes represent data and soft boxes represent functions. IE also uses a short bar across the relationship line to represent a mandatory relationship and a circle on the line to represent an optional relationship. Figure 4.14 shows an example of a one-to-one mandatory relationship to a one-to-many optional relationship between customer and order. This means that in the organization being modelled it is not necessary for a customer to have placed an order, that is, the relationship in this direction is *optional*. In the other direction the relationship is *mandatory*, that is, if an order exists there must be a relationship to a customer, there cannot exist an order not belonging to a customer.

Fig. 4.14. Information Engineering conventions.

Other methodologies use different conventions for representing the degree of the relationship, some use a single arrow to represent a one-to-one relationship and a double-headed arrow to represent a one-to-many relationship, see figure 4.15. However, many people argue that using arrows to represent relationships can easily be thought to represent flow, as in data flow diagrams, whereas there is no connotation of flow in entity models.

Fig. 4.15. Alternative conventions for entity diagrams.

A further variation on entity model conventions is specified by Chen (1976), it is termed the *Entity-Relationship* model, and it is a common representation in the United States. Here, the relationship line has a diamond box in the middle where the name of the relationship is written. The degree of the relationship is specified by figures 1 or *n* (see figure 4.16 for an example). Although this simply looks like another diagrammatic convention, in fact it also embodies a change in principle because Chen allows relationships to have their own attributes. This is not allowed in the entity modelling previously described where all attributes must be 'owned' by entities.

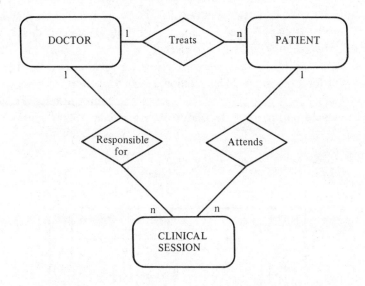

Fig. 4.16. Diagrammatic convention in Chen's entity model.

4.2 NORMALIZATION

Normalization is a technique which is used in a variety of methodologies. Of the methodologies examined in Chapter 6, it is used in Gane and Sarson (STRADIS), Information Engineering, SSADM, and Multiview. It is a technique that was originally developed by Codd (1970) as part of the development of relational theory and relational databases. However, the technique of normalization is applicable irrespective of whether a relational database is envisaged or not. It is often used in its own right as an analysis technique for the structuring of data, it can be used on its own or as a means of cross-checking or validating other models, particularly an entity model. In structured systems methodologies, for example Gane and Sarson, it is used to consolidate all the various data stores that have been identified in a data flow diagram into a coherent data structure.

Normalization is the process of transforming data into well formed or natural groupings such that one fact is in one place and that the correct relationships between facts exist. Normalized data is stable and a good foundation for any future growth. It is a mechanical process, indeed the technique has been automated, but the difficult part of it lies in understanding the meaning — that is the semantics — of the data, and this is only discovered by extensive and careful data analysis.

Normalization results in a set of relations. A relation is a flat file (see figure 4.17 for an example). This relation is called ORDER and it shows that Lee ordered 12 of 'part number' 25, Deene and Smith ordered 18 and 9 respectively of 'part number' 38, and Williams ordered 100 of 'part number' 87.

ORDER

NAME	PART	QUANTITY
LEE	25	12
DEENE	38	18
SMITH	38	9
WILLIAMS	87	100

Fig. 4.17. Relation 'ORDER'.

Each row in the relation is termed a *tuple* and each column is termed an *attribute*. The order of rows and columns is immaterial, and no two tuples can be identical in the relation. A relation will have a number of attributes, and in the ORDER relation, 'name', 'part' and 'quantity' are attributes. All items in a column come from the same domain — there are circumstances where the contents from two or more columns come from the same domain. The relation ELECTION RESULT shown in figure 4.18 illustrates this possibility. Two attributes come from the same domain of Political Parties. The number of attributes in a relation is called the degree of the relation. A relation with two attributes is known as a binary relation. The number of tuples in a relation defines its cardinality.

Each tuple is distinguished from another because one or more attributes in a relation are designated key attributes. In the ORDER relation, the key is 'name', and it is underlined in the column. It might be better to allocate numbers to customers in case there are duplicate names. Customer numbers will be unique. If the customer may make orders for a number of parts, then 'part' must also be a key attribute. 'Name' and 'part' will together make up the composite key of the ORDER relation. What is the key for the ELECTION RESULT relation (figure 4.18)? On first sight, 'election year' would seem appropriate, but there may be two elections in a year. Even if all three attributes were part of the key, this could still bring about duplicate relations as there could be two elections in the same year giving the same result. It is necessary to add another attribute or replace 'year' by 'election date' (there will not be two elections of the same type in the same day) to make each tuple unique. Alternatively the composite key 'election year' and 'election number in year' would be adequate. In some relations there may be more than one possible key. These are known as candidate keys. In this situation one of them is arbitrarily chosen to be the primary key.

ELECTION RESULT

ELECTION YEAR	FIRST PARTY	SECOND PARTY
1972	LABOUR	CONSERVATIVE
1974	LABOUR	CONSERVATIVE
1979	CONSERVATIVE	LABOUR
1983	CONSERVATIVE	LABOUR

Fig. 4.18. Relation 'ELECTION RESULT'.

The structure of the relation is conventionally expressed as shown in the following examples:

ORDER (name, part, quantity)

and

ELECTION-RESULT (elect-year, elect-number, first-party, second-party)

The process of normalization is the application of a number of rules to simplify the relations. The relations formed by the normalization process will make the data easier to understand and manipulate. As well as simplifying the relations, normalization also reduces anomalies which may otherwise occur when manipulating the relations in a relational database.

There are three stages of normalization:

First Normal Form
Ensure that all the attributes are atomic (that is, in the smallest possible components). This means that there is only one possible value for each domain and not a set of values. This is often expressed as the fact that relations must not contain repeating groups.

Second Normal Form
Ensure that all non-key attributes are functionally dependent on (give facts about) all of the key. If this is not the case, split off into a separate relation those attributes that are dependent on only part of the key.

Third Normal Form
Ensure that all non-key attributes are functionally independent of each other. If this is not the case, create new relations which do not show any non-key dependence.

The process of normalization is only made possible by an understanding of the real relationships in the organization, otherwise assumptions have to be made which may be incorrect. A rather flippant, but more memorable, definition of normalization can be given as 'the attributes in a relation must depend on the key, the whole key, and nothing but the key'. This is an oversimplification, but it is essentially true and could be kept in mind as normalization is developed.

A more detailed description of normalization is now given. A key concept is functional dependency. This is defined by Cardenas (1985) as follows:

'Given a relation R, the attribute B is said to be functionally dependent on attribute A if at every instant of time each value of A has no more than one value of B associated with it in the relation R.'

Functional dependency is frequently illustrated by an arrow. The arrow will point from A to B in the functional dependency illustrated in the definition. Thus, the value of A uniquely determines the value of B.

$$A \longrightarrow B$$

(a) COURSE-DETAIL

COURSE	C-NAME	LEVEL	MODULE	NAME	STATUS	UNIT-POINTS
B74	Comp.Sci.	B.Sc.	B741	Programming 1	Basic	8
			B742	Hardware 1		
			B743	Data Proc. 1	Int.	11
			B744	Programming 2		
			B745	Hardware 2	Adv.	15
B95	Comp.Apps.	M.Sc.	B951	Adv.Prog.		
			B952	Micros.		
			B741	Programming 1	Basic	8

(b) COURSE-DETAIL

COURSE	C-NAME	LEVEL	MODULE	NAME	STATUS	UNIT-POINTS
B74	Comp.Sci.	B.Sc.	B741	Programming 1	Basic	8
B74	Comp.Sci.	B.Sc.	B742	Hardware 1	Basic	8
B74	Comp.Sci.	B.Sc.	B743	Data Proc. 1	Basic	8
B74	Comp.Sci.	B.Sc.	B744	Programming 2	Int.	11
B74	Comp.Sci.	B.Sc.	B745	Hardware 2	Int.	11
B95	Comp.Apps.	M.Sc.	B951	Adv.Prog.	Adv.	15
B95	Comp.Apps.	M.Sc.	B952	Micros.	Adv.	15
B95	Comp.Apps.	M.Sc.	B741	Programming 1	Basic	8

Fig. 4.19. First normal form.

Before normalizing the first relation given as figure 4.19, it is necessary to analyse the meaning of the relation. Knowledge of the application area gained from data analysis will provide this information. It is possible to make assumptions about the inter-relationships between the data, but it is obviously better to base these assumptions on thorough analysis. In the relation COURSE-DETAIL, there are two occurrences of 'course', one numbered B74 called computer science at the BSc level and the other B75 called computer applications at the MSc level. Each of these course occurrences has a number of modules occurrences associated with it. Each 'module' is given a 'name', 'status' and 'unit-points' (which are allocated according to the status of the 'module').

First Normal Form: The first stage of normalization includes the filling in of details. This is seen in the example in figure 4.19 (a) and is a trivial task. You may note that in figure 4.19 (a), the order of the tuples in the unnormalized relation is significant. Otherwise the content of the attributes not completed cannot be known. As we have already stated, one of the principles of the relational model is that the order of the tuples should not be significant. The relation seen in figure 4.19 (b) could be in any order. First normal form really converts unnormalized data or traditional file structures into relations or tables.

The key of the relation of figure 4.19 (b) is 'course number' and 'module number' together (a composite key). This is because no single attribute will uniquely identify a tuple of this relation. There were in fact a number of possible candidate keys, for example, 'module name' and 'c-name', but we chose the primary key as above.

Further work would have been necessary if the following was presented as the unnormalized relation:

COURSE, C-NAME, LEVEL, MODULE-DETAILS

'Module-details' has to be defined as a set of atomic attributes, not as a group item, thus it has to be broken down into its constituents of 'module-name', 'status' and 'unit-points':

COURSE, C-NAME, LEVEL, MODULE-NAME, STATUS, UNIT-POINTS

will be the result in first normal form, with all the details filled out.

Second Normal Form: Second normal form is achieved if the relations are in first normal form and all non-key attributes are fully functionally dependent

(a) COURSE-MODULE

COURSE	MODULE	C-NAME	LEVEL
B74	B741	Comp.Sci.	B.Sc.
B74	B742	Comp.Sci.	B.Sc.
B74	B743	Comp.Sci.	B.Sc.
B74	B744	Comp.Sci.	B.Sc.
B74	B745	Comp.Sci.	B.Sc.
B95	B951	Comp.Apps.	M.Sc.
B95	B952	Comp.Apps.	M.Sc.
B95	B741	Comp.Apps.	M.Sc.

(b) MODULE

MODULE	NAME	STATUS	UNIT-POINTS
B741	Programming 1	Basic	8
B742	Hardware 1	Basic	8
B743	Data Proc. 1	Basic	8
B744	Programming 2	Int.	11
B745	Hardware 2	Int.	11
B751	Adv.Prog.	Adv.	15
B752	Micros.	Adv.	15

Fig. 4.20. Towards second normal form: course-module needs further normalization

on all the key. The relation COURSE-DETAIL shown in figure 4.19 (b) is in first normal form. However, the attributes 'status', 'name' and 'unit-points' are functionally dependent on 'module'. In other words, they represent facts about 'module', which is only part of the key. We may say that if the value of module is known, we can determine the value of 'status', 'name', and 'unit-points'. For example, if module is B743, then 'status' is basic, 'name' is Data Proc 1, and 'unit points' is 8. They are not dependent on the other part of the key, 'course'. So as to comply with the requirements of second normal form, two relations will be formed from the relation and this is shown as figure 4.20.

MODULE

MODULE	NAME	STATUS	UNIT-POINTS
B741	Programming 1	Basic	8
B742	Hardware 1	Basic	8
B743	Data Proc. 1	Basic	8
B744	Programming 2	Int.	11
B745	Hardware 2	Int.	11
B751	Adv.Prog.	Adv.	15
B752	Micros.	Adv.	15

COURSE- MODULE

COURSE	MODULE
B74	B741
B74	B742
B74	B743
B74	B744
B74	B745
B95	B951
B95	B952
B95	B741

COURSE

COURSE	C-NAME	LEVEL
B74	Comp.Sci.	B.Sc.
B95	Comp.Apps.	M.Sc.

Fig. 4.21. Second normal form.

But the relation COURSE-MODULE is still not in second normal form because the attributes 'c-name' and 'level' are functionally dependent on 'course' only, and not on the whole of the key. A separate COURSE relation has been created in figure 4.21. The COURSE relation has only two tuples

(a) COURSE-MODULE

COURSE	MODULE
B74	B741
B74	B742
B74	B743
B74	B744
B74	B745
B95	B951
B95	B952
B95	B741

(b) COURSE

COURSE	C-NAME	LEVEL
B74	Comp.Sci.	B.Sc.
B95	Comp.Apps.	M.Sc.

(c) MODULE

MODULE	NAME	STATUS
B741	Programming 1	Basic
B742	Hardware 1	Basic
B743	Data Proc. 1	Basic
B744	Programming 2	Int.
B745	Hardware 2	Int.
B951	Adv.Prog.	Adv.
B952	Micros.	Adv.

(d) STATUS

STATUS	UNIT-POINTS
Basic	8
Int.	11
Adv.	15

Fig. 4.22. Third normal form

(there are only two courses), and all duplicates are removed. Notice that we maintain the relation COURSE-MODULE. This relation is all key, and there is nothing incorrect in this. Attributes may possibly be added later which relate specifically to the course-module relationship. The relation is required because information will be lost by not including it, that is, the modules which are included in a particular course and the courses which include specific modules. The relations are now in second normal form.

Third Normal Form (TNF): Second normal form may cause problems where non-key attributes are functionally dependent on each other (a non-key attribute is dependent on another non-key attribute). This is resolved by converting the relations into TNF. In the relation MODULE, the attribute 'unit-points' is functionally dependent on the 'status' (or level) of the course, that is, given status, we know the value of unit-points. So unit-points is determined by status which is not a key. We therefore create a new relation STATUS and delete 'unit-points' from the relation MODULE. The third normal form is given in figure 4.22.

Sometimes the term transitive dependency is used in this context. The dependency of the attribute 'unit-points' is transitive (via 'status') and not wholly dependent on the key attribute 'module'. This transitive dependency should not exist in third normal form.

Codd developed three nested levels of normalization, and the third and final stage is known as TNF. It is this level of normalization that is usually used as the basis for the design of the data model, as an end result of data analysis. There are a few instances, however, when even TNF needs further simplification, and Kent (1983) and Date (1986) describe these extensions. TNF is usually satisfactory and the model is not developed further in this text.

Relations are normalized because unnormalized relations prove difficult to use. This can be illustrated if we try to insert, delete, and update information from the relations not in TNF. Say we have a new 'module' numbered B985 called Artificial Intelligence and which has a 'status' in the intermediate category. Looking at figure 4.19 (a), we cannot add this information in COURSE-DETAIL because there has been no allocation of this 'module' occurrence to any 'course'. Looking at figure 4.20 (b), it could be added to the MODULE relation, if we knew that the 'status' intermediate carried 11 unit-points. This information is not necessary in the MODULE relation seen in figure 4.19 (c), the TNF version of this relation. The TNF model is therefore much more convenient for adding this new information.

If we decided to introduce a new category in the 'status' attribute, called coursework, having a 'unit-points' attached of 10, we cannot add it to the relation MODULE (figure 4.20 (b)) because we have not decided which 'module' or modules to attach it to. But we can include this information in the TNF model by adding a tuple to the STATUS relation (figure 4.22 (d)).

Another problem occurs when updating. Let us say that we decide to change the 'unit-points' allocated to the Basic category of 'status' in the modules from 8 to 6, it becomes a simple matter in the TNF module. The single occurrence of the tuple with the key Basic, needs to be changed from (Basic 8) to (Basic 6), see figure 4.22 (d). With the unnormalized, first normal or second normal form relations, there will be a number of tuples to change. It means searching through every tuple of the relation COURSE-DETAIL (figure 4.19 (b)) or MODULE (figure 4.20 (b)) looking for 'status' = Basic and updating the associated 'unit-points'. All tuples have to be searched for, because in the relational model the order of the tuples is of no significance. We have ordered them in the text to make the normalization process easier to follow.

Deleting information will also cause problems. If it is decided to drop the B95 course, we may still wish to keep details of the modules which make up the course. Information about modules might be used at another time when designing another course. The information would be lost if we deleted the course B95 from COURSE-DETAIL (figure 4.19). The information about these modules will be retained in the MODULE relation in TNF. The TNF relation COURSE will now consist only of one tuple relating to the 'course' B74.

4.3 DATA FLOW DIAGRAMMING

The data flow diagram (DFD) is fundamental to structured systems methodologies and was developed as an integrated part of those methodologies. However the DFD has been adopted and adapted by a number of other methodologies, not all of the structured systems type, including Multiview and ISAC. In these methodologies the DFD or similar is not the major technique of the methodology but is used in conjunction with other techniques in the functional analysis process. The DFD is thus an important technique in a variety of systems development methodologies and deserves close examination.

The DFD provides the key means of achieving one of the most important requirements of structured systems, that is the notion of structure. The DFD enables a system to be partitioned (or structured) into independent units of a desirable size so that they, and thereby the system, can be more easily understood. In addition it is graphical and concise. The graphical aspect means it can be used both as a static piece of documentation and as a communication tool, enabling communication at all levels — between analyst and user, analyst and designer and analyst and analyst. The fact that the DFD has proved amenable to users means that it is easier to validate for correctness. Thus the probability of a better system resulting is increased. The graphical nature of the DFD also means a more concise document as it is argued that a picture can more quickly convey meaning than more traditional methods, such as textual narrative. The DFD also provides the ability to abstract to the level of detail required. Thus it is possible to examine a system in overview and at a detailed level, whilst maintaining the links and interfaces between the different levels.

The DFD also provides the analyst with the ability to specify a system at the *logical level*. This means that it describes what a system will do, rather than how it will be done. Considerations of a physical and implementation nature are not depicted and it is possible for the logical DFD to be mapped to a variety of different physical implementations. The benefit of this is that it separates the tasks of analysis (what is required) from design (how it is to be achieved). This separation means that the users can specify their requirements without any restrictions being imposed of a design nature, for example, the technology or the type of access method. There exists a logical and physical independence, the hardware can be changed or upgraded without changing the functions of the system. Alternatively, if as often happens a functional change is required, the relevant part of the logical specification is changed and a new mapping to the physical system is designed. The change is thus effected at the logical level, which is the correct place, and the implications of the change are agreed, and only then the necessary design changes made. This improves and speeds up the maintenance process, which currently is such a time and resource consuming activity.

There are a number of other techniques and tools closely associated with DFDs. These are data dictionaries, the process logic descriptions, and the data access diagrams. The data dictionary is the central place where all the details of data flows, data stores and processes are stored in an ordered and logical fashion. The dictionary may be manual or computerized but the important thing is that it must be the centralized resource of the structured analysis project. It is not the same thing as the data dictionary of a database which is concerned with physical aspects of the data, although the two may very well be integrated, and is considered as such in section 5.3.

The way in which process logic is described is by the use of decision trees, decision tables, structured English and action diagrams (described in sections 4.4, 4.5, 4.6 and 4.7). They are alternatives. A particular process is not described using all three techniques but by using whichever is the most appropriate, given the characteristics of the process concerned. Thus each technique has particular strengths and weaknesses. In general however they all provide simple, clear and unambiguous ways of describing the logic of what happens in a particular process.

The data access diagram, called the data immediate access diagram in Gane and Sarson (1979), is a way of depicting the kinds of access that users want to make to a particular set of data. It ensures that this information is captured at the analysis stage and that enough information is provided to the designer so that file and database structures can be designed to provide the kind of access the users want. It also enables trade off decisions to be made between costs of provision and degree of need. The form of the data access diagram differs quite considerably between the various methodologies.

In this section we concentrate on DFDs. The form of DFDs differ between the various proponents of structured systems analysis. The differences are relatively small and the basic concepts are the same. However the symbol used to represent a process differs, Gane and Sarson (1979) use a rectangle with rounded corners (a 'soft box') whereas most other authors use a circle. This means that superficially the DFDs look different but in practice the differences are relatively minor.

A logical DFD represents logical information not the physical aspects. A data flow specifies *what* flows, for example, customer credit details. *How* it flows, for example, by carrier pigeon or via twisted copper wires, is immaterial and not represented in a DFD. A DFD is a graphical representation and is composed of four elements:

The data flow: Data flow is represented by an arrow and depicts the fact that some data is flowing or moving from one process to another. A number of analogies are commonly used to illustrate this. Gane and Sarson suggest that we think of the arrow as a pipeline down which 'parcels' of data are sent, Page-Jones (1980) states that data flow is like a conveyor belt in a factory which takes data from one 'worker' to another. Each 'worker' then performs some process on that data which may result in another data flow on the conveyor belt. These processes are the second element of the DFD.

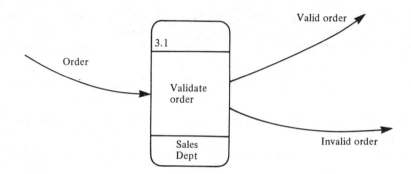

Fig. 4.23. Process box.

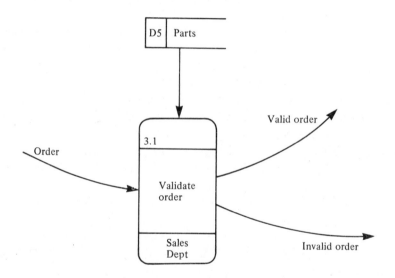

Fig. 4.24. Data store.

The processes: The processes or tasks performed on the data flows are represented in this example by a soft box (see figure 4.23). The process transforms the data flow by either changing the structure of the data or by generating new information from the data. A process might be 'validate order', this has transformed the order data flow by adding new information to the order — whether it is valid or not. It is likely that invalid orders flow out from the validation process in a different direction to valid orders. In this example the conventions used for the process symbol are as follows. The top compartment contains a reference number for the process, the middle compartment contains the description of the process, and the lower compartment indicates where the process occurs.

A process must have at least one data flow coming into it and at least one leaving it. There is no concept of a process without data flows, a process cannot exist independently.

The data store: If a process cannot terminate a data flow because it must output something, then where do the data flows stop? There are two places. The first is the data store, which can be envisaged as a file, although it is not necessarily a computer file or even a manual record in a filing cabinet. It can be a very temporary repository of data, for example, a shopping list or a transaction record. A data store symbol is a pair of parallel lines with one end closed and a compartment for a reference code and a compartment for the name of the data store. For example (see figure 4.24) the process of validating the order may need to make reference to the parts data store to see if the parts specified on the order are valid parts with the correct current price associated with it. The data flow in this example has the arrow pointing towards the process which indicates that the data store is only referenced by the process and not updated or changed in any way. In this example we would expect to find another process somewhere on the DFD which maintained the parts data store. For example, in figure 4.26, if the arrow points to the data store this indicates new information is being added to the store. The manner in which the access to the data store is made is usually regarded as irrelevant. However, it may be information which a designer needs, and therefore in cases where it is not obvious this information *may* be added to the DFD. In the example (figure 4.24) it may be assumed that access to the parts file is via the part number, however if a customer makes an order without specifying the part number flexible access via the part description may be required. This should then be specified (see figure 4.25).

The source or sink (External Entity): The second way of terminating a data flow in a system is by directing the flow to a sink. The sink may, for example, be a customer to whom we send a delivery note. The customer is a sink in the sense that the data flow does not necessarily continue. The customer is a sink down which the delivery note may fall forever. The Inland Revenue may be a sink to which a company may legally be required to provide information but never receive any in return. Sinks are usually entities that are external to the organization in question, although they need not be, another department may be a sink. It depends on where the boundaries of the

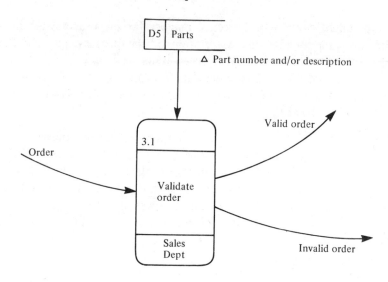

Fig. 4.25. Data store.

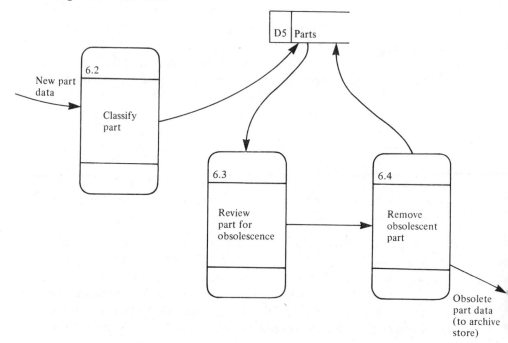

Fig. 4.26. Maintenance of parts data store.

system under consideration are drawn. If a DFD for the sales department is being constructed, any data flows to the production department would be represented as a sink. However, if the whole organization were being depicted, then the same data flows would go to a process within the production department. The original source of a data flow is the opposite to a sink, although it may be the same entity. For example, a customer is the source of an order and a sink for a despatch note. Sinks and sources, are represented by the same symbol which is a rectangle (see for example figure 4.27). Sources and sinks are often termed 'external entities'. Figure 4.28 is an example of a data flow diagram that illustrates the combination of the four elements discussed above.

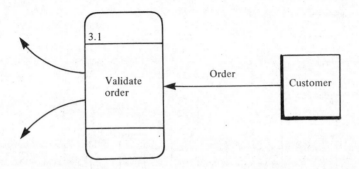

Fig. 4.27. External entity customer (source of order).

One of the most important features of the DFD is the ability to construct a variety of levels of DFD according to the level of abstraction required. This means that an overview diagram can be consulted in order to obtain a high level (overview) understanding of the system. When a particular area of interest has been identified, then this area can be examined at a more detailed level. The different levels of diagram must be consistent with each other so that the data flows present on the higher levels should exist on the lower levels as well. In essence it is the processes which are expanded at a greater level of detail as we move down the levels of diagram. This 'levelling' process gives the DFD its top-down characteristic.

If figure 4.28 is examined we may require more detail of any of the processes on the diagram. Figure 4.29 is the next level down (or an

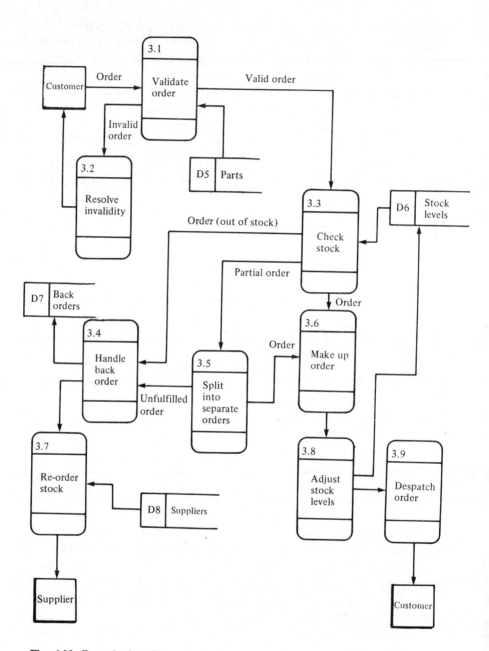

Fig. 4.28. Example data flow diagram.

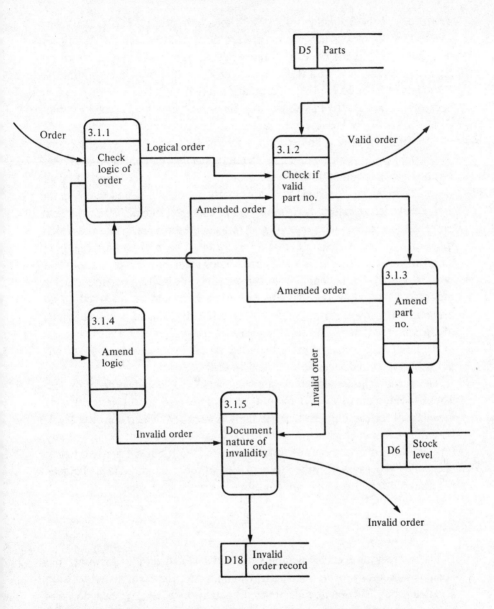

Fig. 4.29. Lower level of detail for 'Validate order' process. (Reproduced from course material from the Warwick University Distance Learning MBA by kind permission of Wolsey Hall, Oxford.)

explosion) of the Validate Order task. The overall process is expanded into five tasks with various data flows between them. However all the data flows in and out of Validate Order (reference 3.1) in figure 4.28 can be found on figure 4.29. The new data flows are either flows that only exist within the Validate Order process, that is they are internal to it and are now shown because we have split this down into separate components (for example, Amended Order), or because they are concerned with errors and exceptions.

The details of errors and exceptions are not shown on high level diagrams as it would confuse the picture with detail that is not required at an overview level. What is required at an overview level is 'normal' processing and data flows. To include errors and exceptions might double the size of the diagram and remove its overview characteristics. For example, figure 4.29 shows new processing concerned with amending an order and even a new data store which did not appear on the higher level diagram. The problem is that it is sometimes difficult to decide what constitutes an error or an exception, and what is normal. Some common guidelines suggest that if an occurrence of a process or data flow is relatively rare, then it should be regarded as an exception. However, if it is financially significant, it should be taken as part of normal processing. Overall, it depends on the audience or use to be made of the DFD as to exactly what is included. At the lowest level, all the detail, including errors and exceptions, should be shown.

The question arises as to how many levels a DFD should be decomposed. The answer is that a DFD should be decomposed to the level that is meaningful for the purpose that the DFD is required. There comes a level, however, when each process is elementary and cannot be decomposed any further. No further internal data flows can be identified. At this point each elementary process is described using a form of process logic. The techniques of representing process logic are described in the next four sections.

4.4 DECISION TREES

Decision trees and decision tables are tools which aim to facilitate the documentation of process logic, particularly where there are many decision alternatives. A decision tree illustrates the actions to be taken at each decision point. Each condition will determine the particular branch to be followed. At the end of each branch there will either be the action to be taken or further decision points. Any number of decision points can be represented, though the greater the complexity, then the more difficult the set of rules will be to follow.

When constructing a decision tree, the problem must be stated in terms of conditions (possible alternative situations) and actions (things to do). It is often convenient to follow a stepwise refinement process when constructing the tree, breaking up the largest condition to basic conditions, until the complete tree is formulated.

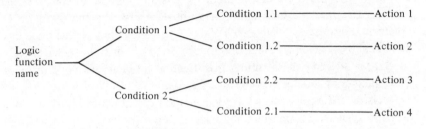

Fig. 4.30. General format of decision tree.

The general format is shown in figure 4.30. An example of a decision tree is given in figure 4.31. At the first decision point, the customer is classified into one of two types, private or trade. If the customer is trade, then a second decision point is reached. Has the customer been trading with us for less than five years or five years or more? If the customer has been trading for five

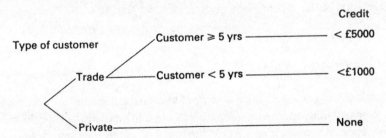

Fig. 4.31. Example of a decision tree.

years or more, then the customer can obtain up to £5 000 credit, otherwise only up to £1 000 credit can be given. If the customer was deemed private at the first decision point, then the action is to offer no credit at all.

Decision trees are constructed by first identifying the conditions, actions, and unless/however/but structures from a narrative statement (or direct from users) of the situation being analysed. Each sentence may form a 'mini' decision tree and these could be joined together to form the version which will be verified by the users. Sometimes it is not possible to complete the decision tree because information has not been given in the narrative or statement. For example, one branch of the decision tree may be identified, but no indication is given on the action to take on this branch. In such cases the analyst has to carry out a further investigation by interviewing staff or by using another method of systems investigation.

Decision trees prove to be a good method of showing the basics of a decision, that is, the possible actions that might be taken at a particular decision point and the set of values that leads to each of these actions. It is easy for the user to verify whether the analyst has understood the procedures.

Sometimes it is possible to associate probability scores for each branch once the decision tree is drawn. With this information it will be possible to compute expected values of the various outcomes and hence to evaluate alternative strategies. For example, in figure 4.31, research may have indicated that trade customers outnumber private customers by 5:1 and that 90% of trade customers are less than five years' standing. By extrapolating these figures with the total number of customers, it will be possible to evaluate the amount of total credit made available to customers. A full description of this technique is given in Crowe and Avison (1980, pp. 171-3).

4.5 DECISION TABLES

These are less graphical, when compared to decision trees, but are concise and have an in-built verification mechanism so that it is possible to check that all the conditions have been catered for. Again, conditions and actions are analysed from the problem situation. Decision tables can be used as computer input, programs being produced directly from them, and there are a number of packages available for this purpose.

When constructing a decision table, the various actions to be executed are listed in the bottom left hand part of the table known as the *action stub*. In the top left-hand part, the conditions that can arise are listed in the *condition stub*. Each condition is expressed as a question to which the answer will be 'yes' or 'no'. All the possible combinations of yes and no responses can be recorded in the upper right-hand part of the table. Each possible combination of responses is known as a *rule*. In the corresponding parts of the lower right-hand quadrant, an X is placed for each action to be taken, depending on the rule of that column.

Figure 4.32 shows the decisions that have to be made by drivers in the UK at traffic lights. The condition stub (upper left quadrant) has all the possible conditions 'red', 'amber' and 'green'. Condition Entries (upper right quadrant) are either Y for yes (this condition is satisfied) or N for no (this condition is

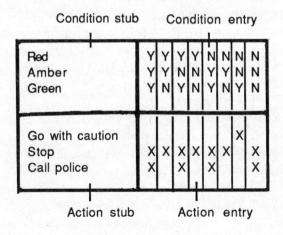

Fig. 4.32. Decision table: UK traffic lights.

not satisfied). Having three conditions, there will be 2 to the power of 3 (2 x 2 x 2 = 8) columns. The easiest way of proceeding is to have the first row in the condition entry as YYYYNNNN, the second row as YYNNYYNN and the final row as YNYNYNYN. If there were four conditions, we would start with eight Ys and eight Ns and so on, giving a total of 2^4 (2 x 2 x 2 x 2 = 16) columns.

All the possible actions are listed in a concise narrative form in the Action Stub (bottom left). An X placed on a row/column coincidence in the Action Entry means that the action in the condition stub should be taken. A blank will mean that the action should not be taken. Thus, if a driver is faced with Red (Y), Amber (Y) and Green (Y), the first column indicates that the driver should stop and call the police (a particular combination of conditions may lead to a number of actions to be taken). All combinations, even invalid ones, should be considered. The next column Red (Y), Amber (Y) and Green (N) informs the driver to stop. Only the Red (N), Amber (N) and Green (Y) combination permits the driver to go with caution.

Once the table is completed, rules which result in the same actions can be joined together and represented by dashes, that is, 'it does not matter'.The result of this is a *consolidated* decision table. Figures 4.33 and 4.34 illustrate an example decision table before and after the consolidation process. In the decision table (figure 4.34), rules (columns) 3 and 4 of decision table seen in figure 4.33 have been merged into a consolidated rule 3, expressing a 'don't care' condition in relation to new customer. This is because the same process needs to be executed whether or not condition 3 is 'yes' or 'no'. This reduces the example table by only one column, but in larger decision tables it may be possible to consolidate many columns.

In systems analysis, there are likely to be requirements to specify actions where there are a large number of conditions. A set of decision tables is appropriate here. The first will have actions such as 'GO TO Decision Table 2' or 'GO TO Decision Table 3'. Each of these may themselves be reduced to a further level of decision tables. The technique therefore lends itself to functional decomposition.

Sometimes the values of conditions are not restricted to 'yes' or 'no', as defined in the limited entry tables described. There can be more than two possible entries, and extended entry tables are appropriate. For example, the credit allowable to a customer could vary according to whether the customer had been dealing with the firm for 'up to 5 years', 'over 5 and up to 10 years', 'over 10 and up to 15 years', and so on. The rule for obtaining the right number of combinations will need to be modified. If condition 1 has two possibilities and condition 2 five possibilities, then the number of columns will be 2 x 5, that is, ten columns.

Invoice > £300	Y	Y	Y	Y	N	N	N	N
Account Overdue by > 3 months	Y	Y	N	N	Y	Y	N	N
New Customer	Y	N	Y	N	Y	N	Y	N
Inform Solicitor	X		X	X	X			X
Write First Reminder Letter		X	X	X	X			X
Write Second Reminder Letter					X			
Cancel Credit Limit			X	X		X	X	

Fig. 4.33. Example decision table.

Invoice > £300	Y	Y	Y	N	N	N	N
Account Overdue by > 3 months	Y	Y	N	Y	Y	N	N
New Customer	Y	N	-	Y	N	Y	N
Inform Solicitor	X		X	X			X
Write First Reminder Letter		X	X	X			X
Write Second Reminder Letter				X			
Cancel Credit Limit			X		X	X	

Fig. 4.34. Example consolidated decision table.

Whereas decision *trees* are particularly appropriate where the number of actions is small (although it is possible to have large decision trees), decision *tables* are more appropriate where there is a large number of actions as they can be decomposed into sets conveniently, in other words decision tables can better handle complexity. However, decision trees are easy to construct and give an easily assimilated graphical account of the decision structure. Decision tables have good validation procedures and, further, can be used to generate computer programs which carry out the actions according to the rules. Here the processing is specified by the analyst in terms of decision tables. These are transferred to computer readable format, and the programs generated automatically.

4.6 STRUCTURED ENGLISH

Structured English is very like a 'readable' computer program, it aims to produce unambiguous logic which is easy to understand and not open to misinterpretation. It is not English, which is ambiguous and therefore unsuitable. Nor is it a programming language, though it can be readily converted to a computer program. It is a strict and logical form of English and the constructs reflect structured programming. It is a useful technique to express logic in a system, though the decision tree or decision table are more suitable tools where the system has many decision points.

CREDIT RATING POLICY

IF the customer is a trade customer
    and IF the customer is customer for 5 or more years
        THEN credit is accepted up to £5000
    ELSE credit is accepted up to £1000
  ELSE (the customer is a private customer)
    SO no credit is given

Fig. 4.35. An example of structured English.

Structured English is a precise way of specifying a process, and is readily understandable by the systems designer as well as being readily converted to a program. It is appropriate to use structured English where sets of operations may be repeated a number of times for certain conditions. An example is given in figure 4.35. Structured English uses only a limited subset of English and this vocabulary is exact. This ensures less ambiguity in the use of 'English' by the analyst. Further, by the use of text indentation, the logic of the process can be shown more easily. (As with all these techniques, however, though the logic can be formally expressed, there is no guarantee that the expression in structured English is correct. That will depend on the investigation in the first place.)

Structured English has an:

> IF condition 1 (is true)
> > THEN action 2 (is to be carried out)
> ELSE (not condition 1)
> > SO action 1 (to be carried out)

construct. Conditions can include equal, not equal, greater than, less than, and so on. The words in capitals are keywords in structured English and have an unambiguous meaning in this context. They include SO, REPEAT and UNTIL, as well as the aforementioned IF, THEN and ELSE keywords. The logic of a structured English construct is expressed as a combination of sequential, decision, case and repetition structures.

Functional decomposition can be supported in structured English by an:

> IF condition
> > THEN do a named set of operations
> > (specified at a lower level)

type construct.

In structured English any logical specification can be written using the four basic structures of :

Sequencing, shows the order of processing of a group of instructions, but has no repetition or branching built into it.

Selection, through the decision process facilitates the choice of those conditions where a particular action or set of actions (or another decision and selection) are to be carried out.

Sequencing:	Statement-1	
	Statement-2	
		Statement-2-1
		Statement-2-2
		Statement-2-3
	Statement-3	
	—	
	—	
	—	
	—	
	Statement-n	

Selection:	IF Condition
	THEN Statements
	ELSE (not condition)
	SO Statements

Repetition:	REPEAT	
		Statements
	UNTIL	
		Condition

Case:	CASE Expression		
	OF	Condition-1 :	Statements
		Condition-2 :	Statements
		—	
		—	
		—	
		—	
		Condition-n :	Statements
		OTHERWISE :	Statements
	ENDCASE		

Fig. 4.36. Structured English — sequencing, selection, repetition and case.

Cases, represent a special type of decision structure (a special kind of selection), where there are several possibilities, but they never occur in combination. In other words, they are mutually exclusive.

Repetition, or loop instructions, facilitate the same action or set of actions to be carried out a number of times, depending on a conditional statement.

The layout of structured English is as follows:

The use of capital letters indicates a structured English keyword such as IF, THEN or ELSE;

Indentation is used to indicate blocks of sequential instructions to be created together, and hierarchical structures can be built by indenting these blocks;

Blocks of instructions can be named and this name quoted in capital letters to refer to the block of instructions elsewhere in the code; and

Any data elements which are included in a data dictionary are normally underlined.

DeMarco (1978) discusses structured English at length and he argues that though there are many advantages of its use, in particular its ability to describe many aspects of analysis, its conciseness, precision and readability, and the speed with which it can be written, there are disadvantages as well. DeMarco highlights the time it takes to build up skills in its use and the fact that it is alien to many users (despite being English-like). Indeed, this aspect might be misleading to users, because the structured English meanings are not exactly the same as their natural language counterparts.

There are alternative languages to structured English such as 'pseudo code', and 'tight English'. These vary on their nearness to the machine or readability to users. For example, pseudo code has a DO-WHILE and END-DO loop structure which is similar to constructs of some conventional programming languages, and is obviously more programming-orientated than structured English. Tight English code can be interpreted by computer programs. When there are a number of decision points, in tight English it is usual to resort to a decision table or decision tree.

4.7 ACTION DIAGRAMS

Action diagrams are also ways of representing the details of process logic and are not dissimilar to structured English. They are designed to represent the detail and the overview levels of a system. Action diagrams were developed by James Martin and Carma McClure (see Martin and McClure 1983 and 1985) and are used in a number of methodologies including Information Engineering.

People have sometimes commented when seeing an action diagram for the first time that 'it doesn't look much like my idea of a diagram', and it has to be said that, compared to a data flow diagram or an entity model, it is rather lacking in diagrammatic features, such as boxes and circles. However, the basic construct of an action diagram is a bracket, which is diagrammatic. A bracket surrounds a group of actions. Actions are broadly defined, and can be parts of program code, a subroutine, a program itself, an operation, a procedure or, at the highest level, a function.

The bracket indicates control. The actions within the bracket are performed in linear sequence like a program, and the brackets may be nested to indicate hierarchical structure.

```
┌─ Admit a student
│
│     Review application
│     Interview student
│     Make decision
│     Communicate decision
└─
```

Fig. 4.37. Action diagram for 'Admit a student'

Figure 4.37 represents the things that have to be done in the function 'admit a student'.

```
┌─ IF AGE > 60
│
│     MOVE 'AGE ALLOWANCE' TO STATUS
│     MOVE AGEIND TO CODE
├─ ELSE
│     MOVE 'STANDARD' TO STATUS
│     MOVE STAIND TO CODE
└──
```

Fig. 4.38. Action diagram illustrating IF....ELSE constructs

Action diagrams support the structured programming constructs of condition, case, repetition, do...while, and do...until. Figure 4.38 shows an action diagram for a part of a program and illustrates the use of an ELSE part of a condition. If there is more than one dash in the bracket this indicates that these parts are mutually exclusive, that is, it represents the CASE structure of structured English. The execution of a loop is indicated by a double dash at the top of the bracket and a thicker than normal line for the bracket. Figure 4.39 illustrates some repeated actions, the arrow indicates a next iteration construct, that is, in certain circumstances skip the remaining actions and go to the next student. The arrow can also be used to indicate an escape from this bracket completely, if it points not to the bracket itself but goes through the bracket to point to an earlier bracket in a nested set.

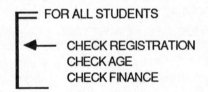

Fig. 4.39. Action diagram — repeated actions.

Do...while and do...until are handled as illustrated in figure 4.40.

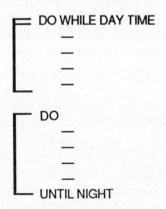

Fig. 4.40. Action diagram — DO loops.

Although brackets indicate sequences of actions, the technique can be used to show the notion of currency. Figure 4.41 illustrates concurrency, the link indicates that the actions in the two brackets can be performed in parallel.

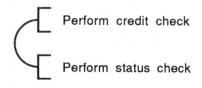

Fig. 4.41. Action diagram-concurrency.

Figure 4.42 extends figure 4.39 and shows a number of the constructs of action diagramming in use.

Many argue that action diagrams are easy to construct and utilize, both by analysts and users. As well as being able to represent and communicate logic in the traditional systems development process, they are also advocated as being useful to end-users when developing their own systems using Fourth Generation Languages and also by information centre staff when working with users. (An information centre provides a source of help (mainly technical) to users developing their own systems.) A particular benefit of using action diagrams is that it is possible to use the same technique for representing high level functions right through to low level process logic.

In order to increase their applicability, action diagrams have been extended in two ways. Firstly, so that the data required for each function or process can be identified, inputs and outputs are added to the diagrams. This requires the brackets to be extended to form a box with the required inputs for the action added to the top right-hand side and the outputs that the action produces added at the bottom right-hand side. Figure 4.43 provides a simple example.

The second extension to action diagrams is to accommodate the fact that actions often need to relate to database operations. The database operations of create, read, update and delete are added to the action diagram conventions and the name of the record that the operation refers to is enclosed in a box. These database operations relate to a single occurrence of the record, more complex operations relate to many occurrences and/or more than one record type, and these are represented by a double box. Searching or sorting, or, in relational

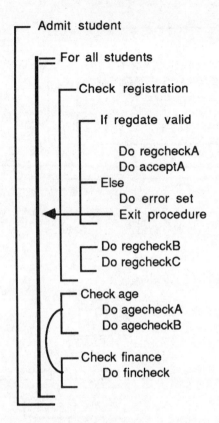

Fig. 4.42. Action diagram with a number of constructs.

environments, select and join, are examples of complex or compound database operations.

Figure 4.44 shows an example of an action diagram using the database conventions. Student records are read and processed a single occurrence at a time, 'read student' is only a single box. If we find an error, we wish to find the corresponding registration record and search the registration file. Thus 'registration' is in a double box.

4.8 ENTITY LIFE CYCLE

The technique of entity life cycle analysis is also common to a number of

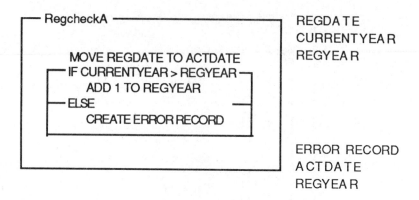

Fig. 4.43. Action diagram including inputs and outputs

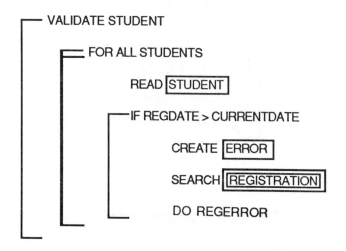

Fig. 4.44. Action diagram incorporating database operations.

methodologies. The technique varies slightly from methodology to methodology and is called by different names, but in essence what is being achieved is substantially the same. The entity life cycle is used at a variety of stages in a methodology and is one of the few attempts to address changes that happen over time in a system (most of the other techniques represent static views of a system).

The entity life cycle is *not*, despite its name, a technique of data analysis, but more a technique of functional analysis. This is because the things that cause the state of the entity to change are functions and events, and it is these changes that are being analysed. The objective of entity life cycle analysis is to identify the various possible states that an entity can legitimately be in. The sub-objectives, or by-products, of entity life cycle analysis are to identify the functions in which the entity type is involved and to discover any functions that have not been identified elsewhere. It may also identify valid (and invalid) sequences of functions, not identified previously, and it can form the outline design for transaction processing systems. Thus, as well as being a useful analysis technique in its own right, it is a useful exercise to perform as a validation of other function analysis techniques.

The documentation of the states of an entity in a diagram is one of the most powerful features of entity life cycle analysis. The diagram provides a pictorial way of communication that enables users to easily validate the accuracy or otherwise of the analysis.

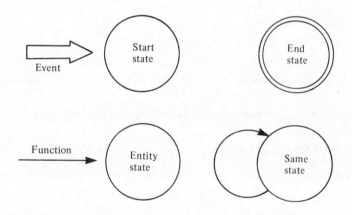

Fig. 4.45. Entity life cycle symbols.

The documentation conventions differ from methodology to methodology but the concepts are fairly consistent. In the following example the conventions used in D2S2, a precursor of Information Engineering, are used. Figure 4.45 shows the different symbols used and figure 4.46 shows a simplified example of an entity life cycle for the entity 'student' in the context of a university environment. There is always a starting point, usually an event, which sets the entity into its initial state. There is always (or

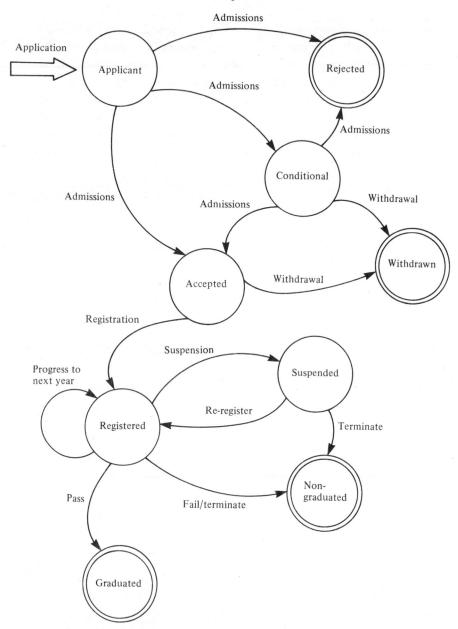

Fig. 4.46. Entity life cycle for the entity student.

should always be) an end or terminating point to finish the life cycle. In between, there may be many different states of the entity.

In the example, the initial state of the entity is as 'applicant'. This is triggered by an event, which in the example is the receipt of an application. The entity changes state as a result of the admissions function which either causes the applicant to be rejected, conditionally accepted (which means that the applicant is accepted provided certain examination grades will be achieved) or unconditionally accepted. The resultant entity states are rejected, conditional or accepted. At any time, conditional or accepted applicants may withdraw their applications.

The accepted applicants start their courses and become registered. They may or may not graduate. Registered students may suspend their registration for a wide variety of reasons at any time, and may either return as registered or terminate as non-graduated. It should be noted that a function can be depicted that does not change the state of the entity. In this case the arrow points back to the same entity state. 'Progress to next year' is an example of this, it is a function that does not change the state of the entity, the student is still registered. Conditional applicants are eventually either accepted or rejected.

In this example there are a number of terminated states, some conventions suggest that there should only be one. In this case we would simply add an extra state, called, for example, archived, and draw arrows from all our terminated states to this archived state.

It can be seen that the technique is useful in identifying the states of an entity, the functions that cause the states of an entity to change, and any sequences that are implied. It is also important to identify the terminating states of the entity. Some systems have not always done this and found that at a later date they have no way of getting rid of entity occurrences.

One example of this is provided by a vehicle spare parts system for a large organization. In this system vehicles require specific parts, but what is not known is which parts support specific vehicles. The result is that when vehicles become obsolete there is no way of withdrawing the parts that support that vehicle only. It is too dangerous to withdraw all the parts required by the obsolete vehicle, as many of these parts will be common to other vehicles. This results in a database which is continually growing as new vehicles and their parts are added. If there had been an entity life cycle analysis performed on the entity part, it would have been discovered that the entity occurrence did not terminate. The likelihood is that the organization would then have designed a function to associate parts with vehicles and thus be able to terminate the entity.

In SSADM the entity life cycle is termed an entity life history. The diagram looks more like a hierarchical structure with the entity under consideration as the root or parent of the tree. This is described, with an example, in section 6.3. The entity life history diagram is also very similar to the structure diagram of Jackson Systems Development (JSD). In JSD this is the central modelling technique used in the methodology. Entity life cycles are discussed further in Palmer and Rock-Evans (1981) and Rosenquist (1982).

Chapter 5
Tools

In this chapter we look at some tools of information systems development. We look at principles and types of product, as the individual products are changing rapidly. Most of these are tools directly related to methodologies themselves, for example, workbenches, fourth generation systems, data dictionaries and project management facilities. The others are either important tools of the systems development environment in general, such as databases and query languages, or tools expected to make an impact in the future, in particular expert systems. Tools, in this context, are restricted to mean software packages.

5.1 DATABASE MANAGEMENT SYSTEMS

A database is an organized and integrated collection of data. It will be used by a number of users in a number of ways. In some methodologies the whole organization (or that part which is of interest in the problem situation) is modelled on a database. A large part of information systems development concerns the best way of using the data resource as a whole, as against designing, creating, validating and updating files especially for a particular application.

There needs to be a large piece of software which will handle the many accesses to the database, because it is a resource that will be used by many information systems applications. This software is the database management system (DBMS). The DBMS will store the data and the data relationships on the backing storage devices. It must also provide an effective means of retrieval of that data when the application systems require it, so that this important resource of the business, the data resource, is used effectively. Efficient data retrieval may be accomplished by computer programs written in conventional programming languages such as Cobol and Fortran accessing the database. It can also be accomplished through the use of a query language which is designed for use by people who are not computer experts. These arrangements are shown in figure 5.1.

There are a number of reasons for adopting the database approach as a basis for information systems development:

Reduce data duplication: Large organizations, such as insurance companies, banks, local councils, and manufacturing companies, have for some time been putting large amounts of data onto their computer systems. Frequently the same data was being collected, validated, stored and accessed separately for a number of purposes. This 'data redundancy' is costly and can be avoided, or at least reduced, by the use of a DBMS. (In fact some data redundancy is

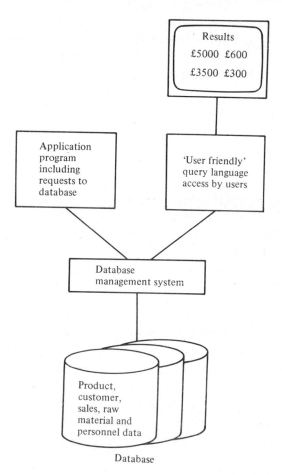

Fig. 5.1. The role of the database management system (DBMS) intercepting the data requests of application programs and users.

reasonable in a database environment, but such redundancy should be known and controlled.) If the data is collected only once, and stored in only one place, there is little chance of inconsistency. With conventional files, the data is often collected at different times and validated by different validation routines, and stored in different places, therefore the output produced by different systems could well be inconsistent. With reduced data duplication, data can be shared but it is essential that good integrity and security features operate in such systems. Furthermore, each application should run 'unaware' of the existence of others using the database. The computer system must therefore be powerful enough that performance is good even when there are a large number of users concurrently accessing the database.

Increase data integrity: In a shared environment, it is crucial for the success of the database system to control the creation, deletion and update of data and to ensure its correctness. Furthermore, with so many users accessing the database, there must be some control to prevent failed transactions leaving the database in an inconsistent state. Again, there must be proper mechanisms to control access by unauthorized users. Although these aspects represent challenges, they also represent an opportunity to increase data integrity and security significantly. These requirements will be easier to effect in a database environment than in one where each application sets up its own files. Because of the possibilities of central administration, standards need only be agreed and set up once for all users.

Increase speed of implementing systems: Information systems ought to be developed and implemented in less time, since systems development staff can largely concentrate on the processes involved in the application rather than on the collection, validation, sorting, and storage of data. Much of the data required for a new application may already be held on the database, put there for another purpose. Accessing the data will also be easier because this will be handled by the data manipulation features of the DBMS.

Ease file access: Early DBMS used well-known programming languages such as Cobol and Fortran as the language which was used to access the database. Cobol, for example, was extended to include new instructions which were used when it was necessary to access data on the database. These 'host language' extensions were not difficult for experienced computer programmers to learn and to use. The query language facilities which will be discussed in section 5.2 extend this impact, because they make access to the database by users possible and help to make information systems development by users possible.

Increase data independence: Data independence is the ability to change the format of the data or the medium on which the data is held or the data structures, without having to change the programs which use the data. Conversely, it also means that it is possible to change the logic of the programs without having to change the files. This separation of the issues concerning processes from the issues concerning data is a key reason for opting for the database solution. It makes changes much easier to effect, and therefore provides for far greater flexibility.

Provide a management view: With conventional systems, management is not getting the benefits from the expensive computing resource that it has sanctioned. Managers are becoming aware of the need for a corporate view of their organization. Such a view requires data from a number of departments, divisions, and sometimes companies in a larger organization. This corporate view cannot be gained if files are established on an applications basis and not integrated as in a database. Thus the database/DBMS facility makes the development of the decision-support aspect of information systems feasible.

Improve standards: In traditional systems development, applications are implemented by different project teams of systems analysts and programmers and it is difficult to apply standards and conventions to run for all applications, especially where applications are developed piecemeal. With a central database, it is possible to impose standards for file access and update and to impose good privacy and security features.

DBMS are software packages which manage complex file structures. DBMS make databases available to a variety of users and the sharing of data can reduce the average cost of data access as well as avoiding duplicate and therefore possibly inconsistent or irreconcilable data. Databases hold large amounts of data and operations required to use the database are complex. Correspondingly, DBMS are large, complex pieces of software. Users of databases do not directly access the database. Instead they access the DBMS which interprets the data requirements into accesses to the database, makes the accesses required, and returns the results to the user in the form that the user requires.

The various users accessing the database via the DBMS may be user department managers and clerks as well as data processing professionals and they may well have different views of the database. They may access the database using 'user friendly' query languages on their workstations. Access may also be made via user programs written in a conventional programming language such as Cobol or PL/1 which act as host languages. Host languages are procedural and the programmer has to know the set of logical procedures required to fulfil a particular request. This requires an in-depth knowledge of the language, but if the knowledge of the language has been acquired, the requests for database access need not be complicated. Query languages are usually non-procedural and are usually suitable for untrained computer users and for 'ad hoc' enquiries of the database. A useful distinction between programming languages and query languages is to look at the former as concerned with the 'how' of an operation, and the latter as being concerned with the 'what'. One area of possible confusion is that 'query' languages are badly named in that they do usually offer ways of updating (changing) the data as well as accessing it in the form of a query. Query languages are discussed further in section 5.2.

Many DBMS provide report generators as an alternative way of using the database. Report generators are usually designed for unskilled users. They are orientated towards providing large volume printed reports rather than displays on the screen although many systems will also display the same report on the screen. The report format should be easy to design. Sometimes the DBMS will also provide program and system generation facilities. These can be used to build more complex systems, containing significant processing facilities. These features are normally associated with fourth generation systems (see section 5.4).

An important human intermediary will be the database administrator (DBA) who will be responsible for the design of the overall data structure and for ensuring that the required levels of privacy, security and integrity of the database are maintained. The DBA, or more accurately the DBA team, could be said to be managers of the database and, because the design of the database involves trade-offs, they will have to balance these conflicting requirements and make decisions on behalf of the whole organization, rather than on any particular user or departmental objective. The DBA can give crucial help to systems analysts designing and developing information systems in a database environment, so that the information system is appropriate to all users.

When setting up the database, the data structures have to be mapped onto the DBMS. In a database environment, data structures may have been formulated using the entity modelling technique described in section 4.1, and the resultant model mapped on to the database. However, DBMS differ in the way that they require the data structures to be formulated. Usually these structures will be hierarchical, network, or relational. These data structures are introduced here, but a more detailed description can be found in Date (1986).

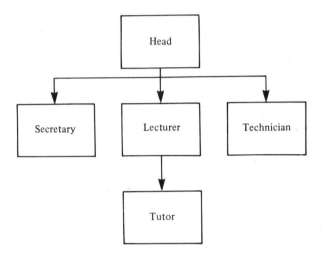

Fig. 5.2. The hierarchy.

A hierarchy is a tree structure and a simple example is shown in figure 5.2. Here a university department is arranged as a hierarchy. Thus, for this particular data structure, the database holds data on each of the secretaries, lecturers, clerks and tutors, which make up the leaves of the tree. The DBMS has to organize the maintenance of a set of pointers (addresses) from the root (head of department) through to the subordinates and back again. In any database structure, there will be a number of these hierarchies held on the database for that particular organization. Another may refer to product information (for example, product category (top level), products (next level) and raw materials going into product (next level)) or reflect the national, regional and local elements of an organization.

A network is a rather more complex relationship. These many-to-many relationships are best illustrated using the example described in figure 5.3. Here, there are more interactions than a hierarchy and they do not form a tree structure. This type of many-to-many relationship is found in many organizations and therefore a DBMS that cannot support them is at a disadvantage. Some hierarchical DBMS have been modified to support a

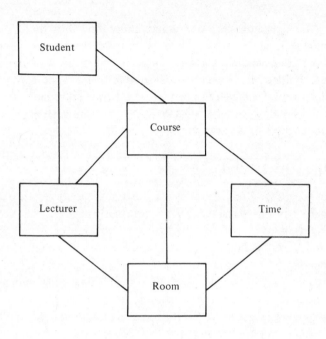

Fig. 5.3. The network

limited network structure. Hierarchical DBMS are rather dated. A network DBMS can also support hierarchies, after all, a hierarchy is a special, simpler, kind of network.

As we saw in section 4.2, relations are tables of data and a relational DBMS supports this view of data. A DBMS must support demands for information stemming from a number of relations. Unlike hierarchies and network DBMS, there are no pointers explicitly relating the elements of the data structure, nor are any pointers stored in the database. When users require access to a number of relations, the links will be set up at run time, that is, when the request is made. This makes the model more flexible, because the links need not be set up when creating the data structure, which requires the user accesses to be predicted. These systems can be slower, however, because of the extra overhead when executing accesses to the database.

The entity model discussed in section 4.1 can be mapped on to any of the above types of database model and therefore proves a good base on which to develop an information system using a DBMS as a tool. Many methodologies assume that the applications will be implemented using a

DBMS. Although those that incorporate entity modelling might claim that the technique is useful whatever tools are used for implementation, the applications are nevertheless usually implemented in this way. Indeed entity modelling gained prominence because it proved to be a very useful preliminary step to database implementation. However, of particular interest to users developing systems in a database environment is the query language, and we look at this in the next section.

5.2 QUERY LANGUAGES

Query languages were originally designed to enable speedy and flexible access to information in a database. They were particularly aimed at non-professional users requiring *ad hoc* access without the necessity of having a special program written for them. Originally query languages enabled only fairly simple queries to be asked but more and more complex searching, sorting and matching facilities are now provided. Further, it is now quite common, given that the user has the correct authorization, for query languages to facilitate updating of the database as well as the retrieval of information.

   An example simple query might be as follows:

'LIST ALL students IN ASCENDING ALPHABETICAL ORDER OF name THAT HAVE AVERAGE OF grade 1, grade 2, grade 3 GREATER THAN 65%'.

This may look very free format and natural language like, but in fact there is a fairly fixed syntax and only a certain number of key words can be used. The words of this particular hypothetical query language are in capitals and the words in lower case refer to elements in the database. This query accesses the student records file, calculates the average of the specified fields (grade 1, grade 2 and grade 3) for each student and lists the students records that satisfy the condition (average greater than 65%) in the specified sequence (ascending alphabetic order of name).

   This is a simple query in that it only requires access to one file (the student file). More complex queries would require access to two or more files or tables in the database.

   Query languages are, in general, non-procedural which means that the users specify what they require from the system rather than how to get it. Most traditional programming languages are procedural and the user has to specify how to achieve what is required, that is, the procedure. Obviously non-procedural languages are easier for non-specialists to use.

Query languages are designed to:

Provide *ad hoc* and on-line access (and update) to information in the database,

Provide an English language-like, non-procedural interface to enable flexible access, and

Handle only relatively small query volumes.

Query languages for non-relational databases differ considerably one from another and are specific to the particular DBMS that they are using. In the case of relational databases the situation is somewhat different. The basic query language of relational DBMS is the relational algebra (see Date 1986). This consists of a basic set of primitives for manipulating relations. It is in fact a procedural language and not particularly easy for non-specialists to use, that is, it does not really meet the criteria required of a query language. For this reason a more fitting query language is often employed that is easier to use and non-procedural, known as the relational calculus. The relational calculus is converted into the relational algebra primitives prior to execution on the relational database.

Relational calculus-based languages differ one from another although there are some common characteristics. So once again there is no standard query language defined for use on all relational databases, although many people now believe that SQL is beginning to emerge as a *de facto* standard now that IBM's DB2, their relational database product, uses it.

When compared to the relational algebra, the relational calculus is more orientated towards expressing the user requests in a way that the user may construct, because it is non-procedural. This means that the user specifies his needs rather than having to construct the procedures to retrieve the required data. 'Pure' relational calculus is difficult for non-mathematicians, but more user-orientated languages which are based on the relational calculus are easier to use. Codd's Data Sub Language called DSL ALPHA (Codd 1971) has the general retrieval format:

GET INTO workspace (target list) option list

where, workspace is the name of an area where the retrieved data is to be put; target list gives detail of the relation; and option list gives the particular restrictions on the target list. In most implementations of the relational calculus, GET INTO is replaced by FIND or RETRIEVE. An example will make this easier to understand:

GET INTO W (ATTENDANCE, STUDENT-NAME, COURSE-NAME)
WHERE (LECTURER-NAME='CLARKE')

Here we are putting into the workspace 'W' the student names of students and the names of courses that they are taking held in the relation called ATTENDANCE who are taught by the lecturer called 'Clarke' (see figure. 5.4). The result in W might be:

STUDENT-NAME	COURSE-NAME
Ashworth	MSc Computer Science
Atkins	MSc Information Technology
Johnson	MSc Computer Science
Smith	MSc Computer Science

Note, in relational query languages, the query response is presented in tabular form. The option list can contain < or > (for less than or greater than) as well as = (for equal to).

If a particular relation is frequently referred to in a particular run, then the use of the 'RANGE' statement can reduce the work of the user. For example:

RANGE ATTENDANCE A and

RANGE LECTURER-MODULE L

will allow the user to specify the ATTENDANCE relation using 'A' and LECTURER-MODULE using 'L' as abbreviations. For example:

GET INTO W (L MODULE) WHERE (L NO-OF-WEEKS>10)

which requests that the module number of those modules which are more than ten weeks long should be placed in the workspace W will give:

MODULE

4

(assuming that, in the example, module 4 is the only module which lasts longer than 10 weeks).

It is possible to search through many relations, indeed the whole database, and the RANGE command can be used to restrict such access by only allowing users to refer to relations defined in a RANGE statement.

DSL ALPHA was specified as a host language system. This means that the

Emp no	Name	Status	Birthday	Tax to date	Salary

(a) Skeleton table for QBE request

Emp no	Name	Status	Birthday	Tax to date	Salary
P.756	P	P			P

(b) Table completed by user:
756: record to be addressed
P: details requested to print

Emp no	Name	Status	Birthday	Tax to date	Salary
756	SMITH	FULL			12,030

(c) Table completed as requested

Fig. 5.4. QBE example.

programs could be written in Cobol (the host language) and when data is to be retrieved from the database, the special DSL ALPHA commands will apply. SQL is not a host language system, but a self-contained query language, that is, all the user requests are written in that language.

SQL, is a calculus-based language which has slowly become a near standard query language. The main operator has the following basic structure:

SELECT/FROM/WHERE

so that a request:

LIST DETAILS OF EMPLOYER NUMBER 756

would be formulated as:

SELECT EMP-NO, NAME, DEPT, SALARY	(data items — a 'target list')
FROM EMPFILE	(a relation involved in the query)
WHERE EMP-NO=756	(qualifier or 'condition')

The qualifications on the data retrieved can include ANDs, ORs and NOTs, along with < (less than), > (greater than), and so on. The results can be ORDERED according to user's requirements and operations such as average, minimum, and maximum values calculated. The user has to know the names of the relevant attributes and key them in explicitly. Alternatively, the sets of commands can be 'programmed' and stored when developing the information system and called in as required when the system is operational. SQL also provides a CREATE VIEW command which sets up alternative views of the data derived from other tables and selected rows and columns. This is useful when setting up different sub-schemas (which adhere to the security and privacy requirements defined by the database administrator), that is apply to different users within the same information system. A full account of SQL is found in Date (1984).

Query By Example (QBE), which was proposed by Zloof (1978), is designed for users with little or no programming experience. This cannot be said of the relational algebra and it is more 'user friendly' than a straight relational calculus language such as SQL. The intention is that operations in the QBE language are analogous to the way people would naturally use tables. Further, as the name implies, the user can use an example to specify his query. The user enters the name of the table and the system supplies the attribute names in a skeleton table. The system details the attributes in which the user has indicated an interest (see figure 5.4).

Many systems are either menu-based (see figure 5.5) or form-based (see figure 5.6) and these prevent even the necessity of recalling the relation names. This means that minimal training is necessary and therefore is usefully associated with informations development by users or with user participation. However there are severe limitations to retain flexibility unless the database is not very complex. Some aspects of a natural language interface, which are still in a somewhat experimental phase, are discussed in Codd (1974).

With database management systems and query languages it becomes easier to translate user requirements into working systems in an information systems methodology. A third piece in this jigsaw of tools in a database

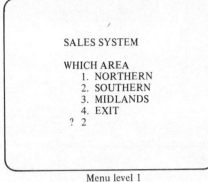

```
        SALES SYSTEM

        WHICH AREA
            1. NORTHERN
            2. SOUTHERN
            3. MIDLANDS
            4. EXIT
          ?  2
```

```
        SALES SYSTEM

        WHICH REP
            1. LONDON
            2. HOME COUNTIES
            3. SOUTH EAST
            4. EXIT
          ?  3
```

Menu level 1
Choosing the sales area
(Southern)
Press 2

Menu level 2
Choosing the representative
(South East)
Press 3

```
        SALES SYSTEM
        SOUTH EAST REGION

        SALES FOR REP: R SMITH (SOUTH EAST)

        WEEK      SALES      EXPENSES
          1       15,400      8,000
          2        7,200      3,000
          3        6,000      3,000
          4        3,500      3,030

        TOTAL     32,100     17,030
```

Report
Obtaining the relevant
information

Fig. 5.5. Enquiry using menu structures

environment is the data dictionary which is discussed in the next section.
These three tools will also be part of a fourth generation system, designed
specifically for applications development. These are discussed in section 5.4.

5.3 DATA DICTIONARIES

There has recently been a significant increase in the use of data dictionary
systems (DDS). This is mainly due to the corresponding growth in the use of
entity analysis techniques, DBMS and fourth generation products. A DDS can

1. Form display

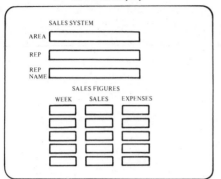

2. Part completed by user using
   one of keys (rep or rep name)

3. Result — completed form

Fig. 5.6. Enquiry using form structures

ensure standard and consistent definitions for all data in the organization, essential if the output from entity analysis is not to cause confusion, as a DDS helps to control and use the information so gathered. Many DDS are integrated with a particular DBMS or offered as a possible 'extra' to a DBMS.

A DDS is a software tool for recording and processing data about the data (*meta data*) that an organization uses and processes. Originally DDS were designed as documentation tools, ensuring standard terminology for data items (and sometimes programs) and providing a cross-reference capability. They have now evolved as an essential feature of the information systems development environment (see Curtice and Dieckman, 1981).

A DDS is a central catalogue of the definitions and usage of the data within an organization. Information systems development is helped by the clear definition of what data is already in the database. The DDS can be accessed by each new information system as it uses the database and therefore the DDS eases the sharing of data. If used alongside a DBMS it could be said to be a directory of the database, 'a database of the database', although this relationship might be better expressed as an 'information source about the database'. Thus DDS are used chiefly as documentation aids and as control points for referencing data. A DDS will hold definitions of all data items, which may be any objects of interest, and their characteristics. It will hold information on how this data is used as well as how it is stored.

A DDS can also be used as a storage base of logical file designs and programming code (sub-programs) and these sub-programs may be used in a number of application programs. Many DDS are therefore more than mere points of reference about data, and they hold information about processes as well as data.

The DDS pervades all aspects of information systems work, and its use could lead to improved documentation and control, consistency in data use, easier entity analysis, reduced data redundancy, simpler programming, the enforcement of standards and a better means of estimating the effect of change. Of course some of these advantages could be equally said to be the result of using a database with a DBMS and an effective database administration team. Indeed, they all contribute to an effective data processing environment.

The DDS, as shown in figure. 5.7 can influence users, managers, and auditors, as well as data processing professionals and the database administrator.

The British Computer Society set up a working party (referred to hereafter as the BCSWP) to suggest a standard for data dictionary systems. Their

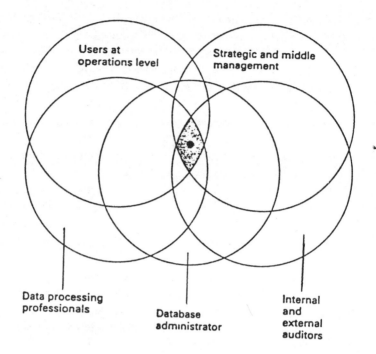

● Data dictionary

Fig. 5.7. Influence and users of data dictionary.

report, British Computer Society (1977), has proved very influential on the design of DDS (see also Gradwell 1983). The BCSWP suggest that a DDS should provide two sets of facilities:

To record and analyse data requirements independently of how they are going to be met, and

To record design decisions in terms of database or file structures implemented and the programs which access them.

These two sets of facilities are referred to as the conceptual data model and the implementation data structure respectively. Some writers refer to these as management use mode and computer use mode.

The conceptual view shows a model of the organization, that is, the entities, their attributes, and the relationships between these entities. This model is the result of the entity modelling process described in section 4.1

and is therefore independent of any data processing implications. The conceptual view can also include details of the events and operations that occur in the organization.

The implementation view gives information about the data processing applications in computing terms. The processes are therefore described as systems, programs and sub-programs (modules), and the data is described in terms of files, records, and fields, or in the terminology of the DBMS used (for example, segments, sets, and data items). Some systems also include an operations view as part of the implementation level. This will include information relating to the operation of the system, such as the schedule for running the system and its hardware requirements.

The BCSWP argue that one of the main functions of a DDS should be to show the relationship between the conceptual and implementation views. One view should map on to the other view. Any inconsistencies between the two should be detected. It should be noted, however, that many DDS currently available only support the implementation view and those which hold a conceptual as well as implementation view do not always map one to the other automatically, nor carry out any checks to ensure their mutual consistency. This feature is significant as it would ease the process of developing information systems.

The conceptual and implementation views for data and processes are shown in figure 5.8. The four quadrants represent the components of the DDS. There is a fifth component which indicates the cross-referencing between components. It will be possible to identify entities, functions, and programs using a simple referencing system which will be an effective tool in maintenance, as well as help when designing the information systems. An example of its use might be in answering the question, 'What processes use this data item?'.

For each data element, the DDS will contain amongst other things, the following:

- The names associated with that element. There may be different names used by the various users and computer programs to refer to one element.
- A description of the data element in natural language.
- Details of ownership (normally the department which creates the data).
- Details of the users that refer to the element.
- Details of the systems and programs which refer to or update the element.
- Details on any privacy constraints that should be associated with the item.
- Details about the data element in data processing systems, such as the length of the data item in characters, whether it is numeric, alphabetic or

another data type, and what logical files include the data item.
- The security level attached to the element in order to restrict access to it.
- The storage requirement.
- The validation rules for each element (for example the range of acceptable values).
- Details of the relationship of the data items to others.

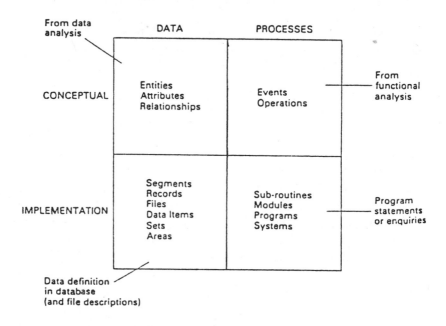

Fig. 5.8. The four quadrants of a data dictionary system

With so much detail needed to be held on the data dictionary, it is essential that a referencing and cross-referencing facility is provided by the DDS. This will help the systems analyst in the design process and it provides a check for completeness.

Earlier DDS concentrated on documentation and on producing reports about the data on the database. In installations where there are no DDS, computer systems can become entangled in a confusion of data. The systems analyst developing a new system in these circumstances is likely to set up new files, because it is difficult to ascertain what aspects of the present applications files might be useful, and this further worsens the situation. Data dictionaries are used to ensure greater discipline.

A pre-printed form usually in fixed format is provided by many DDS. These forms will be used to input data into the system or request reports, in other words, there are well-defined procedures for the systems developers to help them make the best use of the DDS and maintain its integrity. There will also be some form of enquiry language. Where a DDS is associated with a particular DBMS, then this will be the query language supported provided by the DBMS. The DBMS may assist in managing the data dictionary, indeed, the data dictionary will be held on the database, just like any other database file.

Most commercially available DDS now go beyond these basic facilities and the DDS can be seen as a tool with a number of objectives:
1 To provide facilities for documenting information collected during all stages in the development of an information systems project.
2 To provide details of applications usage and their data usage once an information system has been implemented, so that analysis and redesign may be facilitated as the environment changes.
3 To make such access easier by providing cross-referencing and indexing facilities.
4 To make extension of the DDS easy.
5 To encourage systems analysts to follow methodology standards.
This last objective could point, for example, to data dictionaries holding details of the contents of the sources and destinations (sinks) of data flows, outlined in a data flow diagram (section 4.3). In other words, data dictionaries are a tool of process definition as well as data definition.

The scope of a DDS is therefore broad. It is not merely a documenting aid, it provides a support to all stages in the development and maintenance of an information system and the control of the database. A more sophisticated DDS would have a number of extra facilities such as the following:
1 Automatic input from source code of data definitions. These can be copied in at compilation time.
2 The generation of source code relating to items in the data dictionary to an applications program.
3 The recognition that several versions of the same programs or data structures may exist at the same time. The different versions could represent live and test states of the programs or data, or programs and data structures which may be used at different sites or data set up under different software or validation routines.
4 The provision of on-line facilities to aid the interrogation of the database.

Here, an interactive query language needs to be provided as part of the DDS.

5 The provision of an interface with a DBMS.

6 The provision of security features, such as password systems. These may be built in to restrict access to the DDS, for example, users should only gain access to that part of the data dictionary which is relevant to the job in hand. The ability to restrict the type of access, such as read, delete, write, and update, is as important to the DDS as it is to the database.

7 The provision of facilities to generate application programs and produce reports and validation routines and the provision of test file generation facilities. These will help the process of developing information systems.

8 The provision of data definitions and sub-routines for application programs enforce some standards on programming, making programs more readable and consistent. This also removes much of the tedium associated with application program development.

9 The provision of an estimate of costs of any proposed change of use of the data and an estimate of the time scale for making such changes.

Thus, DDS can be used as a dynamic tool of the system development process. The DDS has also become the basis of many analyst and programmer development workbenches. Here, the DDS has had a number of analysis and design functions added to it, and in some cases the addition also of implementation tools. This concept of a DDS has come a long way from its origins as a simple store of data about the data in the database, and, as an indication of this, the term System Encyclopedia or some such grand name is often now used instead of DDS. Many aspects of what we have termed a DDS feature in fourth generation systems and automated workbenches are discussed in the next two sections.

5.4 FOURTH GENERATION SYSTEMS

There is no generally agreed definition on what constitutes a fourth generation system. It is often argued that development work should be carried out by people who are not programmers, and this, perhaps, lies at the heart of the tools which are usually together known as fourth generation systems. But they can be as useful to professional computer people developing information systems. Indeed, Martin (1982a, 1982b, 1983) distinguishes between end user and professional fourth generation systems.

The basic aim of fourth generation systems is to speed up the work of developing new systems and hence reduce any applications backlog — a queue of users' applications waiting to be developed. This queue is long in most data processing installations, surveys show that it commonly varies between three and five years in most organizations. It might be significantly longer if one considers the 'invisible backlog' of applications which are not on the list because users do not think it worthwhile to join the queue. A further benefit accrues to applications developed using fourth generation systems, for they are not just developed more quickly but, when they require changing, as they inevitably will, the changes can be made very speedily and accurately.

As stated above, these tools are sometimes designed for use by users themselves, and sometimes for use by professionals in association with users. In principle there is no difference, but we would expect the systems for users to be simpler, although probably more limited in their facilities.

The term 'fourth generation *languages*' is also used to describe these systems, but the use of 'language' is narrow, even though the non-procedural (compared to high level languages) form of languages used in these systems is a particularly important feature. The term fourth generation language (4GL) inevitably arouses interest in the earlier generations of programming languages. These are:

Machine code (first): this is the language of computers, a pattern of ones and zeros (for on and off states) and therefore very difficult and tedious to use, prone to error and difficult to debug and modify. Such programming requires an intimate knowledge of the physical hardware. This binary coding largely disappeared when assembly languages were developed.

Assembler (second): this is one step away from machine code. Although there is a one-to-one relationship between the two sets of instructions, they represented the instructions using mnemonics (such as MPX for multiply) and symbols for particular items. This language is therefore slightly easier to use and produced code more quickly with fewer errors. However, the programmer still needs to know about the specific hardware on which the program is being developed.

High level procedural (third): these are procedural languages designed to be used for different types of application. Examples include Cobol and PL/1 (for business applications) and Fortran (for scientific applications). One high level language statement can be compiled into several machine code instructions. Programs written in one high level language should in theory be usable on different machines with few changes being necessary, a feature called software *portability*. These languages are easier to use (when compared to their forerunners), though still designed for computer professionals. These languages have contributed greatly to the expansion of computing. However, they are still difficult to learn and use, requiring considerable training. Although English words are used in some of these programming languages, they are far removed from natural languages. Indeed the English words are likely to mislead the naive user. Most importantly, they require considerable time to design and debug.

Non procedural (fourth): where program flow (procedures) are not designed by the programmer but by the fourth generation software itself, in the form of previously constructed, parameterized algorithms. Each user request is one for a result rather than a procedure to obtain this result. Compared to third generation languages, they require less lines of coding, are quicker to write and test and easier to maintain. They are designed for interactive use and the dialogue between user and software enables errors to be corrected as the application is being developed. Mnemonics, which require learning and remembering, are replaced by menus, semi-natural language, and other easy to use facilities. The language is designed so that non-computing people can develop their own systems. This results in more projects being completed more speedily and therefore a smaller applications backlog as well as, in the long term, alleviating the problem of trained programmer shortage.

Most fourth generation systems use a mixture of graphics and text which eases the specification of user requirements. Some use a technique whereby the user 'fills in the blanks' and rapid development is further helped through the sensible setting of default options, which are followed if the user does not specify otherwise. 'Intelligent' defaults, might include, for example, the place and format of the date on a report. If the users specify and implement the fourth generation solution, they can also maintain it without involving the data processing professionals and thereby reduce the large maintenance costs of traditional computing.

The tools that make up a fourth generation system will normally have a common user interface, very often the *WIMP* computer-user interface. WIMP stands for:

     Windows
     Icons
     Mouse, and
     Pull-down (or pop-up) menus,
(or, sometimes, Windows, Icons, Menus and Pointers!)

Windows allow users to work on parts of a number of application areas (for example, different parts of a fourth generation system) at the same time. Each window represents a compartment on the screen and can be moved up and down and the size changed. Thus, whilst the user is working on one part of the system, other parts can be kept in view. The icons represent graphical ways of representing different aspects of the system (filing cabinets, waste-paper baskets, 'in' and 'out' trays, and so on) the meaning of which are easily understood as they represent the *desk top* or whatever the real-world metaphor happens to be. The mouse is a physical box which can be moved around on the desk top and this movement is tracked on the screen. The user moves the mouse as a kind of pointer to arrive at a point on the screen and clicks a switch on the mouse to execute that function. Usually these functions or options are listed in a menu or set of menus. Normally, the name of the menu is given at the top (or bottom) of the screen and the mouse is used to point to that name and then, by dragging the mouse downwards (or pulling up), the full list of options on the menu is displayed.

One obvious advantage of the users developing their own systems is that it avoids some of the communication problems that arose in the past between users and developers. A major criticism that users make of data processing professionals is that they have little understanding of the business and do not pay enough attention to users' requirements. Also, if the development is speeded up, the likelihood of the user requirements changing during the development process is reduced. Further, programming and systems analysis expertise is a scarce resource in most organizations and due to the demand there is frequently a long lead time before projects are implemented. Many of these issues were raised in section 2.3.

Fourth generation systems are designed for 'self help' and the use of these systems has also coincided with the spread of the *information centre* where professional expertise is available to encourage users to help themselves, frequently using their 'private' facilities, usually personal computers in their office. Should more powerful facilities be required, these personal computers might be linked to the organization's mainframe computer, giving an opportunity to use its facilities. An important justification for the information centre is to ensure *some* control over user development. For example, it should prevent a number of users attempting to solve the same problem or purchasing incompatible machines and software. The information centre should help in initiating application development, training users, encouraging efficiency, and encouraging the sharing of data (and ensuring its shareability by helping to establish thorough validation routines and security provisions). This should also ensure that professional computing staff are also committed to the fourth generation environment as they are recognized in the organization as facilitators, important cogs in the wheel.

There are a number of characteristics of a system orientated towards the user to which fourth generation systems would be expected to conform (see also Nelson, 1985):

1 They should be easy to learn and use effectively.

2 As well as good written documentation, there should be on-line 'help' facilities that users can call on when unsure of the next step, also useful and relevant debugging aids should be available to help users when an error has been made.

3 They should be available for use interactively on a terminal connected to a mainframe computer or using a microcomputer. Many fourth generation systems have microcomputer and mainframe versions. Whereas the programmer writing programs in conventional languages wrote the programs which were then compiled and tested, the user and system build the application 'together', with each user request producing a system response.

4 They should be robust, so that they do not 'crash'. Such systems should be designed to be 'tolerant' of mistakes in data entry. However, any errors should be detected by the system and reported to the user in a readily understandable way. Many third generation compilers give an error number and the programmer has to look up its meaning in a handbook only to find a very technical explanation. This would be inappropriate to fourth generation systems.

5 They should self-document any work produced, so that the operational systems are easy to maintain.

As well as producing final applications, fourth generation systems can also be used to generate prototypes (see also section 3.4). Performance criteria are less consequential when developing a prototype, which can be looked on as a working model, a means of refining the exact form of a working model, of the operational system. The system may produce skeletal programs and the user can experiment with various options. Principles and user requirements can be tested for viability so that costly mistakes in solving a complex data processing problem can be avoided. Fourth generation systems can produce fairly cheap and effective prototypes.

We will look at the various parts of a fourth generation system separately. Stand-alone DBMS, query languages and DDS were discussed earlier in this chapter, and we provide here an overview of those aspects particularly relevant to fourth generation systems.

Database Management System

Most fourth generation systems will support their own database. Some will also support an external database, not formed using the fourth generation environment. This is useful as the users can draw on whatever data exists in the computer system already. Most fourth generation database systems are relational. Relational systems allow users to perform operations on the data without knowing its structure, an important feature as users then need only know what is to be done, not how it is achieved. This feature of relational databases, structure independence, means that data relationships implied by user requests are set up dynamically by the system itself. However, the relational database can be slow and so some fourth generation systems offer the facility to set up hierarchies and networks, where the links between data structures are established when setting up the database.

The facilities of a fourth generation DBMS should not be dissimilar from any good stand-alone DBMS, although it is likely to be designed to include an interface that can be used by untrained users. There must also be good security and integrity features so that other users are protected from errors that may be made by inexperienced users. Some operations may be made by filling in a form or by the use of question-and-answer dialogues. Again, defaults will be used wherever possible to minimize this work.

Data Dictionary

The data dictionary is an important element of developing applications in a fourth generation environment. It acts as a reference point for data held in the database, and also describes validation routines. In fact, it can be used to hold details about the applications as well as the data, so that it can represent total system documentation. Many fourth generation data dictionary systems are what is termed *active* systems, that is the data dictionary is automatically updated when relations are created, amended or deleted from the database.

Query Language

The query language is used primarily to interrogate data in the database, originally in retrieval mode only, but now, more commonly, simple update facilities are also provided. Frequently the language used is SQL as this is becoming a standard for relational databases. Some systems offer alternatives, such as Query By Example (QBE) or query by forms, whereby users state their requirements by filling in a soft copy form.

Most systems support a set of standard queries which are stored for regular use, and easily included in particular applications. Results may be displayed in tabular form on a screen or as a number of windows on a screen. *Ad hoc* queries are also supported.

Much fourth generation dialogue is of the question-and-answer type, such as:

System WHICH CUSTOMER RECORD DO YOU WANT TO SEE?

User   PARKES HOLDINGS

This dialogue may be computer initiated (as above) or user initiated.

Report Generator

Report generators retrieve data that is held in the database and format it into reports requested by the users. Again, users specify their requirements in some form of non-procedural language or by filling in a form, they do not program the logic to produce these results. The report generator will set up the page headings, subheadings, totals and detail lines after sorting the information as requested. Most will also carry out arithmetic and logical operations such as working out percentages or maximum and minimum values. For example, customer details in a sales analysis report might only be printed if the total of purchases exceeds a certain amount. Some systems use high resolution graphics to generate reports.

The report writer will normally be used for setting up standard formal reports and is mainly intended for end users. A report lay-out might be 'suggested' by the system and, through a process of refinement, the prototype frames are established. Totals, subtotals, headings and row and column placement may all have default values for the easy creation of standard forms, but can usually be changed easily where necessary.

Screen Generator

Screen painters or generators are a useful tool to set up screen displays quickly and easily. The required design is drawn on screen and the system produces the code to generate the screen as required. This is normally done interactively. Screens can be set up from scratch or by modifying ones already created and held in the database. Screens can be set up which have titles, sets of menus, boxes (for users to fill in) and some of these can be defined through the data dictionary. Once a number of screens have been set up on the database, they can be re-displayed regularly in a pre-defined sequence.

Program Generator

It is frequently possible to purchase application packages which are systems bought 'off the shelf' to do a particular job. Some applications, however, are particular to the firm and do not have suitable application packages readily available. The use of the company's data processing department — if there is one — may result in a long wait, a large cost, or a system that is not exactly what is required. Program generators, designed for users, can assist in the development of these 'tailored' computer applications.

Program generators automate the production of code. They are therefore a development from report generators, producing code for data definition, validation, security, as well as reports. Much time is taken up in conventional programming to screen and report design and data validation routines. Using program generators, generating a program may only involve naming the files to be used and specifying which screen definitions and report layouts are to be output. A more general purpose program might require a menu to be designed so that the user can choose which options they require at run time. Fourth generation systems therefore normally have menu creating facilities.

They may not be able to generate all code, however, and some incorporate facilities to include program statements from a conventional (third generation) programming language. Alternatively, some third generation languages include the added facilities of a program generator. Where object code is produced in a third generation language like Cobol, the trained programmer can pick this up and add to it or amend it as required. It is not always easy to follow the logic of these programs (just as it is not always easy to follow someone else's programs). This obviously needs to be taken into account when time estimates are made for developing these programs, and it must be remembered that any subsequent changes cannot be so easily handled as with 'pure' fourth generation development.

The data for the reports will be either created especially for the new application program (defined, entered, validated and stored) or generated from another subset of the fourth generation system, the database and/or data dictionary. There will be facilities to specify how files are updated on the database and what calculations or logic functions are performed.

Most program generators facilitate the development of programs on-line, and this speeds up the process. Of course the specification of the user requirements must also be thorough and the code generated by a program generator must still be tested thoroughly.

Fourth generation systems may include a specification language that helps enforce rigour when specifying requirements and it is this language that is the input to the program generator. This could be similar to structured English (section 4.6). There is no coding phase as there is when using third generation languages: the specification is converted directly into executable programs.

Other Facilities of a Fourth Generation System

Most fourth generation systems incorporate other facilities such as a graphics (to produce bar charts, pie charts, and scatter diagrams), spreadsheet (for financial analysis), statistical analysis (to calculate averages, variances, standard deviation, linear regression and perform various statistical tests), and may include word processing and even mailing facilities. Some systems may also have tools for specific applications, such as investment analysis. Indeed, a fourth generation system is likely to give the user a comprehensive 'toolkit'.

An Example of a Fourth Generation System

We will look at one particular fourth generation system to gain a feel for a typical product (others include Mimer, Ramis, Oracle and DM). Focus is a product of Information Builders and it is classified as being suitable for end users to develop their own systems as well as professionals. There exist both mainframe and microcomputer versions of Focus which is a family of products that can be purchased in different combinations. The core of the product is the Focus database, which is relational, the Report Generator and Dialogue Manager, in addition there exist a number of optional modules for generating screens, for entering data, for performing various standard statistical functions, for producing graphs, for querying data, for performing financial modelling, for integrating files from non-Focus databases, and so on.

Information Builders claim possible improvements in productivity of over 10:1 by using Focus rather than developing systems using a third generation language. They also state that Focus enables the data processing professional and the end user to perform *ad hoc* queries and create reports in a fraction of the time required with traditional programming languages. 'A few simple English statements replace thousands of lines of equivalent Cobol or PL/1 program code'! Of course, such claims might be appropriate if the application lends itself to this standard approach. As with any tool, it will be costly if used inappropriately.

As a small illustration of its use, examine the two database files in figure 5.9 and suppose a report is required that is sorted by store code, within region, for all order amounts over $1 000. Figure 5.10 shows the Focus request to achieve this and figure 5.11 the result. Any details not specified in the request have automatic default values assigned.

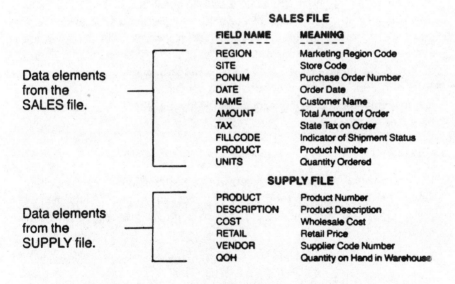

SALES FILE

FIELD NAME	MEANING
REGION	Marketing Region Code
SITE	Store Code
PONUM	Purchase Order Number
DATE	Order Date
NAME	Customer Name
AMOUNT	Total Amount of Order
TAX	State Tax on Order
FILLCODE	Indicator of Shipment Status
PRODUCT	Product Number
UNITS	Quantity Ordered

Data elements from the SALES file.

SUPPLY FILE

PRODUCT	Product Number
DESCRIPTION	Product Description
COST	Wholesale Cost
RETAIL	Retail Price
VENDOR	Supplier Code Number
QOH	Quantity on Hand in Warehouse

Data elements from the SUPPLY file.

Fig. 5.9. Focus database files (Courtesy of Information Builders.)

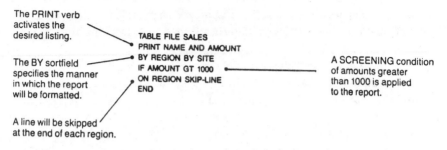

The PRINT verb activates the desired listing.

The BY sortfield specifies the manner in which the report will be formatted.

A line will be skipped at the end of each region.

```
TABLE FILE SALES
PRINT NAME AND AMOUNT
BY REGION BY SITE
IF AMOUNT GT 1000
ON REGION SKIP-LINE
END
```

A SCREENING condition of amounts greater than 1000 is applied to the report.

Fig. 5.10. Focus statements (Courtesy of Information Builders.)

A more complicated example would be a request to know if there are any shortages that will cause problems in supplying products to unfilled orders (an unfilled order has a shipment code of anything other than 'Y'). This requires data from both the Sales file and the Supply file. The JOIN command is used to combine the two files which can then be used as if they were one. The request to achieve this is shown in figure 5.12 and the result in figure 5.13.

All these requests can be saved in Focus as procedures so that they can be executed in the future with a single command. These procedures can call other procedures so that entire applications can be constructed. Additionally the procedure can be interactive so that users can supply run time information to guide the operation of the application. The responses from the users are automatically validated according to a list of acceptable responses. Figure 5.14 is such a procedure and figure 5.15 is the resultant interactive dialogue. Hopefully this illustrates some of the power of a Fourth Generation Language, it would certainly take considerably more code to achieve this in traditional programming language.

Review

In view of the claims made by vendors of fourth generation systems regarding their benefits, it is interesting to ask why they have not currently made a great impact on reducing the application backlog. We suggest possible reasons:

Firstly, they are comparatively new and still in the early development stage.

Secondly, they require a considerable change in the systems development culture of an organization, and not all organizations are yet ready to make this change.

Thirdly, the type of application that successfully used fourth generation

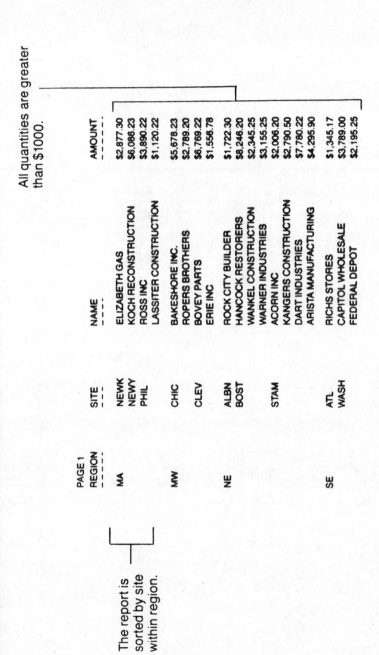

All quantities are greater than $1000.

PAGE 1 REGION	SITE	NAME	AMOUNT
MA	NEWK	ELIZABETH GAS	$2,877.30
	NEWY	KOCH RECONSTRUCTION	$6,086.23
	PHIL	ROSS INC	$3,890.22
		LASSITER CONSTRUCTION	$1,120.22
MW	CHIC	BAKESHORE INC.	$5,678.23
		ROPERS BROTHERS	$2,789.20
	CLEV	BOVEY PARTS	$6,769.22
		ERIE INC	$1,556.78
NE	ALBN	ROCK CITY BUILDER	$1,722.30
	BOST	HANCOCK RESTORERS	$8,246.20
		WANKEL CONSTRUCTION	$2,345.25
		WARNER INDUSTRIES	$3,155.25
	STAM	ACORN INC	$2,006.20
		KANGERS CONSTRUCTION	$2,790.50
		DART INDUSTRIES	$7,780.22
		ARISTA MANUFACTURING	$4,295.90
SE	ATL	RICHS STORES	$1,345.17
	WASH	CAPITOL WHOLESALE	$3,789.00
		FEDERAL DEPOT	$2,195.25

The report is sorted by site within region.

Report lists names, amounts and a line is skipped between each region.

Fig. 5.11. The Focus report. (Courtesy of Information Builders.)

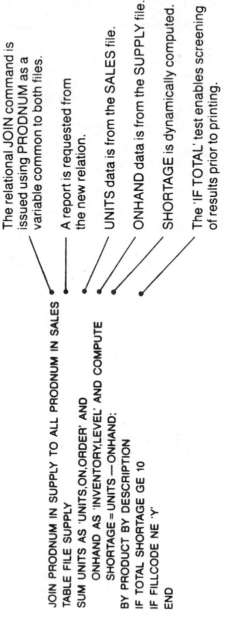

```
JOIN PRODNUM IN SUPPLY TO ALL PRODNUM IN SALES
TABLE FILE SUPPLY
SUM UNITS AS 'UNITS,ON,ORDER' AND
    ONHAND AS 'INVENTORY,LEVEL' AND COMPUTE
       SHORTAGE = UNITS — ONHAND;
BY PRODUCT BY DESCRIPTION
IF TOTAL SHORTAGE GE 10
IF FILLCODE NE 'Y'
END
```

The relational JOIN command is issued using PRODNUM as a variable common to both files.

A report is requested from the new relation.

UNITS data is from the SALES file.

ONHAND data is from the SUPPLY file.

SHORTAGE is dynamically computed.

The 'IF TOTAL' test enables screening of results prior to printing.

Fig. 5.12. Focus report request. (Courtesy of Information Builders.)

system developments has been limited to fairly small, one-off type developments.

Units on order minus inventory level equals shortage.
Only shortages of 10 or more will print on the report.

PAGE 1

PRODNUM	DESCRIPTION	UNITS ON ORDER	INVENTORY LEVEL	SHORTAGE
11275	RADIAL ARM SAW (10 INCH)	570	489	81.00
13938	LATHE	735	689	46.00
14156	ENGINE ANALYZER	797	450	347.00
16394	ALTERNATOR (3000 WATT)	533	367	166.00
17905	PAINT SPRAYER	421	344	77.00
56267	ARC WELDER	1251	244	1,007.00

Fig. 5.13. Focus report derived from request. (Courtesy of Information Builders.)

Fourthly, fourth generation systems are often less efficient in operation than code produced by third generation programming, but any inefficiency, in terms of excess running time and memory required, must be traded off against increased productivity. Some attention is now being paid to efficiency considerations — the final version of the system being converted to fast object code modules by the system. However, with advances in hardware development (for example in very large scale integration and faster logic), these considerations might become less important.

Thus, most large transaction processing systems are still developed in traditional ways. Nevertheless the impact of fourth generation systems will increase, but whether they are ever used for all developments seems unlikely. Indeed, it is somewhat an irrelevant debate because as long as a significant number of developments are undertaken using fourth generation systems, then most objectives will have been achieved. Surveys of fourth generation systems and methodology workbenches can be found in Horowitz (1985), Lobell (1983) and Tozer (1984).

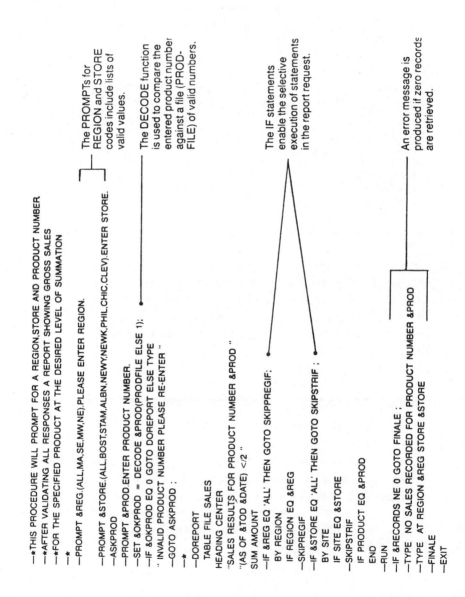

```
-*THIS PROCEDURE WILL PROMPT FOR A REGION,STORE AND PRODUCT NUMBER
-*AFTER VALIDATING ALL RESPONSES A REPORT SHOWING GROSS SALES
-*FOR THE SPECIFIED PRODUCT AT THE DESIRED LEVEL OF SUMMATION
-*
-PROMPT &REG.(ALL,MA,SE,MW,NE).PLEASE ENTER REGION.
-PROMPT &STORE.(ALL,BOST,STAM,ALBN,NEWY,NEWK,PHIL,CHIC,CLEV).ENTER STORE.
-ASKPROD
-PROMPT &PROD.ENTER PRODUCT NUMBER.
-SET &OKPROD = DECODE &PROD(PRODFILE ELSE 1);
-IF &OKPROD EQ 0 GOTO DOREPORT ELSE TYPE
" INVALID PRODUCT NUMBER PLEASE RE-ENTER "
-GOTO ASKPROD ;
-*
-DOREPORT
TABLE FILE SALES
HEADING CENTER
"SALES RESULTS FOR PRODUCT NUMBER &PROD "
"(AS OF &TOD &DATE) </2 "
SUM AMOUNT
-IF &REG EQ 'ALL' THEN GOTO SKIPPREGIF;
BY REGION
IF REGION EQ &REG
-SKIPPREGIF
-IF &STORE EQ 'ALL' THEN GOTO SKIPSTRIF ;
BY SITE
IF SITE EQ &STORE
-SKIPSTRIF
IF PRODUCT EQ &PROD
END
-RUN
-IF &RECORDS NE 0 GOTO FINALE ;
-TYPE  NO SALES RECORDED FOR PRODUCT NUMBER &PROD
-TYPE  AT REGION &REG STORE &STORE
-FINALE
-EXIT
```

The PROMPTs for REGION and STORE codes include lists of valid values.

The DECODE function is used to compare the entered product number against a file (PROD-FILE) of valid numbers.

The IF statements enable the selective execution of statements in the report request.

An error message is produced if zero records are retrieved.

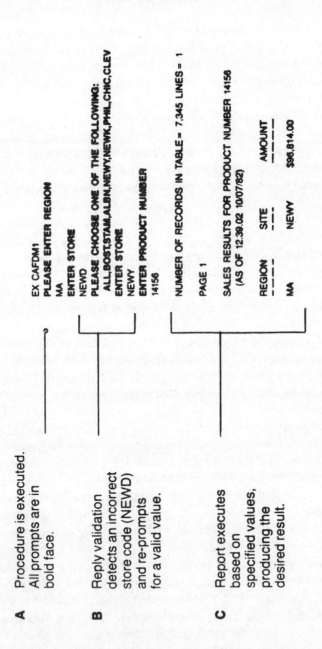

A   Procedure is executed. All prompts are in bold face.

B   Reply validation detects an incorrect store code (NEWD) and re-prompts for a valid value.

C   Report executes based on specified values, producing the desired result.

```
EX CAFDM1
PLEASE ENTER REGION
MA
ENTER STORE
NEWD
PLEASE CHOOSE ONE OF THE FOLLOWING:
    ALL,BOST,STAM,ALBN,NEWY,NEWK,PHIL,CHIC,CLEV
ENTER STORE
NEWY
ENTER PRODUCT NUMBER
14156

NUMBER OF RECORDS IN TABLE = 7,345 LINES = 1

PAGE 1

SALES RESULTS FOR PRODUCT NUMBER 14156
    (AS OF 12.39.02 10/07/82)

REGION      SITE        AMOUNT
------      ----        ------
MA          NEWY        $98,814.00
```

Fig. 5.15. Focus interactive dialogue. (Courtesy of Information Builders.)

5.5 METHODOLOGY WORKBENCHES

Methodology workbenches have been discussed in general terms in section 3.5 under the heading of automated tools for systems development. In this section we look at some of the tools designed to support many of the methodologies of Chapter 6, these tools are generically termed methodology workbenches.

The relationship of methodology workbenches to fourth generation systems often causes confusion. This is because some aspects of a fourth generation system may in fact be included in a methodology workbench and vice versa. The methodology workbench is usually aimed at the technologist rather than the user. Further, they are usually designed to support a particular methodology, although some are more general purpose. The methodology workbench covers a wider range of activities than simply the generation of code for an application, it supports the information and process modelling, the database design, even the strategy planning, as well as the programming or construction of a system which may well include support for fourth generation tools. Some methodology workbenches contain support for the management and control of the development of projects. This is treated as a separate topic in section 5.6.

Methodology workbenches are sometimes separated into two parts and termed analysts workbenches or programmers workbenches. There is no complete agreement on terminology and the term CASE (Computer Aided Software Engineering) is quite common for what we term programmers workbenches, as is IPSE (Integrated Project (or Programming) Support Environment).

Programmers workbenches in general support the design and construction of programs. The objective is to provide an environment in which software can be speedily developed which adheres to the standards of structure and the principles of software engineering. Within this framework there are usually two distinct support features, a code generation facility and a facility to provide sub-programs. A code generation facility generates source code in a traditional third generation language from a high level specification language, such as pseudo code. The second support feature is the provision of building blocks of code that have been pre-written for functions and processes which are frequently required and can be incorporated into a final application.

A workbench is likely to include test tools and diagnostic aids. A subroutine or program can be tested independently of other subroutines or programs. These facilities might be used to trace the execution of the subroutines or programs so that intermediate results can be validated. For this reason, the workbench can also be used to maintain programs and systems as well as creating new ones. Workbenches aim to attack the applications backlog by reducing maintenance time as well as development time.

A programmers workbenches product relating to a particular methodology is PDF (Program Development Facility) from Michael Jackson Systems. It is designed to support JSD and JSP structure diagrams and program designs, as well as generate code. It enables the structure diagrams to be created, saved, and modified by:

- Adding, inserting and naming boxes.
- Deleting boxes and complete substructures.
- Cutting and pasting substructures.
- Saving and restoring substructures.

The screen acts as a window which can be moved over large diagrams and zoomed in on areas of interest. The system organizes the diagrams according to certain standards to ensure consistency and presentability, and it does not allow the construction of invalid diagrams. JSP sequence, selection and iteration components are also supported. PDF enables diagrams to be printed and there are two levels of on-line help available for the user. PDF can generate both pseudo-code (JSP structure text) and program code ready for compilation. Languages supported include Cobol, PL/1, Fortran, Pascal, Ada and C. PDF is available for both mainframe and microcomputer environments.

Analysts workbenches support the systems analysis and design tasks. In particular they usually support the logical data modelling processes by automating the construction and maintenance of entity models, and the conversion to a variety of target DBMS schema designs (including normalized data). On the process modelling side they usually support the construction and maintenance of DFDs and function hierarchy charts of some kind. There may well also be support for screen and report designs and a menu and dialogue design facility. Analyst workbenches will have some kind of data dictionary or system encyclopedia as the central core of the facility. (A review of a number of analyst workbenches is found in Pergamon 1987.)

An example of an analysts workbench is Prokit*ANALYST from McDonnel Douglas which is designed to support application analysts using the Gane and Sarson methodology (STRADIS) (section 6.1). It not only helps the analyst draw (and redraw) DFDs but it simultaneously creates supporting documentation in an integrated data dictionary. The data dictionary can be expanded later as more information becomes available, but the integration of the tools ensures that duplicated entry and storage of data is minimized.

Teamwork/SA is another analyst workbench from Cadre Technologies Inc. It is described as a toolkit that helps analysts and designers to build, store, review and maintain structured specifications quickly and accurately. It is designed for use on a workstation rather than a personal computer and is not tailored to any one particular methodology but to structured methods in general. It features a Project Library Database which keeps all the information required in one central facility. This database includes data dictionaries, data flow diagrams, process specifications, annotations and project management information. The user interface allows multiple windows into all functions, including the library, to enable the user to view and edit several windows together. There is a consistency checker which can be invoked on a complete model or any subset of a model. It checks for accuracy and consistency in the model, detecting errors in and between the data flow diagrams, the data dictionary entries, and the process logic specifications. There is a query function which can answer questions like 'where is a particular term or element referenced?'. Teamwork/SA also includes a project management facility.

Inevitably analyst and programmer workbenches have been combined to form integrated project workbenches which address the whole of the development of a project from analysis through to construction, using a common set of tools and user interfaces.

An example of such a workbench product is the Information Engineering Workbench (IEW) jointly developed by Arthur Young and KnowledgeWare. This is designed to support the Information Engineering Methodology (section 6.2) and so is properly classified as a methodology workbench. The core of the IEW is the Encyclopedia, which contains information about all the objects in the development project, be these entities, processes, relationships, attributes, or whatever. The Encyclopedia is in two parts, one dealing with the organization's information and data, and the other with the organization's functions or activities. Information is also kept that relates one part to the other, for example, what data are used by what function.

At the user end, IEW provides access to a series of diagramming support tools similar to those described above. These are for DFDs, Entity Models, Decomposition Diagrams (which are kinds of structure charts) and Action Diagrams.

Sitting between these diagramming support tools and the Encyclopedia is something called the Knowledge Co-ordinator. This is an 'expert system' containing the rules of the Information Engineering Methodology. It enforces the correct standards for completeness, consistency, and accuracy of the diagram content.

The IEW adopts an interesting approach to the storage of the various diagrams, and unlike most other workbenches it does not store them as diagrams, for example, as DFDs, but as a series of definitions about the objects in the diagrams. This means that objects that appear in more than one diagram are only stored once and that diagrams are generated from the current information in the Encyclopedia, as and when they are needed. When changes are made to one diagram, the effects of that change are automatically reflected when other diagrams in which the object appears are generated. It is the Knowledge Co-ordinator that translates the Encyclopedia information into diagrams and displays, and vice versa. This enables the basic Encyclopedia information to be displayed in a number of ways according to needs. For example, an object may feature in an entity model, a DFD, and an action diagram.

IEW is still in the process of development and features being tested currently include modules for producing physical designs for programs and databases. An automatic code generation feature and a fourth generation language will be available. Ultimately the product will be a full system development environment for the Information Engineering methodology. Other systems of this type include Excellerator (Index Technologies), Information Engineering Facility IEF (James Martin Associates and Texas Instruments) and Application Factory (Cortext/Corvision).

5.6 PROJECT MANAGEMENT TOOLS

One of the most important tasks of a manager of an information systems project is project planning and control. Projects which take longer than scheduled cause a loss of money as well as embarrassment, particularly if they are unexpected or cannot be explained easily. Most methodologies split the information systems task into subdivisions and to activities within these. This ensures that there are a series of checkpoints that can be readily identified so that systems development staff can work to these and hence control the project. These checkpoints can be used to provide the interface to a project control package. The use of a project planning package can ensure that projects are scheduled at the earliest possible date, with the least drain on resources, and that there is a good chance that this date will be met. If there are delays, then at least the managers have information about them.

Project control techniques start with an attempt to break down the large and complex project into tasks, normally called activities. Once the activities have been identified, a time and resource requirement is assigned to each of these, and the inter-relationships between them established. In other words, those tasks which are dependent on the completion of other tasks are identified. These activities, and information about them, can be entered into a project control package. A project control tool may also be a part of the toolkit included in a fourth generation system, or more likely, an analysts workbench.

Using this information, the computer package can draw up a network. In a network, the activities are represented by arrows which join the nodes. These represent events, that is, the completion of activities.

Project control, even with the help of a good computer package, requires careful and detailed work:
- To identify tasks.
- To establish the inter-relationships between tasks.
- Allocate their resource needs.

This is an analytical process which is time consuming.

Figure 5.16 shows a network. The arrows represent the activities, though the length of the arrow does not indicate the time taken for each task. Arrows drawn in parallel indicate tasks that can be carried out simultaneously. Arrows following others indicate tasks that are dependent on the completion of those other tasks.

The manual development of networks is lengthy and project control packages can make the task much easier. They can draw the network and highlight critical activities on which any slippage of time will cause the whole project time scale to suffer. The path of the critical activities joined together forms the critical path, and it is useful for the package to highlight these activities. In figure 5.16, the activities A-B-C-E are on the critical path. If it is possible to reduce the time of these activities, possibly by moving resources allocated from other activities to them, then the overall project time should decrease. Activity D is not on the critical path, and there is a slack of 7 days on this activity. In other words, there can be a delay of up to 7 days on D without delaying the overall project.

Many computer packages will aggregate the various resources, such as the number of people working on the activity, and attempt to level the use of these resources throughout the project. It is usually better to use resources as smoothly as possible in the lifetime of the project. Once this has been done,

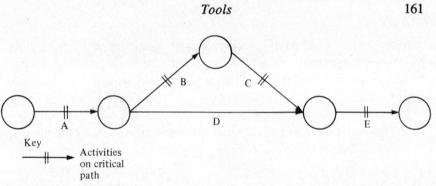

Key

⊢⊣→ Activities
on critical
path

Activity	Dependence	Duration	Start	Finish	Slack
A	–	10 days	–	10	–
B	A	6 days	11	16	–
C	B	16 days	17	32	–
D	A	8 days	11	18	14
E	C, D	6 days	33	38	–

Fig. 5.16. Project control — the network and critical path.

a bar chart showing the resource allocation over time can be displayed and printed (see figure 5.17).

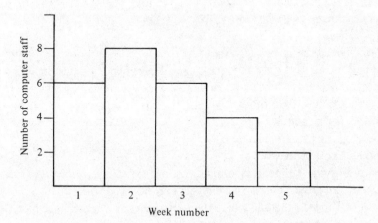

Fig. 5.17. Project control — resource schedule.

Many packages will report on inconsistencies within the network, such as the same resource being used at the same time. The package will normally convert days into calendar dates and to allow for weekends, bank holidays, and other holidays.

Normally there is a trade-off between time and cost, in other words the more resources allocated (and the more costly the project), the quicker it can be finished. The user may like to input:

- The minimum.
- The most likely.
- The maximum,

resource availability so as to get three different results for time/cost comparisons. Such an exercise would be very laborious if drawn by hand.

Project planning packages may permit the user to ask 'what if?' questions so as to see the consequence of certain actions, for example of:

- A re-allocation of staff.
- A holiday period.
- A machine breakdown,

and so on. The user can also use the package to highlight the results of following different work patterns or changing other aspects of the business.

Useful reports from the package include a list of activities presented in order of:

- Latest starting date.
- Earliest starting date.
- By department.
- By resource.
- By responsibility.

Information relevant only to a particular department or sales area can be created so that people are not given unnecessary information. Furthermore, it may simulate the effects of:

- prolonging an activity,
- reducing resources applied to it, or
- adding new activities

to the total project time, and similarly, show the effects of changing these parameters on project costs. The manager may be faced with two alternatives: a resource-limited schedule where the project end date is put back to reflect resource constraints, or a time-limited schedule where a fixed project end date leads to an increase in other resources used, such as human resources and equipment resources.

Once the project has started, there will be progress reporting. This can be used to:

- Compare the schedule with progress made.
- Detect problem areas.
- Provide a historical record which can be used for future project planning.

The system may also give information about how to act so as to put right any deviation from the schedule. This may be achieved by, for example, increasing the resources on some activities and re-scheduling others. This goal-seeking type of analysis, almost impossible manually, is achieved by a number of computer packages.

Any change in a manual system will require the chart to be re-drawn — an inconvenience at best; more often a task left undone, which makes it likely that any previous planning is ineffective.

The development of an information system is likely to be a large scale project, particularly where the overall plan has a number of inter-related sub-systems that need to be completed separately but integrated later. 'Large' here refers to time, cost, people, and equipment resources, as well as to the complexity of the inter-relationships between activities in the project. The use of a project planning tool makes an up-to-date and informative plan far more likely, and such large scale integrated information systems projects feasible. To set against these gains, however, allowance has to be made for the costs of maintaining and updating the project control systems.

Although we have stressed here the need for project planning tools, we must also admit that, according to Grindley (1987), the difficulty of meeting deadlines on computer systems development projects has been *the* major problem concerning information technology managers over the last seven years (when the data were first collected). Although project planning tools help, particularly by enforcing a planning stage, and thereby enabling the discovery of important aspects of the project that would otherwise go unnoticed (such as conflicting objectives), their main effect seems to have been in measuring our lack of success at meeting deadlines.

By providing a number of integrated tools, a fourth generation system, one would expect, would also help by providing workable systems faster. According to Grindley's statistics, however, the problem is worsening. Demand is outstripping the supply of improved information systems. Perhaps the problem is insoluble, the supply of information systems simply feeds further demand. The faster systems are developed using fourth generation tools and others, the faster users will expect them, and want new ones. No project control package can help in a fundamental way to solve this problem. The answer might be to let users develop their own systems and let *them* make the choices. They can then see the repercussions of these decisions. This might make for a more realistic framework for information systems development.

5.7 EXPERT SYSTEMS

An expert system is a system which will simulate the role of an expert. It is distinguished from other applications because its usefulness is derived from the knowledge and reasoning ability of the expert system package and not from number crunching (carrying out large and complex calculations) or the repetitive processing of data, which characterizes most scientific and business computing applications respectively. More formally an expert system has been defined by the British Computer Society's Expert Systems Specialist Group as follows:

'An expert system is regarded as the embodiment within a computer of a knowledge-based component from an expert skill in such a form that the system can offer INTELLIGENT ADVICE or take an INTELLIGENT DECISION about a processing function. A desirable additional characteristic, which many would consider fundamental, is the capability of the system, on demand, to JUSTIFY ITS OWN LINE OF REASONING in a manner directly intelligible to the enquirer. The style adopted to attain these characteristics is RULE-BASED PROGRAMMING.'

Thus, an expert system is basically an intelligent adviser concerning one or more areas or domains of knowledge. This knowledge exists in the minds of human experts, it has been developed and evolved over time by education and experience, and it has to be captured in some way by the expert system, usually in the form of sets of rules and groups of facts. The expert system is then informed about a particular situation of concern to a user, this is usually achieved by the user answering questions posed by the expert system. Then the expert system comes up with intelligent advice concerning that situation. Ideally the expert system should then be able to explain to the user how it has arrived at that particular advice.

Expert systems vary considerably but the most common component parts are as follows:

The knowledgebase: This contains the rules and the facts. The rules are usually as follows:

> If P1 and P2 and ...Pn,
> Then Q1 and Q2 and ...Qn

which reads,

> 'If premises P1 and ... Pn are true,
> Then perform actions Q1 and ... Qn'.

The Ps are sometimes called 'conditions' and the Qs 'conclusions'. The conclusions can sometimes be drawn with certain degrees of confidence by the introduction of probabilities. For example, a rule might be that 'if X is a bird then conclude that X can fly'. This rule is not true in all circumstances because emus are birds but they cannot fly. We might then introduce another rule that states that 'if X is a bird and X is an emu then conclude that X cannot fly' or we might say that 'if X is a bird then conclude with a probability of .99 that X can fly'. The facts contained in the knowledgebase are simply assertions, for example, a robin is a bird.

An inference engine: The inference engine controls the process of invoking the rules that pertain to the solution of the problems posed to the system.

A language: This is the language in which the rules are written. Prolog or LISP are common general purpose languages, but it is quite usual for expert system packages to have their own dedicated languages.

An explanation generator: This is the part of the system that presents the reasoning behind how the system arrived at its conclusions.

A blackboard: This is a temporary workspace that records intermediate hypotheses and decisions that the expert system makes. It usually consists of three elements. Firstly the plan, this is the approach to the current problem, secondly the agenda, which records the potential actions awaiting execution, that is, the rules that appear to be relevant, and thirdly the solution elements, which are the candidate hypotheses and decisions the system has generated so far.

A user interface: This varies widely, but is a very important element in the architecture of an expert system. As well as the interface for the user it also contains the interface for entering and updating the knowledgebase.

A shell: This is addressed later on in this section.

The environment: This is the variety of hardware and software that surrounds the expert system.

So far the major implementations of expert systems have mainly been in the military, scientific and medical world. MYCIN is one of the most famous: it is an expert system designed to carry out medical diagnosis in the domain of blood and meningitis infections. It diagnoses and recommends a course of drug treatment. It is based on a set of about 450 probability rules, as medical diagnosis is not an exact science. It was developed in collaboration with the Infectious Diseases Group at Stanford University in the United States.

Expert systems have developed with the evolution of the *shell* concept. A shell is an expert system with all the inference capability but without any domain specific knowledge. It is thus ready for anybody to input their own rules and knowledge to create their own expert system applications. It is these shell packages that will probably be the basis of most expert systems of the future.

Expert systems have proved of value in scientific and medical applications and many commentators are predicting that they will prove equally valuable in business applications. The reasons are that many areas and applications in business currently rely on the expertise and knowledge of specialists, for example portfolio management, in the same way that medical diagnosis relies on the expertise of specialists. Therefore there is no reason, if an expert system can be built for one, that it cannot be built for the other. Some people have argued that the greatest benefits of expert systems will come when they are applied to the expertise of the strategic levels of management. However, currently, expert systems are better suited to domains away from the strategic level of management where there are fairly firm rules that apply. This is more the case of the professions, for example, the law, or accountancy, than the tasks of Chief Executives. Therefore it is likely that expert systems will be developed for operational business activities first and for strategic and tactical levels of management somewhat later. A short survey of expert systems in business is found in d'Agapeyeff and Hawkins (1987).

Apart from the problem of finding the right applications, the process of knowledge acquisition or knowledge elicitation is proving problematical. This is the process of obtaining the expertise from the human experts. Early expert systems were often developed by the domain experts themselves so the problem was not so difficult, but this cannot usually be the case. The formulation of decision rules is no easy task because the experts themselves do not always structure their decision making in any formal way, they often cannot explain why they know something to be true. The defining of probabilities is also extremely difficult and the views of experts can differ considerably. Even when they are in agreement, the knowledge still has to be formulated into rules for use by the expert system. This problem has often been described as the real bottleneck in the development of expert systems. A related problem is the testing of an expert system. It is difficult to prove that the expertise has been captured correctly and that it will lead to good and accurate results when applied. In fact it is still a very early stage in the development and use of expert systems, indeed perhaps hardly beyond the research stage. There is presently a very limited availability of people who have had experience of implementing expert systems. These systems can take a minimum of three years to be implemented. A further limiting factor has been the range of suitable applications based on our present state of knowledge.

Expert systems relate to information systems methodologies in a number of ways. The systems development process itself may be viewed as a potential application for an expert system. There are clearly people who are experts in some or all aspects, there is a shortage of such people, the process is not algorithmic, and it contains elements of uncertainty. In short, most of the features that would normally be associated with an ideal expert system application are to be found in the case of the systems development process. So the principles of expert systems could be applied. In particular, it is likely that the methodology workbenches of the future will be somewhat akin to expert systems. In fact, it may already have been noticed that in the description of the Information Engineering Workbench (IEW) there was an element which was termed an expert system. This was the Knowledge Co-ordinator which contains over a thousand rules of the Information Engineering methodology in order to be able to perform its task of enforcing standards and translating Encyclopedia entries into diagrams. Thus already the concept of expert systems in workbenches is established.

The area where expert systems are relevant to methodologies, is in the use of methodologies not just to develop standard data processing systems but to develop expert systems themselves. If it is true, as many have argued, that expert systems will see their greatest growth when applied to business problems, then methodologies will need to address themselves to the development of expert systems in the future. There is not much evidence currently that methodologies are evolving in this way, but it is sometimes argued that the knowledge acquisition task is not that significantly different from the standard systems analysis task. Therefore it may be that the current methodologies may not need too much adapting to handle the acquisition of knowledge and its representation as well as the acquisition and representation, of data and processes.

Chapter 6
Methodologies

In this chapter, we look at a number of information systems methodologies which are well used, respected, or typify the approaches described in Chapter 3. These include: a structured approach (STRADIS) based on the work of Chris Gane and Trish Sarson; IE, based on the work of James Martin and Clive Finkelstein; SSADM, a methodology developed by Learmonth and Burchett; JSD, a systems development methodology by Michael Jackson; ISAC, a methodology developed in Scandinavia; ETHICS, a methodology proposed by Enid Mumford; and SSM, a methodology proposed by Peter Checkland. We also look at Multiview, a hybrid methodology, which brings in aspects of other methodologies and adopts techniques and tools which are used as a contingency approach, applied as the application demands. We have not described other similar methodologies, even if they are well used, but reference this similarity where appropriate. The methodologies are described largely uncritically so that the readers can follow their principles and practice, although we have commented on aspects of the methodologies where they reveal important features. However, the descriptions of the methodologies represent interpretations of the methodologies by the authors of this text, and these views may not correspond to those of the methodology suppliers. We look at the methodologies more critically in Chapter 7 and provide a framework in which to assess them.

6.1 GANE AND SARSON (STRADIS)

The major statement of Gane and Sarson's methodology of systems development comes in their book entitled *Structured Systems Analysis* (Gane and Sarson 1979). The development of this structured systems approach to analysis came as a result of the earlier development of a structured approach to design. The structured design concepts were first propounded in 1974 by Stevens, Myers and Constantine (1974) and these ideas were later developed and refined by Yourdon and Constantine (1978), and Myers (1975, 1978). The work of Jackson (1975) was also very influential.

Structured design is concerned with the selection and organization of modules and interfaces that would solve a pre-defined problem. However, it makes no contribution to the defining of that problem. This proves to be a practical limitation as the development of an information system requires both analysis and design aspects to be addressed, and whilst structured design was acknowledged to provide significant benefits, these benefits were wasted if the definition of the original problem was not well stated or inaccurate.

A number of people have therefore attempted to take the concepts of structured design and apply them to systems analysis, in order to develop a method of specifying requirements and to provide an interface to structured design. In this way the techniques of structured analysis were developed. Apart from Gane and Sarson's work, DeMarco (1979) and Weinberg (1978) have also produced books on structured analysis covering some of the same ground and utilizing very similar techniques within the approach.

Gane and Sarson's methodology has been developed over a number of years on a practical basis by providing courses and consultancy in structured systems analysis methods through a company called Improved Systems Technologies (IST). McAuto, a subsidiary of McDonnell Douglas became a client of IST and later bought out IST and now supply structured systems products and training under the name of MCAUTO/IST. The most important product is the methodology itself called STRADIS SDM which stands for STRuctured Analysis Design and Implementation of information Systems System Development Methodology. MCAUTO/IST also market a number of software packages to support the methodology.

Gane and Sarson only relatively briefly outline a methodology of systems development in their book. The majority of the book is devoted to descriptions of the techniques which the methodology utilizes. This is in direct contrast to some other methodologies. ISAC (section 6.5), for example, lays out the steps of the methodology in great detail. Therefore the most important aspect of the Gane and Sarson methodology is the use of many of the techniques which were described separately in Chapter 4 in this book. These techniques are utilized, in some form or other, by many different methodologies, and therefore Gane and Sarson's methodology is not unique but may be regarded as epitomizing those methodologies based on functional decomposition (see section 3.7) and the use of the data flow diagram (DFD), described in section 4.3.

The STRADIS Methodology is still evolving, the method steps are being improved and refined, and the methodology is being expanded into the area of implementation. However, this more recent work has not been formally published and therefore the description given here does not include these developments.

Gane and Sarson's methodology is conceived as being a methodology applicable to the development of any information system, irrespective of size and whether or not it is going to be automated. In practice, however, it has mainly been used and refined in environments where at least part of the information system is automated. The methodology is envisaged to be relevant to a situation in which there is a backlog of systems waiting to be developed and insufficient resources to devote to all the potential new systems.

1 Initial Study

Thus, the starting point of the methodology is an attempt to ensure that the systems chosen to be developed are those that most warrant development in a competing environment. The most important criterion in this selection process being the monetary costs and benefits of each proposal. Systems are viewed as contributing towards increasing revenues, avoiding costs, or improving services. The initial study to discover this information is conducted by systems analysts gathering data from managers and users in the relevant areas. The analyst is to review existing documentation and assess the proposal in the light of any strategic plans relating to systems development that may exist within the organization. The initial study usually involves the construction of an overview DFD of the existing system and its interfaces, and an estimate of the times and costs of proceeding to a detailed investigation. In addition, some broad range of final system development costs might be estimated. The initial study normally takes between two days and four weeks, depending on the size and importance of the application.

On completing the initial study, a report is reviewed by the relevant management and they decide on whether to proceed to a more detailed study or not. If they approve of the proposal, they are committing themselves to the costs of the detailed study but not necessarily to implementing the proposed system.

Gane and Sarson's initial study might be thought to be quite close to the traditional notion of a feasibility study outlined in section 2.2. However, there are some important differences. Gane and Sarson's methodology does not include a review of alternative approaches to the proposal and it is not, perhaps, as major or as resource intensive a task as a traditional feasibility study. Furthermore, a traditional feasibility study, if approved by management, is usually a commitment to the implementation of the complete proposal. Gane and Sarson do address all these aspects, but at later stages within their methodology.

2 Detailed Study

This takes the work of the initial study further. In particular the existing system is examined in detail. As a part of this investigation the potential users of the system are identified. These users will exist at three levels:

1 The senior managers with profit responsibilities, whom Gane and Sarson call the 'commissioners', whose areas will be affected. They initially commissioned the system proposal.

2 The middle managers of the departments affected.

3 The end users, that is, the people who will actually work directly with the system.

Having identified these three sets of users, the analysts ascertain their interests and requirements by interviewing them. Next the analyst prepares a draft logical DFD of the current system. This will usually involve constructing a DFD that extends well beyond the current system under consideration, in order to be clear exactly what and where the boundaries are in relation to other systems, and to identify the interfaces between various systems.

For example, figure 6.1 depicts a data flow of part of a university admissions procedure. The system under consideration is that enclosed by the dotted line but in order to appreciate the context, a larger system is depicted which enables the interfaces to be clearly identified. Any data flow that crosses the dotted line must be addressed by both the external system and the system under consideration. In this case the diagram has highlighted the fact that those applications where the qualifications are not known, require a decision to be made (see the data flow marked with the asterisk). This is a non-obvious interface which may otherwise have been neglected.

The boundary may be drawn in any place and could be moved. It may, for example, be more logical to include other processes within the boundary in order to minimize the number of interfaces to the external system. This is particularly important when the automation boundary is being chosen.

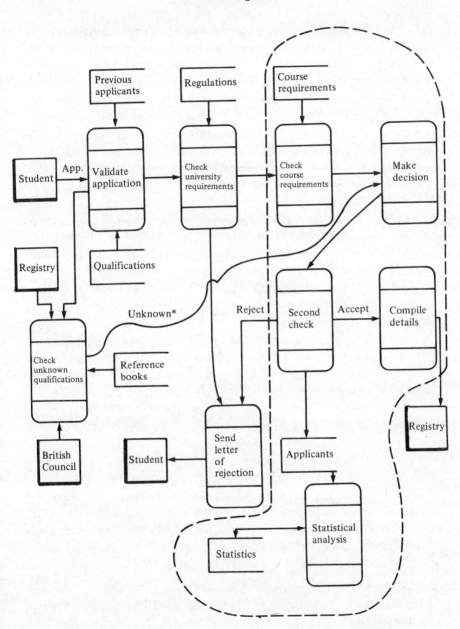

Fig. 6.1. Example of system boundary.

Gane and Sarson describe in detail the drafting of DFDs at various levels, showing how each level is exploded into lower levels through to the level where the logic of each process box in the low level DFD should now be specified using the appropriate process logic representation, for example decision trees, decision tables, or structured English (see sections 4.4, 4.5 and 4.6). They suggest that DFDs and other outputs should be reviewed or 'walked through' with a number of users so as to check their validity and alterations made where necessary.

The detail of the DFDs and the process logic is entered into the data dictionary. The data dictionary can be either manual or computerized. On the DFD, data flows and data stores are defined using a single name which is meaningful. All the details that the name represents must be collected and stored in the central repository which is the data dictionary (see section 5.3).

The extent of detail that the analyst goes to at this stage in the methodology is not made clear, but it appears that not all low level processes are specified in process logic and that not all data flows and data stores are specified in the data dictionary. It is usual to specify in detail only the most significant at this stage.

The initial study estimated the costs and benefits of the proposed system in outline. These estimates are further refined within the detailed study. The analysts need to investigate the assumptions on which the estimates were based, and ensure that all aspects have been considered. They also need to consider the effects and costs of the proposed system from the point of view of organizational impact. In other words they need to have a better estimate on which a final decision can legitimately be made.

In summary the detailed study contains:

A definition of the user community for a new system, that is, the names and responsibilities of senior executives, the functions of affected departments, the relationships among affected departments, the descriptions of clerical jobs that will be affected, and the number of people in each clerical job, hiring rates, and natural attrition rates.

A logical model of the current system, that is, an overall data flow diagram (including the interfacing systems, if relevant), a detailed data flow diagram for each important process, the logic specification for each basic process at an appropriate level of detail, and the data definitions at an appropriate level of detail.

A statement of increased revenue/avoidable cost/improved service that could be provided by an improved system, including: the assumptions, the present and projected volumes of transactions and quantities of stored data and the financial estimates of benefits where possible.

Account of competitive/statutory pressures (if any), including: the system cost and a firm cost/time budget for the next phase (defining a menu of possible alternatives).

The results of the detailed study are presented to management and a decision will be made to either stop at this stage or proceed to the next phase.

3 Defining and Designing Alternative Solutions

The next phase defines alternative solutions to the problems of the existing system. Firstly, the organizational objectives, as defined in the initial study, are converted into a set of system objectives. An organizational objective is a relatively high level objective having an effect on the organization. This could include increased revenue, lower cost, or improved service. A system objective is at a lower level, and relates to what the system should do to help management achieve the organizational objectives.

The system objectives should be strongly stated. This means that they should be specific and measurable, rather than general. So, for example, 'improving the timeliness of information' would be a weakly stated objective and it would be preferable to state this objective more strongly, for example 'to produce the monthly sales analysis report by the fourth working day of the following month'.

The analyst uses these objectives to produce a logical DFD of the new or desired system. The existing system DFD should be used as the basis for this and the desired system may involve the introduction of new or changed data flows, data stores, and processes. The new DFD should be constructed to a level of detail which shows that the most important of the system objectives are being met.

The methodology then enters a design phase. Here analysts and designers work together to produce various alternative implementation designs which meet a variable selection of the identified system objectives. The alternatives should cover three different categories of designs. Firstly, a low-budget, fairly quick implementation which may not initially meet all the objectives; secondly a mid-budget, medium term version, which achieves a majority of the objectives; and thirdly, a higher budget, more ambitious, version achieving all the objectives. Each alternative should have rough estimates of costs and benefits, timescales, hardware, and software.

The report of this phase of the project should be presented to the relevant decision makers and a commitment made to one of the alternatives. The report should contain the following:

- A DFD of the current system.
- The limitations of the current system, including the cost and benefit estimates.
- The logical DFD of the new system.
- For *each* of the identified alternatives:

  The parts of the DFD that would be implemented.

  User interface (terminals, reports, query facilities, and so on).

  Estimated costs and benefits.

  Outline implementation schedule.

  Risks involved.

4 Physical Design

The design team then refines the chosen alternative into a specific physical design which involves a number of parallel activities:

Firstly, all the detail of the DFD must be produced, including all the error and exception handling, which has not been specified earlier, and all the process logic. The content of the data dictionary is completed and report and screen formats produced. This detail should be validated and agreed with the users.

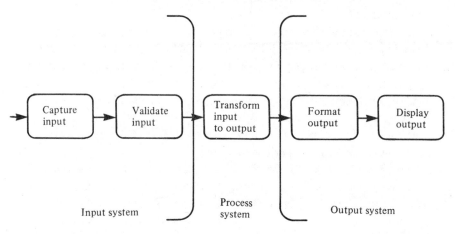

Fig. 6.2. Transform centred system.

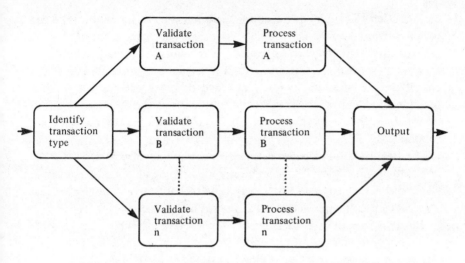

Fig. 6.3. Transaction centred system

Secondly, the physical files or database will be designed. They will be based on the data store contents previously specified at the logical level. Data stores are defined in the DFD as the temporary storage of data needed for the process under consideration. This has the effect of introducing many data stores scattered all over the DFD. Many of these will be very similar in content and have a significant degree of overlap.

Thirdly, the data stores need rationalizing, and the technique of normalization (described in section 4.2) is utilized to consolidate and simplify the data stores into logical groupings. The actual process of mapping and the design of the physical files (or database) are not defined by Gane and Sarson.

Fourthly, derive a modular hierarchy of functions from the DFD. The designer seeks to identify either of two structures that any commercial data processing system is thought to exhibit. The first structure is the simplest. Here all transactions follow very similar processing paths (figure 6.2). Such a system is termed a 'transform' centred system. The second structure is one in which the transactions require very different processing. This is termed a 'transaction' centred system and is illustrated in figure 6.3.

The first step therefore is to identify which type of system is being described. It is recommended that the raw input data flow is traced through the DFD until a point is reached at which it can no longer be said to be input, but has been transformed into some other data flow. The output is traced backwards in a similar fashion until it can no longer be considered to be output. Anything in between is termed the 'transform'. The transform is then analysed to see if it is a single transform or a number of different transforms on different transaction types. Once one or other of these high level functional hierarchy types have been identified from the DFD, the detail of the modules in the hierarchy and the communication between them are constructed.

The final task in this phase is the definition of any clerical tasks that the new system will require. The required clerical tasks are identified according to where the automated system boundary is on the DFD and according to what physical choice of input and output media has been made.

The above activities are pursued to a level of detail at which it is possible to give a firm estimate of the cost of developing and operating the new system. The major components of these costs are identified as:

- The professional time and computer time required to develop the identified modules.
- The machine required.
- The peripherals and data communication costs.
- The professional time required to develop documentation and train users.
- The time of the users who interact with the system.
- The professional time required to maintain and enhance the system during its lifetime.

Subsequent phases of the methodology are not clearly defined by Gane and Sarson as the methodology is effectively concerned mainly with analysis, to a lesser extent design and hardly at all with implementation. However, the following list indicates the remaining tasks that Gane and Sarson envisage as being needed to complete the development of the system:

- Draw up an implementation plan, including plans for testing and acceptance of the system.
- Develop concurrently the application programs and the database/data communications functions (where relevant).
- Convert and load the database(s).
- Test and ensure acceptance of each part of the system.
- Ensure that the system meets the performance criteria defined in the system objectives, under realistic loads, in terms of response time and throughput.
- Commit the system to live operation and tune it to deal with any bottlenecks.
- Compare the overall system facilities and performance to original

objectives and action to resolve any differences, where possible.

Analyse any requests for enhancement, prioritizing these enhancements, and place the system in 'maintenance' state.

6.2 INFORMATION ENGINEERING

The origins of Information Engineering (IE) differ according to which source is referenced. It appears that Clive Finkelstein first used the term to describe a data modelling methodology that he developed in Australia in the late 1970s. In early 1981 he named his consultancy company Information Engineering and wrote a series of articles on the methodology. In the same year he collaborated with James Martin on a two volume book entitled *Information Engineering* (Martin and Finkelstein 1981).

Since that time there rather confusingly appears to exist a number of versions of IE around the world, which, whilst very similar in content, have tended to develop along somewhat different lines. The reason for this is that James Martin has set up a number of independent companies based on the methodology of IE and although the methodologies were originally basically the same, they have evolved in slightly differing ways over the years. The version of IE described here is based on that evolved by James Martin Associates (JMA), London.

This methodology is a synthesis of ideas based on the original IE, and the work of Macdonald and Palmer (1982). They developed the CACI methodology or, as it later became, D2S2 (System Development in a Shared Data environment) (see also Palmer and Rock-Evans (1981). The explanation for this is that they, and a number of others, left the consultancy company CACI and joined JMA. The result was the bringing together of James Martin's ideas, and the data analysis based methodology of D2S2 into one methodology with the name IE. This is claimed to be a comprehensive methodology covering all aspects of the life cycle. Like almost all the methodologies in this book, IE is still evolving and developing in the light of improving technology and experience of use. In particular, it is evolving in the area of automated tools and the development of the methodology to support fourth generation systems development.

IE is viewed as a framework within which a variety of techniques are used to develop good quality information systems in an efficient way. The framework is relatively static, and includes the fundamental things which must be done in order to develop good information systems. The techniques are regarded as the current best way of achieving the fundamentals but are not part of those fundamentals. The techniques can and do change as new and improved techniques emerge. The framework is also designed as a project management tool, which reflects IE's philosophy of 'practicality and applicability'. It is not just a set of ideas but is argued to be a proven and practical approach. This obviously reflects the nature of JMA which is a consultancy house, but also, it is argued, it reflects the needs of their clients. It is also said to be applicable in a wide range of industries and environments. Mitchell (1985) describes a practical application of IE at the British Gas Corporation.

A major philosophical base of IE is the belief that data is at the heart of an information system and that the data, or rather the types of data, are considerably more stable than the processes or procedures that act upon the data. Thus a methodology that successfully identifies the underlying nature and structure of the organization's data has a stable basis from which to build information systems. Methodologies which are based upon processes are likely to fail (the proponents of IE would argue) due to the constantly shifting nature of the base. This is the classic argument of the data analysis school of thought. However, IE does also consider processes in detail, and balances the modelling of data and activity at the appropriate place. But the basis of the information system is data.

A further aspect of the philosophy of IE is the belief that the most appropriate way of communication within the methodology is through the use of diagrams. Diagrams are very appealing to end-users and end-user management, and enable them to understand, participate and even construct for themselves the relevant IE diagrams. This helps to ensure that their requirements are truly understood and achieved. The diagrams are regarded as being rigorous enough on their own to ensure that all necessary information is captured and represented. Each IE technique is orientated towards diagramming, and a diagram is a deliverable of each major stage in the methodology. Support for the diagramming tasks is also a basic goal of the automation of the methodology. The automation of the methodology now forms an important thrust for development. Indeed James Martin has called the automation of the IE process 'the biggest single revolution in the history of computing' and has quoted figures for productivity increases of 4 000 per cent!

The methodology is defined as top-down. Following the overview, as the steps of the methodology are carried out, more and more detail is derived (as in structured methods). However, more importantly, it means that the objectives change as the methodology progresses, each stage having different objectives (though the overall objectives of the project will be stable). Thus progress is controlled by measuring whether the objectives have been achieved at each stage, not how much detail has been generated. The methodology is divided into four levels, within which there are seven stages, each with different objectives (see figure 6.4):

- Planning: The objective here is to construct an information architecture and a strategy which supports the objectives of the organization.
- Analysis: The objective here is to understand the business areas and determine the system requirements.
- Design: The objective here is to establish the behaviour of the systems in a way that the user wants and that is achievable via the technology.
- Construction: The objective here is to build the systems as required by the three previous levels.

Business Planning

This is really the development of the corporate plan and corporate objectives. It is not, strictly speaking, part of the IE methodology, as it would normally be performed by corporate management and planners. However, it is recognized as a fundamental starting point for the methodology. It implies that the organization's information system should be designed to help meet the requirements of the corporate plan, and that information systems are of strategic importance to the organization. The corporate or business plan should indicate the business goals and strategies, outline the major business functions and their objectives, and identify the organizational structure. The plan should ideally be in quantitative terms with priorities between objectives established.

1 Information Strategy Planning

This involves an overview analysis of the business objectives of the organization and its major business functions and information needs. The result of this analysis is what is termed 'information architectures' which form the basis for subsequent developments and ensure consistency and coherence between different systems in the organization. The resulting information strategy plan documents the business requirements and priorities which are the rationale for the development of the information systems. The

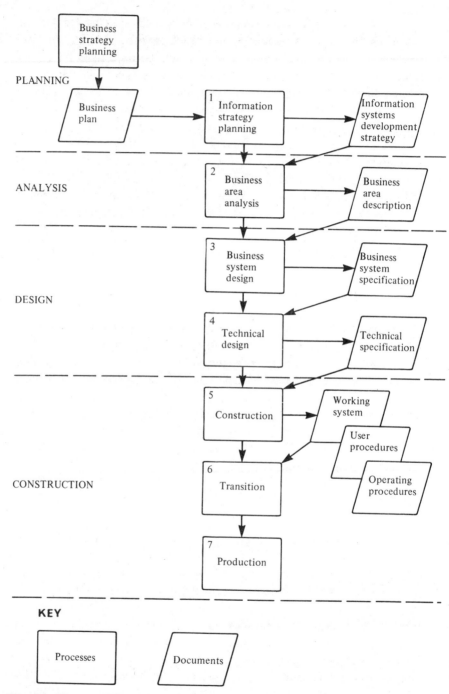

Fig. 6.4. The stage framework of the Information Engineering Methodology™. (Courtesy of James Martin Associates of which Information Engineering Methodology is a trademark.)

plan enables these high level requirements to be kept in view throughout the development of the project. In many other methodologies, it is argued, these needs get lost, if they are ever identified at all. It also provides a means of controlling changes to assumptions, priorities, and objectives should it become necessary. Apart from such changes, the information strategy plan should remain relatively static. Information strategy planning is a joint activity of user management and information system staff. It involves the performance of four tasks as follows:

Current Situation Analysis. This is an overview of the organization and its current position, including a view of the strengths and weaknesses of the current systems. This overview will include an analysis of the business strategy, an analysis of the information system organization, an analysis of the technical environment, and a definition of the preliminary information architecture (data subject areas, such as customer or product, and major business functions).

Executive Requirements Analysis. Here, managers are provided with an opportunity to state their objectives, needs and perceptions. These factors will include information needs, priorities, responsibilities and problems.

Architecture Definition. Again, this is an overview of the area in terms of information architecture (identification of global entity types and the decomposition of functions within the subject areas described in the preliminary information architecture in the current situation analysis above), an analysis of distribution (the geographic requirements for the functions and the data), a definition of business systems architecture (a statement of the ideal systems required in the organization), a definition of technical architecture (a statement of the technology direction required to support the systems including hardware, software, and communications facilities), and a definition of information system organization (a proposal for the organization of the information systems function to support the strategy).

Information Strategy Plan. The creation of the information strategy plan includes the determination of business areas (divides the architectures into logical business groupings, each of which could form an analysis project in its own right), the preparation of business evaluation (evaluates strategies for achieving the architectures, including migration plans for moving from the current situation to the desired objective), and the preparation of the information strategy plan (a chosen strategy including priorities for development and work programs for high priority projects).

2 Business Area Analysis

The business areas identified in the information strategy plan are now treated individually and a detailed data and function analysis is performed. Maximum involvement of end users is recommended in this stage. The tasks of business area analysis are as follows:

Entity and Function Analysis. This is the major task of the stage. It involves the analysis of entity types and relationships, the analysis of processes and dependencies, the construction of diagrammatic representations of the above (such as entity models (section 4.1), function hierarchy diagrams similar to that shown as figure 3.2, and process dependency diagrams (a kind of data flow diagram (section 4.3) but without data stores)) and the definition of attributes and information views.

Interaction Analysis. This examines the relationship and interactions between the data and the functions, that is, the business dynamics. This phase includes an analysis of entity type life cycles (see section 4.8), an analysis of process logic (see section 4.3, 4.4 and 4.5), and the preparation of process action diagrams (see section 4.7).

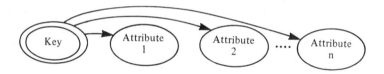

Fig. 6.5. A bubble chart.

Current Systems Analysis. This models the existing systems in the same way as for the entity and function analysis task in order that the models can be compared in the confirmation task (below), and so that smooth transition from one to the other can be achieved. The phase includes the construction of procedure data flow diagrams (see section 4.3) and the preparation of a data model by *canonical synthesis*. Because this is a technique not described previously, an example of its use will be provided. Canonical synthesis is a technique for pulling together all the data identified in separate parts of the organization, whether they be reports, screens, forms, diagrams and so on, in fact all sources, into a coherent structure, which is the entity model. The

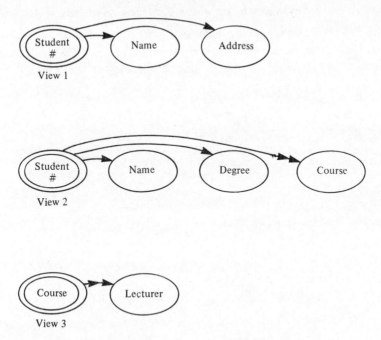

View 1

View 2

View 3

Fig. 6.6. Three user views. (Courtesy of James Martin Associates.)

technique involves the drawing of bubble charts (user view analysis) and synthesizing all the data into an entity model. A bubble chart is a graph of directed links between data-item types (see figure 6.5). A double ellipse represents a key, an arrow represents a one-to-one dependency, and a double arrow represents a one-to-many dependency. In this case the key completely determines (or identifies) the attributes, therefore the data is normalized. A separate bubble chart is constructed for each separate user view of the data. Figure 6.6 shows an example of three user views in a university environment. View 1 might be a secretary's view, view 2 a registrar's view, and view 3, a course manager's view. The process of canonical synthesis combines the separate views into one data model. Each view is normalized (section 4.2) and combined with another, and any duplications in the graph are eliminated. Figure 6.7 is the result of the combination of views 1 and 2 and figure 6.8 is the synthesis of all three views.

Confirmation. This is the cross-checking of the results of the above, in terms of completeness, correctness and stability. Hypotheses concerning business changes are also examined to see what effects these might have.

Planning for Design. This step includes the definition of design areas (which identifies those parts of the model to be automated), the evaluation of implementation/transition sequences and the planning of design objects.

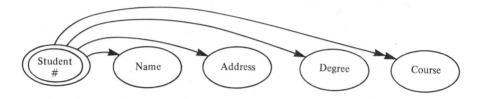

Fig. 6.7. Synthesis of views 1 and 2.

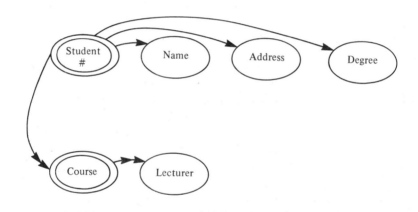

Fig. 6.8. Synthesis of all three views.

The output from business area analysis is the business area description which contains the business functions, and each function is broken down into its lower level processes and the process dependencies. On the data side, the entity types, relationships and attributes are described, along with their properties and usage patterns. The level of detail here is much greater than that arrived at during the construction of the architectures performed during the information strategy planning stage. This information provides the basis for the broad identification of business processes requiring computer support.

3 Business Systems Design

For each design area identified at the previous stage (planning for design) the facts gathered are used to design a system to fulfil the identified business requirements. The design is taken up to the point at which technical factors become involved, thus it is the *logical* design. The steps involved are as follows:

Preliminary Data Structure Design. In order to ensure integration and compatibility for all systems in the business area, this step is performed at the level of the whole business and not just the design area. It involves a first attempt at converting the entity model to the structure of the chosen database management system. This includes a summary of data model usage (basically an analysis of the way the data is used by the functions to produce a quantifiable view, sometimes referred to as *volumetrics*) and the preparation of the preliminary data structure.

System Structure Design. This involves the mapping of business processes to procedures and the interactions are highlighted by the use of data flow diagrams. This phase therefore involves the definition of procedures and the preparation of data flow diagrams.

Procedure Design. This stage involves the development of data navigation diagrams (access path analysis, which examines the types and volumes of access required to particular entity types), the preparation of dialogue flows (that is, the various hierarchies of control of user interaction), and the drawing of action diagrams (section 4.7).

Confirmation. Again, as part of business systems design there is a stage to confirm completeness, correctness and usability. Matrices are used to analyse completeness. For correctness, the question 'does it follow the IE rules?' is asked. For usability, verification is normally achieved by the users commenting on a prototype.

Planning for Technical Design. The final phase of this stage involves the definition of implementation areas and the preparation of technical design plans.

At the end of this stage a business systems specification is produced which details, for each business process, the information flows and user procedures, and for each computer procedure, the consolidated and confirmed results of business area analysis, plus the dialogue design, screens, reports and other user interfaces. The scope of the proposed computer systems is defined along with the work programmes and resource estimates for the next stage.

4 Technical Design

The computerized aspects of the business systems identified above are designed at a technical level such that the final construction and operation of the systems can be costed. The tasks are as follows:

Data Design, which includes preparation of data load matrices, refinement of the database structure, design of data storage, and the design of other files.

Software Design, which includes the definition of programs, modules, and integration groups, the design of programs/modules, and the definition of test conditions.

Transition Design, which includes the design of software and procedures for bridging and conversion, the planning of system *fanout* (the phases in which it should be implemented by location), and the definition of user training.

Operations Design, which includes the design of the security/contingency procedures, the design of operating and performance monitoring procedures, and the design of software for operations.

Verification of Design, which includes benchmark testing and performance assessment.

System Test Design, which includes the definition of system tests and acceptance tests.

Implementation Planning, which includes a review of costs and the preparation of the implementation plan.

The output from this stage is the technical specification, including the hardware and software environment, its use, standards and conventions. It also includes the plan and resources for the subsequent construction and transition stages.

5 Construction

Each defined implementation unit is created at this stage. The stages are:

System Generation, that is construction of the computing environment, preparation of development procedures, construction of database/files, generation of modules, generation of module test data, performance of integration tests, and generation of documentation.

System Verification, that is generation of system test data, performance of system tests, generation of acceptance tests data, performance of acceptance tests and obtaining approval.

The stage is completed once the acceptance criteria are satisfied.

6 Transition

This is the controlled change-over from the existing procedures to the new system. The tasks are:

Preparation, that is, prepare transition schedule, train users, and install new local hardware.

Installation of New Software, that is, perform conversion and execute trial runs.

Final Acceptance, that is, agree terms and transfer fully to the new system.

Fanout, which means install at a location.

System Variant Development, which is to identify requirements, revise analysis and design, and perform construction and transition where a particular location requires a variance from the norm.

Transition is regarded as complete when the system operates for a period at defined tolerances and standards, and passes its post-implementation review.

7 Production

Production is the continued successful operation of the system over the period of its life. The tasks are to ensure that service is maintained and that changes in the business requirements are addressed.

Evaluate System, that is, perform a measurement of benefits and costs, and make a comparison with the design objectives.

Tune, that is monitor performance, tune software, and reorganize databases.

Carry Out Maintenance, that is, correct bugs and modify system as required.

The stage framework outlined above is one view of IE which highlights the tasks that need to be performed and the sequence relationships. There are other ways that the methodology can be viewed and figure 6.9 presents a technique orientated view of IE which emphasizes the important role of automated support.

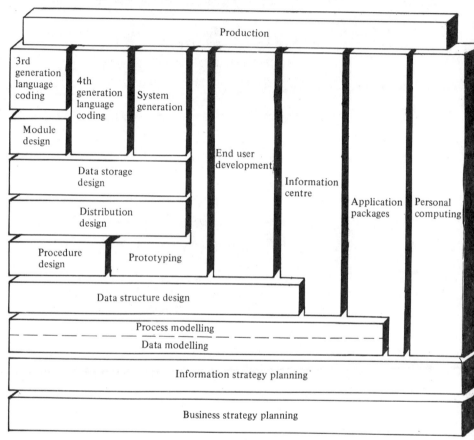

Fig. 6.9. Information Engineering — the building blocks (Courtesy of James Martin Associates).

The increasing automation of the systems development process is an ultimate goal of IE and to this end a framework for automation has been defined. The framework is the encyclopaedia, which in concept is a sophisticated data and functional dictionary, designed to be able to support information types at a variety of levels of detail to reflect the different levels required in the methodology. The encyclopaedia stores object types and their associated properties. There must be an encyclopaedia maintenance function which enables the creation and maintenance of the objects and properties, this can be through the use of the graphics tools. There must also be an encyclopaedia analysis function to perform an impact analysis of potential changes. There must be a systems generation function capable of translating the systems design information in the encyclopaedia together with the technical information held, into a full working application. There must also be a project management function in the encyclopaedia to provide information on progress, quality, and scheduling.

This kind of automation is in progress but not yet fully complete, although some of the diagramming interfaces have been demonstrated and are illustrated in Olle *et al.* (1986). See section 5.5 for a discussion of automated workbenches.

There are presently two different sets of automated tools to support IE. One is called the IEF (Information Engineering Facility) and is being produced by JMA in association with Texas Instruments, and the other is called IEW (Information Engineering Workbench) produced by KnowledgeWare and Arthur Young.

6.3 STRUCTURED SYSTEMS ANALYSIS AND DESIGN METHODOLOGY (SSADM)

SSADM, sometimes known as ISDM or LSDM (although these are not exactly the same), is a data driven methodology developed originally by UK consultants Learmonth and Burchett Management Systems (LBMS) and the Central Computing and Telecommunications Agency (CCTA) which is responsible for computer training and some procurement for the UK Civil Service. It has been used in a number of government applications since 1981 and its use has been mandatory in many Civil Service applications since 1983. Thus it is an important methodology, particularly in the UK, and it has had proven success over some years. A description of the methodology can be found in Downs *et al.* (1988).

The methodology provides project development staff with very detailed rules and guidelines to work to. These are contained in a set of manuals (NCC 1986). One reason for its success has been in the standards provided (often exercised by completing pre-printed documents) when following the methodology. This pervades all aspects of the information systems project. In many ways it is the true successor to the conventional approach described in Chapter 2, but includes the new techniques and tools developed in the 1970s and 1980s.

The question of maintenance is also addressed in SSADM. Where an operational system requires enhancement, a set of procedures known as *Maintenance SSADM* can be followed. A system not written using SSADM needs to be documented to follow SSADM standards first. This is likely to be a tedious task. The methodology is, perhaps, most appropriate to medium and large projects, though there is a version of the methodology, called *Micro SSADM*, which is designed for small-scale applications.

The methodology proper starts with an initial statement of requirements and terms of reference, and produces as its final outputs:
• Program specifications.
• User clerical procedures.
• Operating schedule.
• File design or database schema (as appropriate).
• Plan for testing and quality assurance.

The methodology has six phases with each phase sub-divided into sub-phases. The activities of each phase are precisely defined as are their associated end-products (or deliverables), thus facilitating the use of project management techniques.

The six phases of the methodology have been classified into two areas, three phases of systems analysis and three phases of systems design. Sometimes systems analysts not following a methodology like SSADM might find it difficult to decide on the level of detail being sought when reviewing the current system. This can cause a kind of 'paralysis by analysis', where a vast amount of information can be gathered but no conclusions ever reached. By separating the systems analysis activities from the systems design activities, SSADM makes it easier to judge the proportion of time spent on analysis. This separation also marks the separation of the application area from implementation considerations (the logical/physical split). The importance of this split is discussed in section 7.6.

1 Analysis of the Current System

The current operational system, which may be computer-based or manual, is investigated, and any problems such as system bottlenecks or dissatisfaction amongst users are identified. The traditional techniques of interviewing, questionnaires, sampling, observation and studying records are used for this information gathering process. It is recommended that data flow diagrams (section 4.3) and data structure diagrams (a type of entity model, section 4.1) are constructed at the time in order to help this analysis process. This is followed by the identification of any new services requested by the users and some of the options that might be available in the new system. Finally an ideal model of the present system is constructed and agreed with the users. There will be some circumstances where there is no current system. In this case the environment for the new system is studied. By the end of this phase, there is a general understanding of what happens now, its strengths and weaknesses, and an overview of the possible options regarding the new system.

2 Specification of the Required System

The logical view of an ideal current system is extended to include the new requirements of the many users, so that a logical view of the ideal required system can be formed. Although it is mainly a specification in narrative, data flow diagrams are also used at this stage. This logical view looks at data and process aspects and includes requirements for audit, security, and system controls (including error handling routines). Thus the views of such users as the auditors, as well as general users, are considered at this stage. This will help ensure that the requirements analysis has not been interpreted too narrowly. This view is documented as a brief explanation of the aims and services of the new system in general terms. It will represent a consolidation of many people's views.

3 User Selection of Service Levels, Including Technical Options

This phase can be carried out either as part of a feasibility study or as a full study. Its activities will vary according to which kind of study it forms a part. In a *feasibility study* the various options for implementation are presented to users. Such options might be presented as a 'menu' of possibilities and could include the high level technical options, such as a centralized, distributed, batch processing or on-line systems. On the other hand, it could relate to such aspects as the siting of terminals. The participation of users in these decisions will, hopefully, encourage acceptance of the system when it is implemented. Users are expected to choose from the options presented. In a *full study*, the options tend to be at a more detailed level, such as particular response times required. In either case, users are made aware of the implications of any option on issues such as staffing levels and skills and other resources required, as well as the standard of service provided. Although this third stage is considered as a logical phase in the logical/physical split, it is obvious from the preceding description that some discussions regarding the physical options are made at this time.

These three analysis phases described above will normally be carried out twice (particularly on medium to large projects). In the first run through they will be carried out in outline and then again for full analysis studies, which will be much more detailed. The latest version of SSADM (version 3) has formalized this requirement, by adding a feasibility study stage to the approach, itself consisting of two phases, problem definition and project definition. *Problem definition* concerns itself with a review of the problem area, the current system, and future needs. *Project definition* concerns itself with an evaluation of the different project options for tackling the problems defined at the problem definition phase. This two-phase feasibility study, which will be very helpful when project decisions are not clear-cut, is not expected to be used for small projects nor ones where the project forms part of a strategic plan. In the latter case the feasibility studies will relate to the strategic plan, rather than each time to the smaller projects within it. By adding this feasibility phase, we see that this methodology, as with most others, has changed with experience in its use.

4 Detailed Data Design

The purpose of this phase is to define in detail the data and data relationships and ensure that this model supports the processes. One sub-phase is a data analysis carried out to produce third normal form (TNF) relations (see section 4.2). This process looks at the data requirements implied by the screen formats, report layouts, and input forms selected by users in the previous phase. This analysis of documents to produce TNF relations is frequently referred to as document-driven data analysis. It is a bottom up approach, because the detail on the documents is used as the basis of the data model, via normalization.

A second sub-phase, known as logical data structuring (LDS), is created to meet processing requirements, and carried out independently of document-driven data analysis. This consists of entity modelling (identifying the entities and relationships between entities) and converting the model into a data structure with data groups and relationships defined (see section 4.1). This is a top-down method of analysis. The format of the results is the same as the end product of the first sub-phase, but they may contain different facts as they are arrived at by different techniques. Document driven data analysis and entity modelling are discussed and compared in Avison (1981). Although document-driven data analysis is slow and sometimes tedious, it is argued that the resulting data model will be accurate and result in time savings in the long run.

A composite logical design (CLD) is produced which is so called because it is a composite data structure of the TNF and LDS data structures. The CLD is then converted to a 'first-cut' file or database design, the mapping of a logical data structure to a physical data structure. The information contained in the CLD is described in a data dictionary.

5 Detailed Procedure Design

Since the users have chosen the version of the system to be implemented (in phase 3), the required functions are catalogued and checked against the CLD so as to ensure that the logical design will meet all the system requirements. A prototype version may be developed at this phase. This is a trial design for the system including file or database designs, dialogue designs and supporting processes, such as validation routines and update processing. The prototype may be a 'paper prototype' for assessment by project teams or users. It may also take the form of a trial version of the system on a microcomputer, using a fourth generation package. No consideration will have been given to performance considerations nor maintenance aspects in this trial version.

6 Physical Design Control

This phase is concerned with the production of a plan for building and testing the system, program specifications, operating procedures and file layouts or database definitions (as appropriate). These aspects are analysed on paper and refined to maximize performance, before being developed on computers. Alternatively, a prototype system may be built up at this phase or developed from the previous phase, so that it now conforms to acceptable performance criteria. Another alternative route to physical design is to use conversion rules which convert the CLD to any widely-used DBMS. The methodology is therefore suited to a database environment, but not exclusively so. Performance predictions will be verified at this stage and the design tuned for best performance of both data and process aspects. It is essential that at the end of this phase, documentation is consolidated and checked for completeness. This documentation will include test plan, operations guide, implementation plan and user guide.

The six phases are subdivided into the sub-phases as shown in figure 6.10. The methodology documentation does describe in some detail all the steps in these sub-phases. Its well-defined structure makes it teachable. Many UK polytechnic and university courses in information systems have used this methodology for in-depth treatment and discuss other methodologies in overview only, for comparative purposes. Although only an overview can be provided here, the methodology documentation contained in NCC (1986), gives specific help on, for example, when and how each technique and tool should be used.

Along with these well-defined tasks, and guidance with the techniques and tools, the methodology defines the outputs expected from the stage, and gives time and resource management guidelines. Many of the techniques and tools were described in Chapters 4 and 5, indeed one of the requirements of the CCTA was for a methodology that used techniques that had been well used and tested. Data flow diagrams (see section 4.3) provide a picture of how data moves around the information system and how it moves between the system and the external world. These are used in the early stages of the methodology to understand the current system and to specify the required system. The diagram conventions are slightly different from that described in section 4.3, in that an external entity is represented by a rounded symbol and a process by a box (see figure 6.11). The logic of the processes named in the lowest level data flow diagrams can be represented on decision trees (section 4.4) or decision tables (section 4.5). Other documentation techniques are included in the methodology. For example, there is a dialogue design chart which is used to model screen displays to help ensure that the human—computer dialogues are well designed.

We have already discussed the use of document-driven (TNF) data analysis, entity modelling and data flow diagrams in SSADM. The technique of constructing an entity life cycle (section 4.8) provides another view. This is a historical view and therefore shows the effects of time on the system (data flow diagrams and entity models represent static views of the system).

1 Analysis of the current system
Carry out detailed investigation Create current data flow Create ideal current data flow Create logical structure overview
2 Specification of the required system
Define audit control and security Extend logical data structure overview Create required data flow Define process outlines
3 User selection of service levels
Create user options Assist user in selection Set performance objectives
4 Detailed data design
Carry out TNF data analysis Create detailed logical data structure Build composite data structure Set up data dictionary Define first-cut physical data structure
5 Detailed procedure design
Carry out physical design control Design manual procedures
6 Physical design control
Design system test plan Create program specifications Create operating schedule Create file or data base definitions Write user manuals

Fig. 6.10. The SSADM methodology.

As we mentioned in section 4.8, although the technique uses entities, it is a technique for analysing processes. For each major entity identified in the entity modelling phase, a diagram is produced showing all the events which affect or update the data. The origin of each transaction is identified and its

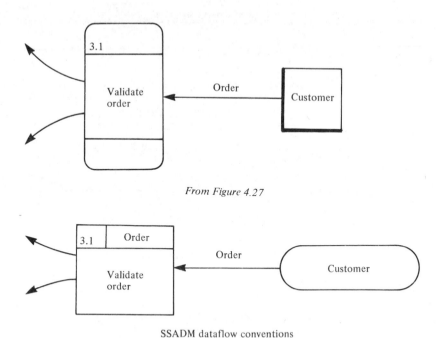

From Figure 4.27

SSADM dataflow conventions

Fig. 6.11. DFD conventions.

processing defined. The construction of a function/event matrix (figure 6.12(a)) and an entity/event matrix (figure 6.12(b)) help in this process. Further detail such as error recognition and processing, and the identification of exception conditions, are added to the model. Entity life cycles are used to validate previous results.

The diagramming conventions used in drawing entity life cycles (called in SSADM entity life histories) are rather different than those described in section 4.8, making the diagrams look very different. They are very similar to the entity structure step conventions of JSD (section 6.4) and the technique is described in more detail there because it is of such crucial importance in JSD. In SSADM, the diagrams look like hierarchies, but they are meant to be read from left to right, and, in so doing, progressively suggest the different states of the entity. Using an example from the academic world, figure 6.13(a) shows how the entity 'student' changes over time, as an applicant, registered student and graduate (there will be other intermediary states). Figure 6.13(b)

EVENTS	FUNCTIONS	Process enquiries	Counselling	Enrolment	Accounts	Mark exam paper	Give result to tutor	
Student enquires		X						
Student registers				X	X			
Student completes exam script						X	X	

(a) Function/event matrix

ENTITIES	EVENTS	Student enquiries	Student registers	Student completes	
Student		X	X	X	
Lecturer		X			
Examination					
Admin staff		X	X		

(b) Entity/event matrix

Fig. 6.12. Example matrices.

(a) Sequence

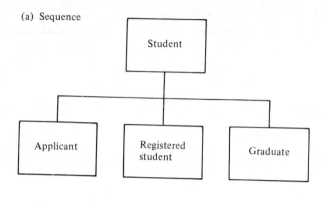

(b) Selection

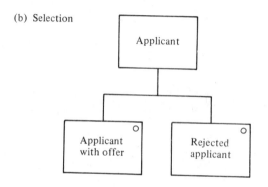

(c) Iteration

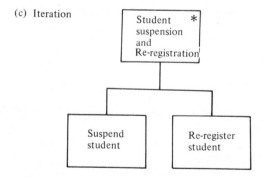

Fig. 6.13. SSADM entity life history constructs.

shows the use of the selection construct, whereby the 'o' in the 'applicant with offer' and 'rejected applicant' boxes denote alternative conditions (these are mutually exclusive). Figure 6.13(c) shows the iteration construct, marked with an asterisk, which shows an event that may repeat (in this example, the possible repeated suspension and re-registration of a student who might regularly pay fees late).

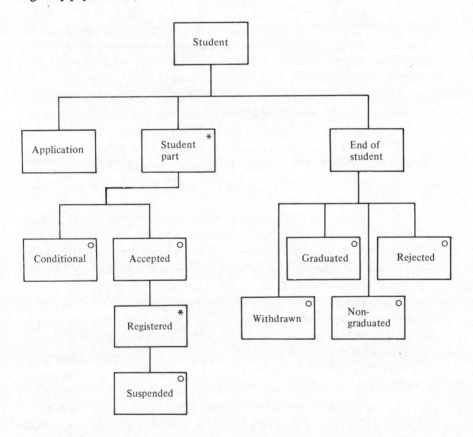

Fig. 6.14. Entity life history.

Figure 6.14 presents an SSADM entity life history. The first level contains the events that cause an entity to be initiated into the system and those events that terminate the entity from the system. There is an iteration construct relating to whether the student is accepted conditionally or not, and to reflect suspended or registered states. There are four states for the end condition: withdrawn, graduated, non-graduated or rejected. These are all mutually exclusive (the selection construct). Notice that in this model it is not possible to show that 'graduated' can only happen from registered and that 'suspended' can only terminate with non-graduated. Thus, some information is lost when compared to the earlier entity life cycle representation described in section 4.8, and seen in figure 4.46.

SSADM is expected to be used along with computer tools. Along with the general computer tools, and in particular a data dictionary system, are the computer packages Auto-Mate and Data-Mate which help when drawing entity models and data flow diagrams. Auto-Mate and Data-Mate are marketed by LBMS and are designed specifically for the methodology. For example, it is possible to produce and maintain entity model pictures on the screen using a microcomputer using these packages. Entity, relationship and attribute details can be added to the model. The system can be used to guide the user through the normalization process to TNF and automatically produce a TNF structure diagram, greatly reducing the clerical effort that is usually associated with this process. It is also possible to integrate Data-Mate with the particular data dictionary system adopted by the organization. The package LEAP, which gives help on overall project planning, and PROMPTII for detailed planning, use the techniques discussed in section 5.6 and are often used as tools of SSADM. There are also available tools such as test data generators, database utilities, and utilities to check and collect statistics for operational systems which, as with the project planning packages, can be used along with the methodology. Downs *et al.* (1988) propose ways in which the methodology can be used with application generators, such as ICL's Quickbuild.

The proponents of the methodology also recommend 'Quality Assurance Reviews' based on structured walkthroughs, described in section 3.7. They are meetings held to review identifiable end products of the various phases of the methodology such as data flow diagrams, entity life histories, and process details. Usually the end product is presented by the authors and reviewed by personnel from related project teams (helping good communication between project teams and ensuring a common standard of work), specialist quality assurance teams, or the user area. The purpose of the meetings is to identify errors in the product. Solutions are resolved outside the meeting. Post implementation feedback is also encouraged and there is an audit at this time.

SSADM does not itself address the problem of project control and estimating costs directly through the incorporation of project management tools, though the framework provided should help in these aspects of systems development. Nevertheless, as mentioned above, it has been interfaced with a number of project control products such as PROMPTII which is the UK government standard package. However, it does provide flexibility in situations where there is a short timescale. Here there is likely to be a 'one-pass analysis', where the preliminary and detailed run through the analysis phases are merged. The solution may not be optimal, but it may cure an urgent problem, and it would be implemented with the expectancy that it would have a short working life.

The successful implementation of the methodology relies on the skills of key personnel being available, though the techniques and tools are widely known and the project team method of working, along with systems walkthroughs, encourages good training procedures and participation. Analysts trained in the conventional approach, discussed in section 2.2, will recognize many features of the SSADM approach, particularly the emphasis on documentation standards, clear and detailed guidelines and thorough quality assurance.

6.4 JACKSON SYSTEMS DEVELOPMENT (JSD)

Michael Jackson's program design methodology, Jackson Structured Programming (JSP), which is described in Jackson (1975), has had a profound effect on the teaching and practice of commercial computer programming. Jackson (1983) on JSD, argues that system design is an extension of the program design task, and that the same techniques can be usefully applied to both. Aspects of JSP are diffused throughout JSD, so that the JSD methodology is a significant development on its precursor, and therefore should not be seen as a 'front end' to JSP but an extension of it, so that JSP is the core. 'In principle', says Jackson, 'we may think of a system as a large program'. The primary purpose of JSD is to produce maintainable software, and its emphasis is on developing software systems. This leads to a potential criticism of JSD in that, in the context of this text, it is orientated towards software and not to organizational need.

Given this comment, therefore, it is not surprising that JSD does not address the topics of project selection, cost justification, requirements analysis, project management, user interface, procedure design or user participation in the text. Further, JSD does not deal in detail with database design or file design. *At least as described in his book*, Jackson's methodology is not comprehensive in the sense that it does not cover all aspects of the life cycle. The commercial version of JSD, because of practical necessity, has now been extended to include some of these aspects.

The emphasis in the methodology is solving what Jackson terms the *hidden path problem*, that is the path between the presentation of a specification to the design/programming group and the completed implemented system, which could be described as a 'bundle' of documentation, listings and executable programs. Jackson asks, 'What reasons do we have to support the claim that we have delivered what is required in the specification?' The traditional answer is the processes of testing and checking. But there are two problems here. We cannot be sure that the tests are complete and, in any case, when testing is possible, the system is already complete and it is usually rather too late and too costly to repair the damage. A second answer is to apply formal methods, and the JSD methodology does have some links with formal methods (see section 3.6). However, Jackson is aware of the problem of their inaccessibility, and the difficulty of communication.

JSD uses transformation through process scheduling as the answer to the hidden path problem and the contribution of JSD lies in the areas of process scheduling and real-world modelling. JSD deals with the problem of time in systems modelling and systems design in a way that most other systems design methodologies do not.

The major phases of JSD are:
- Entity action step.
- Entity structure step.
- Initial model step.
- Function step.
- System timing step.
- Implementation step.

The first four steps relate to specification (*modelling*, that is, what is happening in the real world and how this might be connected to the computer world, and *function*, that is, what outputs are needed from the system, and what processes and operations must be added to produce these outputs) and steps five and six to implementation factors, that is, how can the specification (model plus function) be transformed to run on the hardware.

In the *entity action step* the systems developer defines the real world area of interest by listing the entities and actions with which the system will be concerned. In the *entity structure step* the actions performed or suffered by each entity are ordered by time. In the *initial model step* communications between entities are depicted in a process model linked to the real world. In the *function step* functions are specified to produce the outputs of the system, and this may give rise to new processes. In the *system timing step* some aspects of process scheduling are considered which might affect the correctness or timeliness of the system's functional outputs. In the *implementation step* the system developer applies techniques of transformation and scheduling that take account of the hardware and software that is available for running the system. JSD is applied iteratively, and as increasing detail is revealed, data and functions will also be revealed. Each of these stages will be looked at in turn.

1 Entity Action Step

JSD aims to model the real world. In the entity action step, real-world entities are defined. These might include SUPPLIER, CUSTOMER or PART, but unlike the data analysis approaches, JSD is concerned with the behaviour of the entity, not about its attributes or its relationships with other entities. Entity modelling presents a static view of the real world, whereas JSD is concerned with modelling system dynamics.

To be defined as an entity in JSD, an object must meet the following criteria:

1 It must perform or suffer actions in a significant time ordering.
2 It must exist in the real world outside the system that models the real world.
3 It must be capable of individual instantiation with a unique name.

Entities may also be collective (for example, BOARD OF DIRECTORS) if the instantiation has objective reality without considering its component objects. Entities may be generic (for example, SPARE-PART) thus supporting the abstraction of classification, or specific (for example, INNER-FAN-SHAFT). Entities that exist in the world may be ignored if it is impossible or unnecessary to model their behaviour. Thus, only a relevant subset of the real world is modelled.

Since the distinctive feature of JSD entities is that they perform or suffer actions, it is necessary to specify the criteria for something to be an action. These are as follows:

1 An action must be regarded as taking place at a point in time, rather than extending over a period of time.
2 An action must take place in the real world outside the system and not be

an action of the system itself.

3 An action is regarded as atomic and cannot be decomposed into sub-actions.

The end result of the entity action step is a list of entities and a list of actions. The list of entities is liable to be much shorter than that produced by an equivalent data analysis process, particularly if the latter normalizes the entities, because the functional components of the system are excluded at this stage.

2 Entity Structure Step

The actions of an entity are ordered in time and are expressed diagrammatically in JSD. This is similar to the technique of entity life cycles (see section 4.8), although there are differences. They show the structure of a process in terms of sequence, selection, and iteration. The diagram shown as figure 6.15 is read from top to bottom as a hierarchical decomposition. Each structure diagram is intended to span the whole lifetime of an entity, including therefore an action that causes the entity to come into existence and one that causes it to cease to exist. The model must illustrate time ordering of these elements. The lifetime of an entity may span many years in the real world.

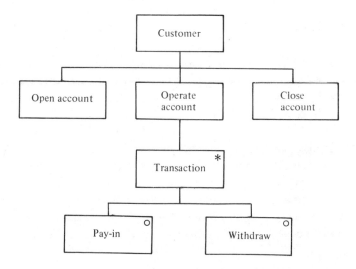

Fig. 6.15. JSD structure — diagram sequence.

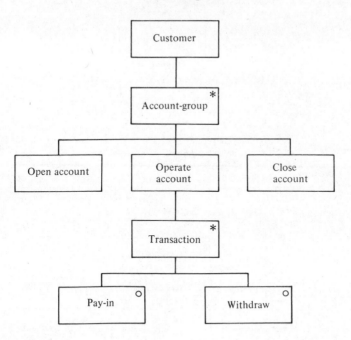

Fig. 6.16. JSD structure diagrams — customer with more than one account.

JSD structure diagrams do not support concurrency. For example, the entity CUSTOMER in a banking system, an example discussed fully in Jackson (1983), might have been specified as a sequence (as in figure 6.15) of OPEN-ACCOUNT, OPERATE-ACCOUNT and CLOSE-ACCOUNT. OPERATE-ACCOUNT is an iteration of TRANSACTIONs, each of which is a selection of either PAY-IN or WITHDRAW. Such a structure would constrain a customer to having only one account. To relax this constraint, the systems developer may be tempted to re-draw the structure diagram as in figure 6.16. It now appears that the customer may have many accounts each being operated as in figure 6.15. The diagram now specifies that the customer can have more than one account, but not more than one at the same time. A customer may only open a new account after an existing account has been closed. The JSD structure diagram cannot show the simultaneous operation of many accounts. The answer to this problem is to specify a new entity ACCOUNT whose life history proceeds in parallel to the life history of the CUSTOMER entity. CUSTOMER now appears as in figure 6.17(a) and ACCOUNT as in figure 6.17(b).

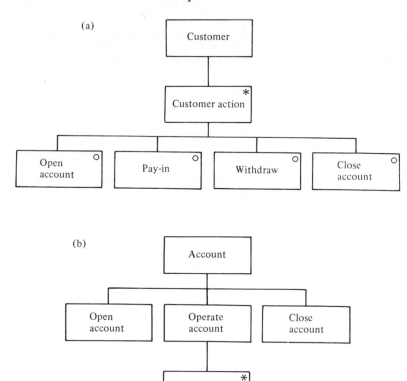

Fig. 6.17. JSD structure diagrams — simultaneous operation of many accounts.

In JSD, discrimination between entity roles is necessary if an entity can play more than one role simultaneously. Jackson provides an example using the entity SOLDIER. A soldier enlists in the army and may be promoted to a higher rank at various parts of his career. Soldiers are also given training and may attend training courses, which they may or may not complete successfully. If successful completion of a course always leads to promotion, then these facts can be accommodated in one structure diagram. If there is no necessary connection between training and a career, then two structure diagrams are required, one for the soldier's promotion career and one for his training career. The soldier in this example is playing two roles, one as a person being trained and one as a person being promoted to a higher rank. Multiple roles may be synthesized into another structure diagram showing a selection of the possible activities in the possible roles that can be played.

Entity structure diagrams represent a sequence of activities ordered in time, without concurrency, from the 'birth' of an entity to its 'death'. One final problem addressed by the methodology in this step is that of the premature termination of the life cycle. In the real world, events may occur that prevent an entity making an orderly progression through its life cycle. For example, a soldier may be killed in battle without proceeding to retirement. It may not be feasible to draw a structure diagram for every possible variation on a prematurely terminated life cycle. JSD allows for a general specification of premature termination. This recognition of such a circumstance is an example of backtracking, from JSP.

It is possible to use tools which support the methodology. Drawing and redrawing design structures can be somewhat tedious, and the Program Development Facility (PDF) is a Jackson diagram editor which eases this process.

The end result of the entity structure step in JSD is a set of structure diagrams. New entities and multiple roles for the same entity may have been generated during this phase.

3 Initial Model Step

In this third step the systems developer creates a model that is a simulation of the real world. For each entity defined in the preceding two phases a sequential process is defined in the model that simulates the activities of the entity in such a way that it could be implemented on a computer. This is not to say that the implementation necessarily has to be computerized, merely that it could be if this were required.

In the model there will be a sequential process for each instance of an entity type, not one process for all instances. Thus if there are a hundred instances of entity type CUSTOMER there will be one hundred sequential processes in the model. Moreover the processes notionally execute at exactly the same speed as the real-world processes. Thus if a customer has a bank account for fifty years, the matching processes will also execute for fifty years.

The sequential processes specified in the initial model step are documented both by a diagram showing the interconnection of processes and by a pseudo code definition of each model process. Pseudo code is a language similar to structured English, which was described in section 4.6, but nearer to a programming language in type. The pseudo code is known as structure text in JSD, and resembles a high-level Algol-like programming language. Structure text exactly matches a corresponding entity structure diagram and major constructs are sequence, selection and iteration. The value of structure text is that it may be elaborated in later phases of the JSD methodology in a manner similar to the program design technique of stepwise refinement. This process should be straightforward. An example of structure text for the ACCOUNT entity is provided in figure 6.18.

Process connection in JSD is achieved by either data stream connection or state vector connection. In data stream connection one process writes a sequential data stream, consisting of an ordered set of messages, and the other process reads this stream. This is similar to process connection in a data flow diagram (section 4.3).

In state vector connection, one process inspects the state vector (the internal local variables) of another process. State vector connection has no equivalent in data flow diagramming because the data flow technique permits process connection via logical files. There are no logical files in a JSD System Specification Diagram (SSD). An example of an SSD is provided in figure 6.19. CUSTOMER-0 is intended to represent a real-world instance of a customer, sending messages about his actions to a process that simulates this behaviour (CUSTOMER-1). A circle in an SSD indicates data stream connection. CUSTOMER-1 is sending a stream of messages to ACCOUNT-1. Since a customer can have many accounts, a double bar is used on the diagram to represent this multiplicity. Data stream connection is appropriate in the banking example, as it is not practical to telephone the customer every ten minutes to find out if he or she had paid in or withdrawn money. Jackson (1983) also gives the example of a lift system that finds out whether a button has been pressed in a lift, by linking the button via a state vector to a process that models the button's behaviour. State vector connection is appropriate here because the button is essentially a switch, denoting on or off states.

Data stream connection is considered to be buffered, so writing processes are never blocked; reading processes may lag behind writing processes. State vector connection is also unbuffered and again no blocking occurs. State vector inspection therefore depends on the relative speeds of the processes involved. This is not true of data stream connection. If there is more than one

```
ACCOUNT-1 seq
    read data-stream
    OPEN-ACCOUNT; read data stream
    OPERATE ACCOUNT itr while (PAY-IN or WITHDRAW)
        TRANSACTION sel (PAY-IN)
            PAY-IN; read data stream
        TRANSACTION att (WITHDRAW)
            WITHDRAW; read data stream
        TRANSACTION end
    OPERATE-ACCOUNT end
    CLOSE-ACCOUNT;
ACCOUNT-1 end
```

Fig. 6.18. JSD structure text.

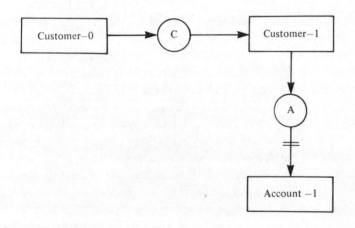

Fig. 6.19. JSD system specification diagram.

input to a process, rules must be specified for determining which input is to be taken next. The determination may be made by fixed rules (fixed merge), or specified as part of the message stream (data merge), or determined simply by the relative availability of messages (rough merge). Such careful attention to synchronization details is absent from most other methodologies. JSD also allows for time grain markers to indicate the arrival of particular points in real world time.

The end result of the initial model step is a systems specification diagram depicting a set of communication processes each of which is specified by a pseudo code structure text.

4 Function Step

The model created in the first three phases of JSD has no outputs; it models the dynamic behaviour of the real world. In the function step, functions are added to the model to ensure that the required outputs are produced when certain combinations of events occur. The addition of functions may require no change to the SSD, in which case structure text is elaborated to specify the functions required. Alternatively, it may be necessary to create new processes, which are added to the SSD and specified with new structure text.

To give an example, we may wish to provide the facility in the banking application to interrogate customer balances on demand. Thus functions must be added to the existing SSD and structure text that record and display account balances. The elaboration of the ACCOUNT text is shown in figure 6.20. Clearly now the state vector of ACCOUNT includes knowledge of the customer's balance, because the structure text has been elaborated to update that balance. The SSD can now be amended (as in figure 6.21) to show the new interrogation process. INTERROGATE can inspect the state vector of any ACCOUNT-1 process (as indicated by a diamond symbol). It will do so when it receives a message specifying an account enquiry, and it will produce an output showing the balance of the customer's account. Thus, the addition of function to an initial model may cause the elaboration of existing structure texts, and/or lead to the specification of new processes with their own structure texts.

The examples in figures 6.20 and 6.21 are close to Jackson's in Jackson (1983). They pose a problem however. The data stream input to the INTERROGATE process is apparently unconnected to the real world. Suppose that we decide that it is the customer that is allowed to interrogate the balance of his account via an automatic teller machine (ATM). We now link CUSTOMER-1 to data stream 1. This implies redrawing the structure diagram and text for CUSTOMER-1 to allow the selection of an enquiry input. Necessarily we must also amend the structure of CUSTOMER-0 (the real-world customer) to reflect the new behaviour. Apparently, then, the addition of a function to an SSD can change the real world — and this is not supposed to happen in JSD. It might be argued that our initial modelling of customer

```
ACCOUNT-1 seq
   read amount-deposited;
   OPEN-ACCOUNT seq
      balance:= amount-deposited;
   OPEN-ACCOUNT end
   read transaction;
   OPERATE ACCOUNT itr while (PAY-IN or WITHDRAW)
      TRANSACTION sel (PAY-IN)
         PAY-IN seq
            balance := balance + amount;
         PAY-IN end
         read transaction;
      TRANSACTION alt (WITHDRAW)
         WITHDRAW seq
            balance := balance - amount;
         WITHDRAW end
         read transaction;
      TRANSACTION end
   OPERATE ACCOUNT end
   CLOSE ACCOUNT;
ACCOUNT-1 end
```

Fig. 6.20. Addition of functions to structure text of figure 6.18.

behaviour was at fault, but it does appear that the strict separation of real-world modelling and model function may not always be sustainable in JSD.

The end result of the function step is an amended System Specification Diagram with associated structure texts.

5 System Timing Step

The JSD modelling process so far described has not yet explicitly raised the question of speed of execution. Implicitly, the model must lag to some extent behind the real world because input must take some time to arrive. In the System Timing Step explicit consideration is given to permissible delays between receipt of inputs and production of outputs. Different parts of the system may be subject to different time lags.

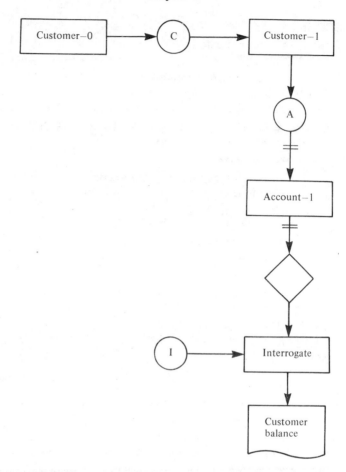

Fig. 6.21. System specification diagram with interrogation process.

Time constraints will derive either from user requirements (for example, for a monthly report or for an immediate response to an enquiry) or from technical considerations. Examples of the latter are state vector retrievals that must be sufficiently frequent to capture changes of state (as in a process control application) but not so frequent that they capture many instances of the same state. The System Timing Step will gather information usable in the next phase when decisions are made. These decisions may concern questions such as on-line, real-time, or batch implementation of aspects of the model system.

The end result of the System Timing Step is a largely informal specification of timing constraints. The step does allow for the addition to the SSD of synchronization processes whose sole function is to ensure that certain actions have been completed satisfactorily before a further process is initiated.

6 Implementation Step

Jackson's account of systems implementation is not a comprehensive treatment of all implementation considerations. Moreover 'implementation' in JSD includes activities that would be regarded in other methodologies as 'systems design', for example file and database design — not that JSD describes these processes in any depth. The JSD Implementation Step concentrates on one particular issue — the sharing of processors among processes. A System Specification Diagram can be directly implemented by providing one processor for each sequential process. Since there is one sequential process for each instance of an entity type (for example one for each customer of a bank) this might imply many thousands of processors. If this is an unacceptable implementation of the model, then the Implementation Step provides techniques for sharing processors among processes.

The direct opposite of providing one processor for each process is to provide one processor for all processes, which could be provided by a centralized mainframe computer. In this case JSD provides for a transformation of the model into a set of sub-routines. JSD is not recommending computer users to write their own operating systems and teleprocessing monitors, however. If these items of software are available on a machine and match the process scheduling requirements of a system, then Jackson would recommend using them. In fact, most computer-based systems are scheduled by a mixture of administrative, clerical and software action. The JSD Systems Implementation Diagram (or SID) is, in a way, an abstraction of all these real-world scheduling possibilities. The structure diagram for a scheduler can be drawn to alternatively represent an on-line system, a batch system or a mixture of these, together with actions that may, in fact, be performed by human beings.

The system may be implemented by one or more real processors, thus giving rise to possible implementations that range from completely centralized to completely distributed. In general, multiple instances of common processes would share process texts (that is, programs) as well as processors. To make process text sharing possible, it is necessary to separate the state vectors of processes from the shared process text. A concatenation of state vectors is then transformed into a file or a database. Thus the Implementation Step in JSD can give rise to perfectly conventional data processing solutions.

JSD's strength as a methodology lies in its determined and detailed attempt to model the dynamic aspects of real-world systems. Its treatment of concurrency, timing and process scheduling is more comprehensive than any other methodology discussed, the model is, as far as possible, kept up-to-date so that it is always a fair reflection of the real world that this abstract model represents. In this way it is possible to see what is happening in the real world and address it in the decision-making process. Data modelling, it is argued, only represents a static view of the real world, whereas this process-orientated approach is dynamic.

It is, however, self consciously incomplete as a methodology. Jackson wishes to say nothing about areas that are satisfactorily treated by other methodologies, only those that are not. Jackson is critical of methodologies that rely on structured decomposition, on the grounds that they confuse a method of documenting a design with the design process itself. JSD is not top-down design. Jackson is similarly critical of entity modelling approaches: 'It is not much more sensible to set about designing a database before specifying the system processes than it would be to declare all the local variables of a program before specifying the executable text: the two are inextricably intertwined' (Jackson 1983).

6.5 INFORMATION SYSTEMS WORK AND ANALYSIS OF CHANGES (ISAC)

The ISAC methodology has been developed since 1971 by a research group at the Department of Administrative Information Processing at the Swedish Royal Institute of Technology and at the University of Stockholm. The methodology has been developed by use and experience in a number of commercial organizations and Swedish Government agencies. Most users of the methodology are Scandinavian, although a number of users are claimed in other parts of Europe and North America. The methodology is closely associated with Mats Lundberg of the University of Stockholm and it is papers by Lundberg and others that form our source material for this methodology (see Lundberg *et al.* 1979a, 1979b, 1982 and Lundberg 1982, 1983).

The methodology covers all aspects of information systems development, although some users only apply the analysis and design parts of the methodology, which are probably its best known aspects. ISAC is a problem orientated methodology and seeks to identify the fundamental causes of users' problems. The approach is designed to analyse users' problems and to solve aspects of them where appropriate. The methodology begins at an earlier stage than most methodologies and does not assume that the development of an information system is necessarily the solution to the problem. If a need for an information system is not identified then the role of the methodology terminates. Need is established only if it is seen that an information system benefits people in their work, so that pure financial benefit to the organization, or some other benefit, is not thought to be an indication of need for an information system. An information system is thought to have no value in its own right and without benefitting people should not be developed. Thus it can be seen that ISAC is a people-orientated approach.

People, and the problems they have, are seen as the important factors in organizations. The term people includes all people in an organization; users, managers, workers, as well as people usually thought of as outside the organization, such as customers, and funders. People in an organization may have problems concerning the activities they perform. These problems may be overcome, or the situation improved, by analysis of these activities and the initiation of various changes. ISAC believes that the people best equipped to do this analysis, in terms of their knowledge, interest, and motivation, are the users themselves. The methodology attempts to facilitate this by providing a series of work or method steps and a series of rules and techniques which, it is claimed, can be performed by these users. For ISAC, an important part of this process is the education of the users to better understand the organization and to improve the communication between people in the organization.

If the need for an information system is established then the methodology emphasizes the development of a number of specific information sub-systems rather than one 'total' system. The sub-systems are local systems tailored to groups of individual needs, and these sub-systems may well overlap in content and function. However, it is argued that the benefit that accrues is in the specific relationship to the local needs. The assumption is therefore that solutions to sub-problems will give solutions to the organization's problems as a whole (which perhaps conflicts with the holistic, systems view described in section 3.1).

In ISAC terms, an information system is an organized cooperation between human beings in order to process and convey information to each other, it does not necessarily involve any form of automation.

The major phases of ISAC are:
- Change analysis.
- Activity studies.
- Information analysis.
- Data system design.
- Equipment adaptation.

The first three phases are classified as problem-orientated work, and focus on users and their problems, whereas the latter two phases focus on data processing-orientated work. Within each phase a number of work steps are identified and within these work steps various techniques concerning documentation are employed.

1 Change Analysis

Change Analysis seeks to specify the changes that need to be made in order to overcome the identified problems. Change analysis begins with the analysis of problems, the current situation, and needs. The following method steps are used:

Problem listing: This is a relatively unstructured, first attempt, look at current problems and any anticipated future problems.

Analysis of interest groups: ISAC acknowledges that problems do not usually have objective status, they are relative to the viewpoint of the participants in the system. At this stage, the different interest groups are identified. These interest groups may be system end-users, public users, departmental managers, and so on.

Problem grouping: Here the identified problems are grouped into related sets or categories.

Description of current activities: The activities that the identified problems relate to, plus the activities undertaken by the concerned interest groups, are now modelled. This activity model is a functional view and shows processes performed on inputs to produce outputs. These aspects are not just concerned with information, but include physical activities, such as the loading of a lorry. The activity model is documented in the form of an A-graph (an Activity-graph).

An A-graph depicts three things.
- Firstly *sets*, these can be real or physical sets, concerning for example, people or lorries or stock, or they can be message sets, containing only information, or they can be a combination of both.
- Secondly A-graphs depict *activities*.
- Thirdly they depict *flows*, which can be shown in detail or in overview.

Activities are transformations of sets into new sets, and flows represent the movement of sets to and from activities. They are really very similar to data flow diagrams (see section 4.3), except that they also represent physical objects as well as data flows. Figure 6.22 shows an example of an overview A-graph concerned with the despatch of goods. The message set 'orders' flows into the activity 'produce shipping list' which results in a message set 'shipping list'. This itself flows to an activity called 'load lorries' which has input flows of real sets 'empty lorries' and 'goods'. A-graphs exhibit a hierarchical structure capable of showing an overview picture which can then be broken down to show the detail at lower levels. The A-graph is supplemented by narrative or descriptive text and property tables. The property tables show quantitative information such as volumes.

Description of objectives: The previously identified interest groups are perceived to have a variety of different general objectives and desires. Here firmer and more specific objectives are defined and these are unified into a single set of objectives via a process of negotiation and compromise. An attempt is made to reach a situation where the achievement of a set of agreed objectives solves the problems that have been identified.

Evaluation of current situation and analysis of needs for changes: This is where all the previous work comes together and enables the methodology to progress. What is wanted (the objectives) is compared to what is available. What is available is described by the activity model, but this is tempered by the problems that have been identified. The differences between what is wanted and what is available are defined as the *needs for changes*. These needs are then evaluated and prioritized according to the values of the different interest groups involved. This evaluation of the importance of the various needs for changes leads directly into the next stage which is the generation and study of different change alternatives.

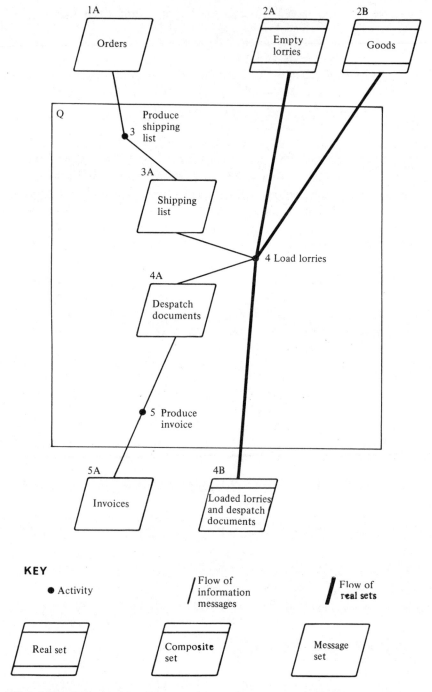

KEY

● Activity

∕ Flow of information messages

▮ Flow of **real sets**

Real set

Composite set

Message set

Fig. 6.22. A-graph.

ISAC gives no guidance on how to generate ideas for changes since this requires creativity in the context of the situation rather than the use of techniques, except to say that an analysis of flows and activities might be helpful. ISAC does not presuppose that the solution to the problems lies in automation or indeed in the construction of any form of information system. The type of solution is not constrained and may involve purely organizational and physical changes that do not result in the generation or modification of information systems. Once possible changes have been generated they are described through a new A-graph. The changes and the models are then analysed and evaluated from human, social, and economic feasibility viewpoints.

The final part of Change Analysis is to choose the most appropriate change approach based on the previous evaluations and to document the reasons for the choices made. If the recommended changes do not involve information systems then the role of ISAC ceases, more likely however is that the recommendations involve a combination of types of changes, and a plan is made concerning the necessary development measures for each type. An analysis of the effect and consequences of these parallel development measures is also made.

2 Activity Studies

The starting point for activity studies is a proposal for a new system modelled and described in a number of ways, in particular as an A-graph. The activity models that were produced in change analysis for the purpose of identifying needs for changes were at a relatively high, overview level, and these need to be expanded and investigated at a more detailed level (see figure 6.23, which is a decomposition of process 4 on figure 6.22). The object is to get to the level at which the information system is separated from the human activities which it supports, such that each process on the graph has inputs and outputs that are unequivocally either information or some other flow (for example, materials).

The next step is to identify potential information sub-systems relating to groups of users. The sub-systems are not supposed to be identified in relation to artificial criteria, such as some common technical aspect, but only in relation to commonality in use. ISAC is not interested in identifying any overall information system totality and believes that it is more relevant to identify a number of sub-systems. These information sub-systems are then

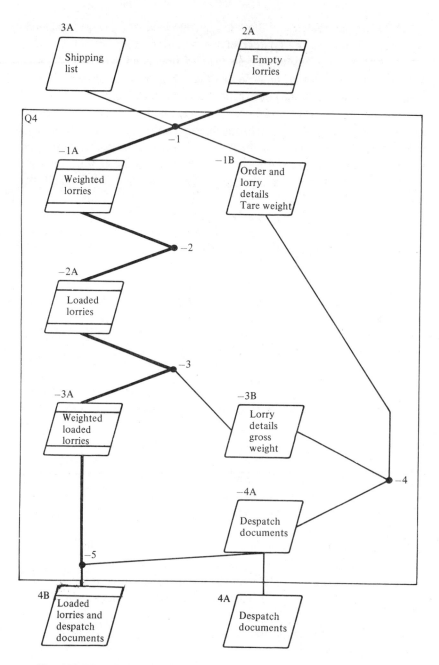

Fig. 6.23. More detailed A - graph.

classified according to whether they are formalizable or not. An unformalizable information system might be one concerning qualified decisions, informal contacts, know-how, and so on. The formalizable sub-systems are divided into those that are sensible to automate, in terms of cost, social desirability, and so on, and those that are not. The automated ones are further classified according to whether they involve calculations or simply involve storing and retrieving information. These classifications are the basis for subsequent parts of the methodology.

Each information sub-system is now studied separately in terms of its costs and benefits. ISAC attempts to do this cost-benefit analysis without making assumptions about technical implementation. To do this ISAC refers to ambition levels for an information system, rather than particular technologies for implementation. For example, two different ambition levels for the same sub-system might be a one second response time compared with a three hour one. Each ambition level will have a different cost-benefit associated with it.

The steps in this phase are as follows:

Analysis of contributions: This is a study of the benefits (not quantified) expected to accrue from the change. It is a refinement of the earlier work done in change analysis and the results are documented in a property table. It is emphasized that this analysis must be performed in the context of the environment and the way in which the environment uses the information. This may require a more detailed analysis of the environment than has been done up to this point.

Generation of alternative levels of ambition: A number of alternatives are generated for each sub-system and documented. The alternatives must be realistic, there is no point in generating ambition levels that do not fulfil minimum requirements in terms of, for example, frequencies or volumes.

Test of ambition levels: Here the ambition levels are tested to see if they are practical. ISAC envisages a number of ways that they might be tested, for example, if similar information systems exist elsewhere, then it is likely that such a system can be created. Prototyping is also suggested, but not a prototype of the technology, rather one of the provision of information to the user.

Cost-benefit analysis: This is a conventional cost-benefit study of each identified level of ambition.

Choice of ambition level: The results of the cost-benefit analyses are evaluated in conjunction with the human and social analyses performed at an earlier stage, and a choice of ambition level made. One result may be that the development of an information system is discontinued.

The next stage concludes the activity studies and is the *Co-ordination of Information Sub-systems*. This is in effect the project plan. Special emphasis is given to the inter-relationships between the different sub-systems in order that they are sensibly co-ordinated. Priorities, resources, and schedules are allocated for the developments and the plans documented.

3 Information Analysis

The transition from change analysis to activity studies was not made unless the agreed proposal for change included the development of an information system. Similarly the transition from activity studies to information analysis is made only if one or more information systems have been identified as formalizable. The techniques used in information analysis assume a formalizable and automatable information system, although it is indicated that a limited degree of information analysis might be appropriate for non-automatable systems.

For each information system the input and output information sets are extracted from the A-graphs for the system. Then an iterative process of function and data analysis is performed.

The ISAC term for functional analysis is *precedence analysis*, because ISAC recommends that it be performed by reasoning about the precedents for each information set. If the output information set from an information system is clearly derivable from its input set then precedence analysis stops. If, however, the derivation is not clear, then the information set that immediately precedes the output information set must be deduced. If the derivation of this set from the inputs to the system is not clear, then precedence analysis continues. The precedents from each information set are analysed until the input sets are reached. At each stage of precedence analysis the information system (considered as a set of processes) has been refined to a lower level of detail. Precedence analysis is in this way equivalent to functional decomposition in other methodologies. The reasoning process, however, is different, in that instead of enquiring about the logical structure of a process, ISAC concentrates on the transformation that must have been necessary to produce the output information set currently being studied. If this transformation is not clear then a simpler problem must be solved. The question is asked, 'what was the nature of the information set that immediately preceded the transformation of the current output set?'. In this way the definition of processes is implicit; at any stage a process is always a black box (or using ISAC notation a black dot).

The result of precedence analysis is a set of information precedence graphs (I-graphs). I-graphs describe information sets, and precedence relations between information sets. They are more precise than A-graphs in that they not only show input and output sets but also show relationships between sets. Figure 6.24 shows an example of an I-graph derived from the A-graph of figure 6.23. It shows the input and output information sets and the precedence relations, for example it shows that in order to derive the 'accepted despatch' information set we first need the 'order details', 'customer details', and 'product details' information sets.

Reasoning about the transformations that need to be performed on information sets requires knowledge of the structure of information, and that is why component analysis is performed at the same time as precedence analysis.

In component analysis the structure of the information sets is studied. An information set is either a data-flow or a data store. So an information set will either have been specified as a basic input to, or output from, the information system being studied; or will have been from a preceding process or a set of permanent information. An information set may be compound, that is it may itself contain information sets. An elementary information set consists of one or more messages, where each message consists of an identification term and one property term. An 'almost elementary' information set consists of a number of elementary information sets with common identification terms. Thus an almost elementary information set corresponds to a logical record with a key (identification term), and a number of data-item types (property terms).

ISAC documents information sets by means of a C-graph (component graph). This graph is a hierarchy showing the decomposition of an information set into subsets. Figure 6.25 is an example of a C-graph for the 'despatch document' information set. The lowest level on the graph shows either elementary or almost elementary sets.

A further step in information analysis concerns process logic analysis. This has been ignored by ISAC during precedence analysis in order not to complicate things, but must now be addressed. Process analysis means the detailed description of the information processes in the information system.

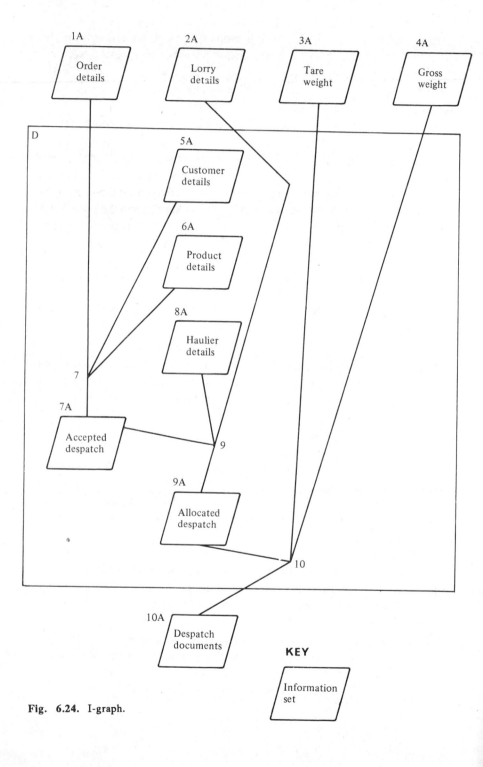

Fig. 6.24. I-graph.

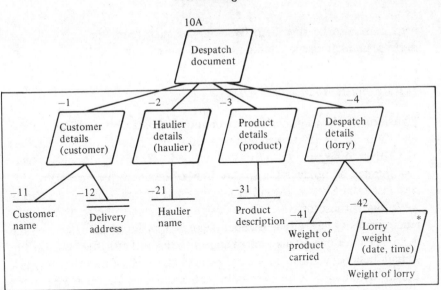

10A

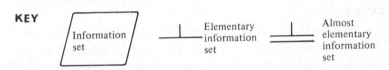

KEY

Information set — Elementary information set = Almost elementary information set

Fig. 6.25. C-graph.

An information process is the transformation of one or more information sets into some other information set, or sets. These transformations are at the logical level and do not depict representation or implementation aspects.

The processes which have previously appeared simply as nodes or black dots on the I-graphs are now identified and named. The relationships between the processes have already been described in the C-graphs so that all that needs doing is for the content of the process to be specified individually. This is done via a process table that defines the prerequisites for the process, the conditions, permitted states for conditions, and required actions. A process table is effectively a decision table (see section 4.5) constrained by prerequisites.

The final stage of information analysis is property analysis. Precedence and component analysis are structural descriptions of an information system. Requirements that are specific to the environment in which the system is used must also be specified. Examples of such properties are volumes, response times, frequency, and security requirements.

4 Data System Design

Transition to data system design implies a fundamental change in the application of the ISAC methodology. Up to this point the ISAC activities of Change Analysis, Activity Studies, and Information Analysis have concentrated on producing a specification of requirements for information systems. Data System Design is the first part of data orientated systems work, the purpose of which is to design a technical solution to meet the requirements specification. A data system is a means of implementing the requirements of one or more information systems. A data system will usually contain both manual and automated parts, both of which must be designed. Data System Design is followed in ISAC by an activity known as Equipment Adaptation. Data System Design, therefore, assumes types of equipment but not specific equipment.

The design activity starts with a study of processing philosophy. Processes that are to be performed on a computer are differentiated from those that are not. A decision is made on the mix of batch and on-line processing, and centralized versus distributed processing. The results of Activity Studies are particularly relevant to the determination of processing philosophy, and the identification of processes performed in information analysis enables preliminary 'process collections' to be made grouped by some common requirement (for example, response time).

The next stage of Data System Design is data structure design and program delimitation and design. Information Analysis has typically decomposed data and functions below the level of files and programs, and appropriate groupings are now made.

The design of a permanent data set is performed by consolidating or aggregating more primitive objects (for example, elementary information sets) into higher level groupings, on the basis of functional dependency, and secondly by considering access requirements and search paths for efficient retrieval and storage.

Program delimitation consists of putting a boundary around a group of processes defined on an I-graph. The number of processes so grouped will clearly partially determine the size and complexity of the program, and these two factors are a constraint on the delimitation. The other important constraint is the nature of the decisions that have been made about file and database design.

Once programs have been delimited and files or a database have been designed the overall structure of the system can be recorded in a D-graph (a form of program run-chart). The next step is to specify each program, which is completed in some detail in the ISAC approach, and the JSP method is recommended.

The final stage in data system design is the design of manual routines. Some information processing activities are naturally manual, and all computer based systems will have associated manual routines. ISAC recommends that users design their own work routines.

5 Equipment Adaptation

The preceding phase of data system design has produced an 'equipment-independent' solution. This is now adapted to fit particular equipment. Equipment Adaptation consists of equipment study, adaptation of computer based routines, and creation of side-routines.

The equipment study involves collecting and evaluating technical specifications and cost and performance characteristics, and formulating an equipment strategy. Possible options might be, for example, the use of existing computer facilities, the purchase or rent of new equipment, or the use of bureau facilities. Accurate sizing of the configuration required is performed at this stage. The final choice of equipment is documented in an E-graph, which is a mapping of the D-graph onto a particular machine configuration.

Adaptation of computer-based routines consists of two tasks. Firstly, physical data structures must be designed, and secondly the program specifications must be adapted. Files and databases are mapped to specific storage devices and retrieval and linkage mechanisms specified. Outputs are mapped to specific output peripherals, such as displays or printers. Input formats are mapped to specific methods of data capture. Any of these mappings may alter the data structures of computer programs and thus the structure of the programs must be adapted. Finally side-routines are specified. These are work-routines that are a necessary consequence of the choice of a particular set of equipment. For example, side-routines might be specified for data preparation, output handling, or computer operation.

The emphasis on the methodology is placed on analysis and design aspects of information systems development where appropriate. The methodology seeks to identify the fundamental causes of users' problems in the present system. These problems may be overcome or the situation improved by analysis of these activities and the initiation of various changes. The methodology authors believe that the people best equipped to do this analysis, in terms of their knowledge, interest, and motivation, are the users themselves. The methodology attempts to facilitate this by providing a series of work or method steps and a series of rules and techniques which, it is claimed, can be performed by these users. It is accepted that this might lead to a series of self-contained application systems which might be regarded as 'inefficient' from some points of view.

The methodology does not assume that the development of a computer information system is necessarily the solution to the problem. Need is established only if it is seen that an information system benefits people in their work. It is traditional in Scandinavian countries, sometimes backed-up by legislation, that technology is only implemented with the approval of the workers in that workplace. This people-orientated methodology has a wide view of the stakeholders of an information system, including users, managers, workers, and also those usually thought of as outside of the organization, such as customers and funders.

6.6 EFFECTIVE TECHNICAL AND HUMAN IMPLEMENTATION OF COMPUTER-BASED SYSTEMS (ETHICS)

ETHICS is a systems design methodology and, as well as being an acronym, the name is meant to imply that it is a methodology that embodies an ethical position. ETHICS has been devised by Enid Mumford (see Mumford and Weir 1979) over the past fifteen years or so although the name ETHICS is more recent, and is a methodology based on the philosophy of the participative approach (discussed in section 3.3). In addition, it encompasses the socio-technical view, that for a system to be effective the technology must fit closely with the social and organizational factors. In particular, this means that an improved quality of working life and enhanced job satisfaction of the users must be a major objective of the systems design. This is not simply to guard the interests of the users in the introduction of computing and technology, although this is obviously of major importance, but it is an essential prerequisite to achieve effective systems as far as the organization and its management is concerned. To support her case Mumford points to the failure of many traditionally performed system implementations, where technical and economic objectives were the only consideration.

The philosophy of ETHICS is different from most information system methodologies and is also explicitly stated, which is not common amongst authors of methodologies. The philosophy is one which has evolved from organizational behaviour and perceives the development of computer systems not as a technical issue but as an organizational issue which is fundamentally concerned with the process of change. It is based on the socio-technical approach of the social sciences as developed by a number of authors, one of the most influential being Davis (1972). Mumford (1983a) defines the socio-technical approach as

'one which recognizes the interaction of technology and people and produces work systems which are both technically efficient and have social characteristics which lead to high job satisfaction'.

Elsewhere, in Mumford and Weir (1979), job satisfaction is defined as

'the attainment of a good "fit" between what the employee is seeking from his work — his job needs, expectations and aspirations — and what he is required to do in his job — the organizational job requirements which mould his experience'.

In order to ascertain how good this fit is, a theory for measuring job satisfaction has been developed based on the various views of what is important in job satisfaction and these have been integrated into a framework derived from Parsons and Shils (1951). Five areas of measurement are identified as follows:

The knowledge fit — a good fit exists when the employees believe that their skills are being adequately used and that their knowledge is being developed to make them increasingly competent. It is recognized that different people have widely different expectations in this area, some wanting their skills developed, others wanting to remain static and opt for an 'easy life'.

The psychological fit — a job must fit the employee's status, advancement and work interest (some of the Herzberg (1966) motivators). These needs are recognized to vary according to age, background, education, and class.

The efficiency fit — this comprises three areas. Firstly, the effort-reward bargain, which is the amount an employer is prepared to pay (as against the view of the employee about how much he is worth). Although, to management, this is probably the prime area of importance, it is in practice sometimes way down the list of employee needs. Secondly, work controls, which may be tight or loose but need to fit the employee's expectations. Thirdly, supervisory controls, such as the necessary back-up facilities, such as information, materials, specialist knowledge, and supervisory help.

The task-structure fit — this measures the degree to which the employee's tasks are regarded as being demanding and fulfilling. Particularly important are the number of skills required, the number and nature of targets, plus the feedback mechanism, the identity, distinctiveness, and importance of tasks, and the degree of autonomy and control over the tasks that the employee has. This measure is seen to be strongly related to technology and its method of employment. Technology can affect the task-structure fit substantially and, it is argued, has reduced the fit by simplification and repetitiveness. However, it is also seen as a variable which can be improved dramatically by design of the technical system to meet the requirements of the task-structure fit.

The ethical fit — this is also described as the social value fit and measures whether the values of the employee match those of the employer organization. In some organizations performance is everything, whilst others value most other factors, for example, service. Some firms are paternal or welfare orientated, others have characteristics of 'success', and so on. The better the match of an organization's values with those of the employee, the higher the level of job satisfaction.

A second philosophical strand of the ETHICS methodology is participation. This is the involvement of those affected by a system being part of the decision making process concerning the design and operation of that system. Those affected by a system includes not only direct users but indirect users, management, customers, suppliers, and so on. Of course there are limits to this. For example, competitors will be affected, but it is unlikely that they will be asked to participate. Participation is of course important in many methodologies, but has been described as not just important, but vital, in ETHICS (see Hirschheim 1985a). In other methodologies participation is sometimes simply regarded as 'allowing the users to chose the colour of the terminals that they use', in ETHICS users are involved in the decisions concerning the work process and how the use of technology might improve their job satisfaction.

In ETHICS the development of computer-based systems is seen as a change process and therefore will involve conflicts of interest between all the participants or actors in that process. These conflicts are not simply between management and worker but often between worker and worker and manager and manager. The successful implementation of new systems is therefore a process of negotiation between the affected and interested parties. Obviously one of the major affected and interested parties are the users themselves and if these people are left out of the decision making process, the process of change is unlikely to be a success. This is not just because of resulting disaffection amongst the user group but, more positively, because they have so much to contribute to make the implementation a success. They are probably the most knowledgeable about the current workplace situation and the future requirements. Mumford (1983a) summarizes:

'all change involves some conflicts of interest. To be resolved, these conflicts need to be recognized, brought out into the open, negotiated and a solution arrived at which largely meets the interests of all the parties in the situation....successful change strategies require institutional mechanisms which enable all these interests to be represented, and participation provides these'.

It is recognized in practice that participation means different things to different people and that the parties involved may have quite different reasons for wanting participation and quite different expectations concerning the benefits. Management may see it as a way of achieving changes that would otherwise be rejected. This is perhaps not the ideal view for management to take but if the resulting participation is real then so be it, although the end result may not turn out exactly as they assume. The point being that it is not a pre-requisite for everybody to hold the view that participation is a moral or ideological necessity, enlightened self-interest will do just as well.

The philosophical commitment to participation outlined above begs the question of exactly how it is to be achieved. There appears to be quite a degree of freedom involved and although there exists 'ideal' types of participation, in practice, a variety of forms are acceptable for it still to be 'ETHICS'. In fact, it can be used by an expert group to design a system for another, non-participating, group. However, this is not recommended. This debate does illustrate that ETHICS is a methodology that has quite a level of flexibility. It is better, Mumford argues, to use it in some form, rather than not at all. The implication being, that its use, even stripped of some of its most important participatory trappings, is better than using other more traditional methods which concentrate purely on technical and economic objectives.

Mumford distinguishes between structure, content, and process. Structure is the mechanism of participation which, as discussed in section 3.3, can be consultative, representative or consensus. Consultative involves the participants giving evidence to the decision makers which, hopefully, will influence the decision makers but does not bind them in any way. This is the weakest form of participation and not recommended for detailed design. Representative participation is a structure where selected or, preferably, elected representatives of the various interests are involved in the decision making. This is most appropriate for the tactical or middle management type of decision making. In computing terms this might be at the system definition stage where the system outline and boundaries are discussed and a fairly wide spectrum of interests are involved. The third form of participation is consensus, where all the constituents are involved in the decision making. This is most suitable at the detailed design stage where the decisions probably affect the day to day work practices of the people involved. Clearly it is difficult to involve everybody in everything, and what usually happens is that design groups are formed to do the work and present alternatives to the whole constituency, which takes the final decisions.

The content of participation concerns the issues and the boundaries of activities that are within the remit of participation. Generally, prior to any participation, management will want to keep certain things as their own prerogative. One objective of the process of participation is the gaining of the relevant knowledge and information by the participants. In general, the users involved in participation will not have previously had the necessary knowledge, information, and perhaps confidence to discuss issues and make decisions. Without this, the participation is only of a very limited kind. The users must have as much information and knowledge as is necessary to make informed decisions, or at least as much as anyone else. Without the acquisition of this information and knowledge they will be at a disadvantage and subject to undue influence from more powerful groups. True participation means equal knowledge and thus, it might be argued, equal power for all groups. The training and education of the users is therefore a very important aspect of ETHICS.

Participation usually involves the setting up of a steering committee and a design group or groups. The steering committee sets the guidelines for the design group and consists of senior managers from the affected areas of the organization, senior managers from management services and personnel, and senior trade union officials (if the organization is unionized). It is recommended that the steering committee and the design group meet once a month during the course of the project. The design group designs the new system including:

- Choice of hardware and software.
- Human—computer interaction.
- Workplace re-organization.
- Allocation of responsibilities.

All major interests should be represented, including each section and function, grade, age group, and so on. The design group includes systems analysts, although their role is not the normal one of analysis and design, but one of educator and adviser. This often involves the analysts in a learning process themselves. If the area of the design is large, involving many departments or sections, then a design group may first design in outline, and then hand over to detailed design groups. A participative design requires the appointment of a facilitator to help the design group manage the project and educate the group in the use of ETHICS. The role is multi-faceted and concerns motivation and confidence building of the design group, it is not one of decision making or persuading. For this reason the facilitator must be neutral and preferably external, if not to the organization then to the department. The role is very important. In one situation, the facilitator withdrew, and the confidence of the design group declined and the importance of the group in the eyes of the management also declined.

Depending on which sources are referred to, the actual steps of ETHICS differ somewhat in their names and numbers, however the content remains much the same. The fifteen step version outlined here corresponds to those described in Mumford (1983a). A six-stage, twenty-five step version of ETHICS is described in Hirschheim (1985a). The major difference is that there is a greater separation of the technical and social issues. This might mean that the technical issues of design could be addressed by a separate, more technically experienced, design group. ETHICS has also been amended slightly, although the principles are the same, for use by small businesses thinking of purchasing a computer system for the first time. This version is described in Mumford (1986). Unless stated otherwise the work in the steps that follow are performed by the design group or groups themselves.

1 Why Change?

The first meeting of the design group considers this rather fundamental question and addresses the current problems and opportunities. The result should be a convincing statement of the need for change. Presumably, if no convincing statement is arrived at for change, the process stops there, although this is not made explicit.

2 System Boundaries

The design group identifies the boundaries of the system it is designing and where it interfaces with other systems. Four areas are considered: business activities affected (for example, sales, finance and personnel); existing technology affected; parts of the organization affected (for example, departments and sections); parts of the organization's environment affected (for example, suppliers and customers).

3 Description of Existing System

This is to educate the design group as to how the existing system works. In practice, it is found that people will know the detail of their own jobs and those that they interact with directly, but will have little knowledge of the whole system. In this step, two activities are undertaken. Firstly, a horizontal input/output analysis is described with inputs on the left, activities in the middle, and outputs on the right. Secondly, a vertical analysis of the design area activities is made at five different levels. The lowest level is of the operating activities, that is, the necessary activities of a day to day nature — these should have appeared in the horizontal analysis. The problem prevention/solution activities are also identified. These are the key problems or variances that occur and how they are corrected. Thirdly, the co-ordination activities are identified. These are activities that have to be performed together or in a particular sequence or at a particular time. These are both inter- and intra-departmental co-ordinations. Fourthly, the development activities are recorded. These are the things or areas that need improving. Fifthly, the control activities are identified indicating how the system is controlled, how it is judged to be meeting targets or objectives, and how it is monitored.

4, 5 and 6 Definition of Key Objectives and Tasks

Three questions are asked in order to help define the key objectives. Firstly, why do particular areas exist, what is their role and purpose? Secondly, given this, what should be their responsibilities and functions? Thirdly, how far do their present activities match what they should be doing? From this, the key objectives can be listed and these form the design objectives of the new system. In addition, the key tasks that need to be performed to achieve the key objectives are defined in outline, along with their key information needs.

7 Diagnosis of Efficiency Needs

Weak links in the existing system are identified and documented. Mumford talks about them as variances, which is a '...tendency for a system or sub-system to deviate from some desired or expected norm or standard' (Mumford 1983a). Mumford identifies two types of variance. Firstly, systemic or key types, which are inherent in the system and cannot be completely overcome, but only eased. An example is provided by the variances connected with the *financial desire* to keep stocks small and the *service desire* to be able to supply customers with what they want. The second type of variance is operational, these are variances due to poor design or lack of attention to changing circumstances, and can usually be completely eliminated in the new system. Examples could include bottlenecks, insufficient information and inadequate equipment.

8 Diagnosis of Job Satisfaction Needs

This step measures the job satisfaction needs. The principles and measures used have already been described. This is achieved by use of a standard questionnaire provided by the ETHICS methodology. The design group may alter the questionnaire to fit their organization and requirements. The results are discussed democratically and the underlying reasons established for any areas where there are poor job satisfaction fits. In addition, formulations for improving the situation in the new design are made and everybody is encouraged to play a major part in this design work. Where there have been knowledge or task-structure problems of fit, these are susceptible to improvement by a redesign of the system. Other areas of poor fit, such as effort-reward or ethical, may be improved somewhat in this way, but will probably require changes in personnel policies, or more radically, organizational ethos.

9 Future Analysis

The new system design needs to be both a better version of the existing system and able to cope with future changes that may occur in the environment, technology, organization, or fashion. Thus an attempt is made to try and identify these changes and to build a certain amount of flexibility into the new system. This may involve the design group in interactions with people outside the organization in order to identify and assess some of the potential changes.

10 Specifying and Weighting Efficiency and Job Satisfaction Needs and Objectives

Of all the steps, Mumford identifies this as the key step in the whole methodology. Objectives are set according to the diagnosis activities of the three previous steps. The achievement of an agreed and ranked set of objectives can be a very difficult task and must involve everyone, not just the design group itself. Often objectives conflict and the priorities of the various constituencies may be very different. These differences may not all be resolved, but one of the stated benefits of ETHICS is that at least these differences are aired. Ultimately, a list of priority and secondary objectives is produced. The criteria for the systems design is that all priority objectives must be met and also as many of the secondary ones as possible. At this stage a certain amount of iteration is recommended, to review the key objectives and tasks from steps 4 and 5.

11 The Organizational Design of the New System

If possible this should be performed in parallel with the technical design of step 12, because they inevitably intertwine. The organizational changes which are needed to meet the efficiency and job satisfaction objectives are specified. There are likely to be a variety of ways of achieving the objectives, and between three and six organizational options should be elaborated. The design group specifies in more detail the key tasks of step 5 and addresses the following questions — the answers forming the basic data for the organizational design process:

* What are the operating activities that are required?
* What are the problem prevention/solution activities that are required?

- What are the co-ordination activities that are required?
- What are the development activities that are required?
- What are the control activities that are required?
- What special skills are required, if any, of the staff?
- Are there any key roles or relationships that exist that must be addressed in the new design?

Each organizational option is rated for its ability to meet the primary and secondary objectives of step 10, and should identify the sections, sub-sections, work groups and individuals, their responsibilities and tasks. In order to meet the job satisfaction objectives it is almost inevitable that the design group will have to consider the socio-technical principles of organizational design and be provided with information and experience in relation to design. The socio-technical approach is the antithesis of Taylorism (see Taylor 1947) which is to break each job down into its elemental parts and rearrange it into an efficient combination. The traditional car assembly line which requires its operators to perform small, routine, repetitive jobs is regarded as the ultimate example of Taylorism in action. The requirements of the machine are given priority over the requirements of the human being. This has, it is argued, inevitably led to a bored, disaffected, and ultimately inefficient workforce.

Although ETHICS uses aspects of socio-technical design, the socio-technical school assumes a given technology, whereas, in ETHICS, the technology is part of the design. Further, they assume shop-floor situations, rather than the office and high level organizational situations, which concern ETHICS.

Mumford recommends the consideration of three types of work organization patterns. The first is *task variety* and involves giving an individual more variety in work by providing more than one task to be performed or by rotating a person around a number of different tasks. This is the more traditional approach, but is limited especially where the expectations of job satisfaction are more sophisticated. In this case the principles of *job enrichment* might be appropriate. This is where the work is organized in such a way that a number of different skills, including judgemental ones, are introduced. In particular, it involves the handling of problems and the organization of the work by the individual without supervision. This may require an increased skill level on behalf of the individual, but leads to enhanced job satisfaction. A further stage in job enrichment is the incorporation of development aspects into a job. This means that the individual has the freedom to change the way the job is performed. This leads to constant review and the implementation of new ideas and methods. Obviously this cannot be introduced into every job, but there are probably more opportunities than at first imagined.

As important as individual jobs is the concept of what Mumford calls *self-managing groups*. Here groups are formed that have responsibility for a relatively wide spectrum of the tasks to be performed. These groups are preferably multi-skilled so that each member is competent to carry out all the tasks required of the group, they are encouraged to organize themselves, their work, and their own control and monitoring, which may include their own target setting. This can provide a very stimulating and satisfying work environment for the group members. Again self managing groups are not always possible and require a good deal of management goodwill at first, but nevertheless can prove very effective.

12 Technical Options

The various technical options that might be appropriate, including hardware, software and the design of the human—computer interface, are specified. Each option is evaluated in the same way as the organizational options, that is, against efficiency, job satisfaction, and future change objectives. As mentioned in step 11, the organizational and technical options should be considered simultaneously, as often one option implies certain necessary factors in the other. It is advised that one option should exist which specifies no change in technology so as to be able to see how much could be achieved simply with organizational changes.

The organizational and technical options are now merged to ensure compatibility, and are evaluated against the primary objectives and the one that best meets the objectives is selected. This selection is performed by the design group with input from the steering committee and other interested constituencies.

13 The Preparation of a Detailed Work Design

The selected system is now designed in detail. The data flows, tasks, groups, individuals, responsibilities and relationships are defined. There is also a review to ensure that the detail of the design still meets the specified objectives. Obviously, the design detail includes the organizational aspects as well as the technical.

14 Implementation

The Design Group now applies itself to ensuring the successful implementation of the design. This involves planning the implementation process in detail, the strategy, the education and training, the co-ordination of parts, and everything needed to ensure a smooth change-over.

15 Evaluation

The implemented system is checked to ensure that it is meeting its objectives, particularly in relation to efficiency and job satisfaction, using the tools of variance analysis and measures of job satisfaction. If it is not meeting the objectives, then corrective action is taken, indeed as time progresses changes will become necessary and design becomes a cyclical process.

Quite a common reaction to ETHICS is for people to say that it is impractical. Firstly, it is argued, that unskilled users cannot do the design properly, and secondly, that management would never accept it, or that it removes the right to manage from managers. In answer to the first problem Mumford argues that users can, and do, design properly. They certainly need some training and help along the way, but this can be relatively easily provided. More importantly, they have the skills of knowing about their own work and system, and have a stake in the design. This is much more than many traditional analysts and designers. To answer the second point, managers have often welcomed participation and can be convinced of its benefits. There are many success stories. It is not always the management that needs to be convinced, sometimes it is the users who are sceptical about participation, seeing it as some sort of management trick. The job of a manager is to meet the corporate objectives, not simply oversee people and make every last decision. This is often counter-productive to achieving those objectives, often resulting in very high staff turnover rates, which is not productive.

Mumford does admit that it will not be easy, quite the reverse, but the benefits are, she claims, worth it. Mumford has produced some publications relating to experiences using ETHICS. They illustrate many of the problems that are encountered and the solutions, they show how users can design their own systems and how they come to terms with their design roles. The first book shows how a group of secretaries at Imperial Chemical Industries (ICI) in the UK designed new work systems for themselves in the wake of the introduction of word processing equipment (Mumford, 1983c). The second example shows how a group of Purchase Invoice clerks helped design a major on-line computer system (Mumford, 1983b). One of the most interesting aspects, and most telling concerning the power of ETHICS that emerges from this study, is the fact that the clerks designed three different ways of working with the computer system to do essentially the same thing. Which one is used depends on the clerk. It is interesting to consider whether any professional systems design team would have dreamt of doing such a thing.

6.7 SOFT SYSTEMS METHODOLOGY (SSM)

As discussed in section 3.1, general systems theory attempts to understand the nature of systems. Scientific analysis breaks up a complex situation into its constituent parts for analysis. Although this works in the physical sciences, it is less successful in the social sciences and in management science. One tenet of systems thinking is that the whole is greater than the sum of the parts: properties of the whole are not explicable entirely in terms of the properties of its constituent elements. Human activity systems are more complex and the human components in particular may react differently when examined singly to when they play a role in the whole system. Something is lost when the whole is broken up in the 'reductionist' approach of scientific analysis.

The systems principle also implies that we must try to develop application systems for the organization as a whole rather than for functions in isolation. It may take only a few hours by Concorde to cross the Atlantic, but this progress may be lost if it takes as many hours to get from the centre of London to Heathrow Airport and from JFK Airport to the centre of New York. It is the transport system we should be looking at, not the airline system in isolation. Another aspect of this is that organizations are 'open systems' and therefore the relation between the organization and its environment is important. We should always be looking at 'the system' in terms of the wider system of which it is part. Systems theory would also suggest that a multi-disciplinary team of analysts is much more likely to understand the organization and suggest better solutions to problems. After all, specialisms are a result of artificial and arbitrary divisions. In the information systems context, a systems approach prevents an automatic assumption that computer solutions are always appropriate. It will also help in problem situations which have been studied from only one narrow point of view. Such an approach is not appropriate in the study of large and complex problem situations.

Checkland (1981) has attempted to adapt systems theory into a practical methodology. By methodology he means the study of methods to achieve certain purposes. 'For any particular problem situation, the study will lead to a subset of principles which can be applied for that particular situation.' He argues that systems analysts apply their craft to problems which are not well defined. These 'fuzzy', ill-structured or *soft* problem situations are common in organizations. The description of one category of systems, Human Activity Systems, also acknowledges the importance of people in organizations. It is relatively easy, it is argued, to model data and processes (the emphasis placed in many methodologies), but to understand the real world it is essential to include people in the model, people who may have different and conflicting objectives, perceptions and attitudes. This is difficult because of the unpredictable nature of human activity systems. There is no such thing as a repeatable experiment in this context. The claims for the soft systems approach are that a true understanding of complex problem situations is more likely using this approach than if the more simplistic structured or data orientated approaches are used, which address mainly the formal, 'hard' or scientific aspects of systems.

Wilson (1984) gives an analogy. He considers two examples of problems. The first is a flat tyre. The solution is clear. The second is 'What should the UK government do about Northern Ireland?' The solution is not clear and it would be difficult to find any solution that satisfied all the interested parties. Wilson suggests that hard methodologies, that may be suitable for solving 'burst tyre type problems' are inappropriate for organizational problem situations. It is not only a question of techniques and tools, but also concepts, culture and language.

Another difference between hard and soft systems thinking is that in hard systems thinking a goal is assumed. The purpose of the methods used by the analyst (or engineer) is to modify the system in some way so that this goal is achieved in the most efficient manner. Hard systems thinking is concerned with the 'how' of the problem. In soft systems thinking, the objectives of the system are assumed to be more complex than a simple goal that can be achieved and measured. Systems are argued to have purposes or missions rather than goals. Understanding is achieved in soft systems methods through debate with the actors in the system. Emphasis is placed on the 'what' as well as the 'how' of the system. The term 'problem' in this context is also inappropriate. There will be lots of problems, hence the term 'problem situation' — 'a situation in which there are perceived to be problems' (Wilson 1984).

The methodology of Checkland has been developed at Lancaster University. It was developed through 'action research' whereby the systems ideas are tested out in client organizations by ISCOL (a consultancy company owned by the University). The analysts neither dictate the way the action develops nor step outside as observers: they are participants in the action and results are unpredictable. The practical work provides experience which can be used to draw conclusions and to modify these ideas. This proves to be a successful approach, because, as we have said, it is not possible to develop a good 'laboratory model' of human activity systems and set up repeatable experiments.

Each action research project therefore furthers knowledge which can be used in future soft systems work, as well as provide some benefits in a particular problem situation. Change is therefore achieved through the learning process as theory and practice meet and affect each other. Checkland's book is aptly titled *Systems Thinking, Systems Practice*!

Checkland has carried out extensive studies, both theoretical and practical, on the analysis of organizations in his action research projects. The central focus of the methodology is the search for a particular view (or views). This Weltanschauung (Assumptions or World View) will form the basis for describing the systems requirements and will be carried forward to further stages in the methodology. The world view is extracted from the problem situation through debate on the main purpose of the organization concerned — its *raison d'être*, its attitudes, its 'personality' and so on. Examples of world view might be : 'This is a business aimed at maximizing long term profits' or 'This is a hospital dedicated to maintaining the highest standards of patient care'.

Firstly, the problem solver, perhaps with extensive help from the problem owner, forms a *rich picture* of the problem situation. The problem solver is normally the analyst or the project team. The problem owner is the person or group on whose behalf the analysis has been commissioned. The 'picture' represents both subjective and objective perceptions of the problem situation in diagrammatic and pictorial form, showing the structures of the processes and their relation to each other. Elements of this rich picture will include the clients of the system, the people taking part in it, the task being performed, the environment, and the owner of the system. This picture can be used as an aid to discussion between the problem solver and the problem owner, or may simply help the problem solver better understand the problem situation. This stage is concerned with finding out about the problem situation.

The rich picture is mainly intended as a communication tool between the analysts and the users of the system and therefore uses the terminology of the environment. It will usually show the people involved, problem areas, controlling bodies and sources of conflict. From the rich picture the problem solver extracts problem themes — things noticed in the picture that are, or may be, causing problems. The picture may show conflicts between departments, absences of communication lines, shortages of supply, and so on. Rich pictures are intended to help in problem identification, not in the process of recommending solutions. In general, SSM concentrates on understanding problem situations, rather than developing solutions.

Rich pictures prove to be a very useful way of getting the user to talk about the problem situation. They may stimulate the drawing out of some of the parts of the 'iceberg' which normally lies hidden when using traditional methods of investigation. Figure 6.26, an example rich picture chart (from Avison and Catchpole 1988) highlights areas of conflict and concerns in the problem situation, a branch of the community health service in the UK.

Although mainly intended as a communication tool between the analysts and the users of the system, it will be possible to glean a lot of information about the system, including the main people involved (the 'people' figures in figure 6.26), problem areas (the 'question bubbles'), controlling bodies (the 'big eyes') and sources of conflict ('crossed swords'), by looking at the rich picture. This interpretation of rich pictures is developed from Wood-Harper *et al.* (1985).

Taking these problem themes, the next stage of the methodology involves the problem solver imagining and naming relevant systems that may help to relieve the problem theme. By relevant is meant a way of looking at the problem which provides a useful insight, for example:

Problem theme   =   conflicts between two departments

Relevant systems   =   system for redefining departmental
                                          boundaries.

Several different relevant systems should be explored to see which is the most useful. It is at this stage that debate is most important. The problem solver and the problem owner must decide which view to focus on, that is how to describe their relevant system. For example, will the conflict

Chapter 6

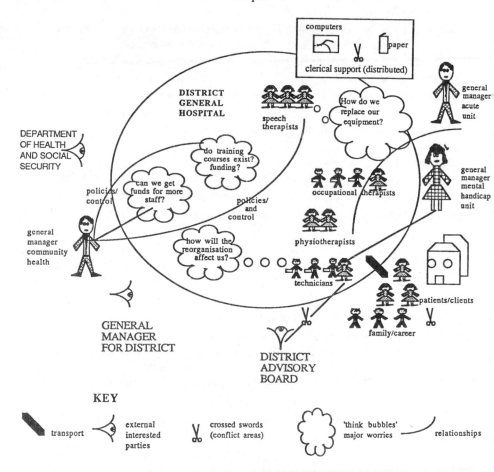

Fig. 6.26. Rich picture chart (early draft) for part of paramedical services.

resolution be 'a system to impose rigid rules of behaviour and decision-making in order to integrate decisions and minimize conflict' or will it be 'a system to integrate decisions of actors through increased communication and understanding between departments' or even 'an arbitration system to minimize conflict between departments by focussing disagreements through a central body'?

After constructing a rich picture, a root definition is developed for the relevant system. A root definition is a kind of hypothesis about the relevant system, and improvements to it, that might help the problem situation:

'The root definition is a concise, tightly constructed description of a human activity system which states what the system is' (Checkland 1981).

Using the checklist technique called the CATWOE criteria, the root definition is created. There are six elements of the CATWOE criteria and all must be included. Put into plain English, these six elements are *who* is doing *what* for *whom*, and to whom are they *answerable*, what *assumptions* are being made, and in what *environment* is it happening? If these questions are answered carefully, they should tell the analysts all that is needed.

There are technical terms for each of the six parts of the CATWOE list (the order having been changed from that of the explanation above):
- *Client* is the 'whom' (the beneficiary, or victim, affected by the activities).
- *Actor* is the 'who' (the agent of change, who carries out the transformation process).
- *Transformation* is the 'what' (the change taking place, the 'core of the root definition' (Smyth and Checkland 1976)).
- *World view* (or Weltanschauung) is the 'assumptions' (the outlook which makes the root definition meaningful).
- *Owner* is the person 'answerable' (the sponsor or controller).
- *Environment* is kept as the 'environment' (the wider system of which the problem situation is a part).

A root definition for a hospital administration system could be: 'to provide a service which gives the best possible care to the patients and which balances the need to avoid long waiting lists with that to avoid excessive government spending'. But alternative root definitions could have been 'a system for employing medical and administrative staff', 'a system to generate long waiting lists to illustrate the high status of consultants', or 'a system to encourage private health facilities'. One root definition of a prison might be 'a system to rehabilitate criminals', another 'a system to train criminals', and yet another 'a storage system for people'.

When the problem owners and the problem solvers are satisfied that the root definition is well formed, a conceptual model can be developed using this root definition (see figure 6.27). In this context the conceptual model is a diagram of the activities showing what the system, described by the root definition, will do. This stage in the methodology is about model building, but the model is meant to describe something relevant to the problem situation, it is not meant to be a model of the situation itself.

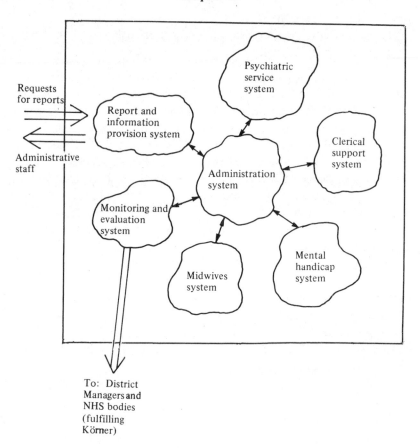

Fig. 6.27. Community health — conceptual model (early draft).

This interpretation is different to that implied in a mathematical model, or an architect's model. The conceptual model, such as that shown in figure 6.27, is used as a debating point so that the actors can relate the model to the real world situation. Usually there is a conceptual model drawn for each root definition and the drawing up of several root definitions and conceptual models becomes an iterative process of debate and modification towards an agreed root definition and conceptual model. An agreed statement is never easy to achieve as the process described is meant to draw out the different ideologies and conflicts, so that the final version represents an understanding of the problem situation. Similar processes were described in the ETHICS methodology. There is a danger that these final versions represent a conservative compromise. This is not what is intended. In SSM, if the ideological conflict is central to the problem situation, it has to be represented in the solution. The approach is meant to represent a holistic view to consider a complex problem, not a simplistic view representing a 'political' compromise.

The processes of developing rich pictures, root definitions of relevant systems and conceptual modelling gives the actors the wherewithal to understand the problem situation and to discuss possible changes and thereby actions to improve the problem situation. The next stage is therefore about comparisons of views, and since these views are those of human activity systems, made by people, we may not be comparing similar things. On assimilating these views, the last stage concerns recommending action to help the problem situation. Note that the methodology does not describe methods for implementing solutions. The methodology helps in understanding problem situations rather than provide a scheme for solving a particular problem.

Figure 6.28 (from Checkland 1981) summarizes the stages of Checkland's methodology. *Stages 1 and 2* are about finding out about the problem situation. This unstructured view gives some basic information from the views of the individuals involved. The application of the CATWOE criteria gives some structure to the expressions of the problem situations and in *stage 3* the analyst selects from these those views which which he or she considers give insight to the problem situation. *Stage 4* is to do with model building, that is, what the systems analyst might *do* (as against what the system *is* — the root definition). There must be one conceptual model for each root definition. *Stage 5* compares the conceptual models from stage 4 and the root definitions formed at stage 2. This comparison process leads to a set of recommendations regarding change, and *stage 6* analyses these recommendations in terms of what is feasible and desirable. *Stage 7*, the final phase, suggests actions to improve the problem situation, following the recommendations of stage 5.

Although we have discussed rich pictures, root definitions and conceptual models, the methodology relies much less on techniques and tools than most other methodologies, particularly 'hard' methodologies. These provide tools for use in particular situations at particular times in the development of the information systems project. SSM provides all actors, including the analysts, opportunities to understand and to deal with the problem situation. The analysts are perceived as actors involved in the problem situation, as much as those of the client and problem owner — they are not perceived

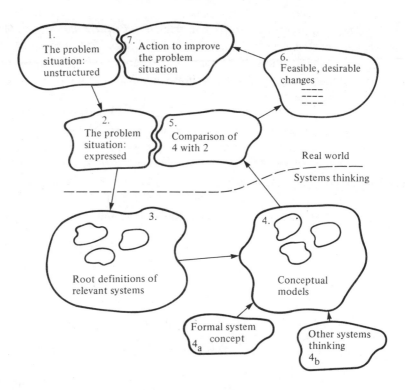

Fig. 6.28. The methodology in summary (after Checkland 1981).

as outside onlookers providing objectivity.

The process is iterative and the analysts learn about the system and are not expected to follow a laid down set of procedures. This does present problems: it is difficult to teach and to train others, and it is difficult to know when a stage in the project has been satisfactorily completed. However, these features are also its strengths, because it does not have any pre-conceived notions of a 'solution' and use of the methodology gives a better understanding of the problem situation.

One possible way that SSM can be fitted in the information systems development process is by using it as a 'front end' before proceeding to the 'hard' aspects of systems development. This would seem to be appropriate because SSM concerns analysis whereas the harder methodologies tend to emphasize design, development and implementation. Thus attempts are being made to develop a combination of SSM and SSADM. The Multiview

methodology, discussed next, also draws on SSM in the early parts of the
systems definition process.

6.8 MULTIVIEW

Multiview perceives information systems development as a hybrid process
involving computer specialists, who will build the system, and users, for
whom the system is being built. The methodology therefore looks at both
the human and technical aspects of information systems development. In this
aspect and others, it has been greatly influenced by the work of Checkland and
Mumford, but has fused these ideas with those found in 'hard' methodologies.
The approach adopted has been used on a number of projects, and the
methodology itself has been refined using 'action research' methods, that is
the application and testing of ideas developed in an academic environment
into the 'real world', also mentioned in the context of SSM. Further, unlike
many of the methodologies discussed in this chapter, it has mainly been used
for small scale computing projects, particularly for microcomputer
applications using software packages rather than developing 'bespoke'
systems, which is the intention of users of most information systems
methodologies.

The main text detailing the methodology (Wood-Harper, Antill and Avison
1985) tells the story of one particular project. This aspect of the book is at
least as important as the theoretical content and the descriptions of its general
application. Although the project is used to illustrate particular techniques,
the case study is not put forward as a 'textbook' example, showing how the
application of the Multiview methodology 'worked perfectly'. The search for
a perfect methodology, it is argued, is somewhat illusory. On the contrary,
the text exposes some of the difficulties and practical problems of
information systems work.

The authors are concerned to show that information systems development
theories should be contingent rather than prescriptive because the skills of
different analysts and the situations in which they are constrained to work
always has to be taken into account in any project. Avison and Wood-Harper
(1986) describe Multiview as an *exploration* in information systems
development. It therefore sets out to be flexible: a particular technique or
aspect of the methodology will work in certain situations but is not advised
for others.

The methodology will be seen by readers of this text as truly 'multi-view', because it can be clearly seen to include many of the techniques used by the other methodologies, and also the stages parallel those of other methodologies. The authors of Multiview claim, however, that it is not simply a hotch-potch of available techniques and tools, but a methodology which has been tested and works in practice. It is also 'multi-view' in the sense that it takes account of the fact that as an information systems project develops, it takes on different perspectives or views: organizational, technical, human-orientated, economic, and so on.

The five stages of Multiview are as follows:
• Analysis of human activity systems.
• Information modelling.
• Analysis and Design of the socio-technical system.
• Design of the human—computer interface.
• Design of the technical sub-systems.

They incorporate five different views which are appropriate to the progressive development of an analysis and design project so as to form a system which is complete in both technical and human terms. The five stages move from the general to the specific, from the conceptual to hard fact and from issue to task. Outputs of each stage either become inputs to following stages or are major outputs of the methodology. The Multiview methodology is shown in outline as figure 6.29. The two analysis orientated stages are shown in boxes and the three design orientated stages in circles. The arrows represent information passing between stages and the dotted arrows represent outputs of the methodology.

The first stage looks at the organization — its main purpose, problem themes, and the creation of a statement about what the information system will be and what it will do. The second stage is to analyse the entities and functions of the problem situation described in stage one. This is carried out independently of how the system will be developed.

The philosophy behind the third stage is that people have a basic right to control their own destinies and that if they are allowed to participate in the analysis and design of the systems that they will be using, then implementation, acceptance and operation of the system will be enhanced. This stage emphasizes the choice between alternative systems, according to important social and technical considerations. The fourth stage is concerned with the technical requirements of the user interface. The design of specific conversations will depend on the background and experience of the people who are going to use the system, as well as their information needs.

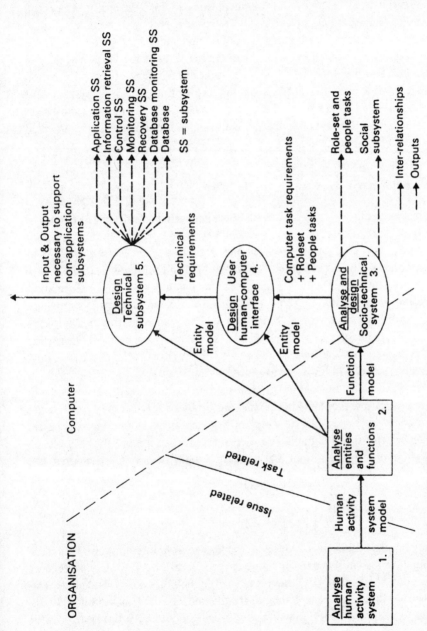

Fig. 6.29. The multiview methodology.

Finally, the design of the technical sub-system concerns the specific technical requirements of the system to be designed, and therefore to such aspects as computers, databases, control and maintenance. Although the methodology is concerned with the computer only in the latter stages, it is assumed that a computer system will form at least part of the information system. However, the authors do not argue that the final system will necessarily run on a large mainframe computer. This is just one solution, in fact the system described in the project discussed in the text is implemented on a microcomputer.

1 Analysis of Human Activity Systems

This stage is based on the work of Checkland. He has carried out extensive studies, both theoretical and practical, on the analysis of human activity systems. The very general term human activity system is used in SSM to cover any sort of organization, but is restricted in Multiview to include only those organizations which might consider using a computer information system. Information systems problems in human activity systems are frequently not precise nor well-defined. This stage in the methodology addresses these 'fuzzy' or soft problems. The technique (or craft) of developing rich pictures, root definitions using the CATWOE criteria, and conceptual models described in SSM, are also used in the first stage of Multiview.

In some cases the output of this stage is an improved human activity system and the problem owner and the problem solver may feel that the further stages in the Multiview methodology are unnecessary. In many cases, however, this is not enough. In order to progress to a more formal systems design exercise, the output of this stage should be a well formulated and refined root definition.

2 Analysis of Entities and Functions

The purpose of this stage, which is also known as 'information modelling', is to analyse the entities and functions of the system described, independent of any consideration of how the system will eventually be implemented. The stage is similar to those found in the IE and SSADM methodologies. Its input will be the root definition/conceptual model of the proposed system from the previous stage.

Two phases are involved:

1 The development of the functional model, and

2 the development of an entity model.

The first step in developing the functional model is to identify the MAIN function. This is always clear in a well formed root definition. This main function is then broken down progressively into sub-functions, until a sufficiently comprehensive level is achieved. This occurs when the analyst feels that the functions cannot be usefully broken down further. This is normally achieved after about four or five sub-function levels, depending on the complexity of the situation. This idea of functional decomposition has been described in section 3.7 and elsewhere. Data flow diagrams are developed from this hierarchical model. The hierarchical model and data flow diagrams are major inputs into stage 3 of the methodology — the analysis and design of the socio-technical system.

In developing an entity model, the problem solver extracts and names entities from the area of concern. An entity is defined in Multiview as anything that it is relevant to keep records about, for example, customers, sales, patients, hospital beds, and hotel reservations. Relationships between entities are established, such as 'patients occupy beds' and 'doctors treat patients'. These processes can be very subjective and depend on a good understanding of the problem situation in order to decide which entities and relationships are important. The preceding stage in the methodology — analysis of the human activity systems — has already given this necessary understanding and has laid a good foundation. The entity model then becomes an input into stages 4 and 5 of the Multiview methodology.

3 Analysis and Design of the Socio-Technical System

This stage leans heavily on the work of Mumford, seen in the ETHICS methodology (section 6.6). It takes the view therefore that human considerations, such as job satisfaction, morale and so on, are just as important as technical considerations. The task for the problem solver is to produce a 'good fit' design, taking into account people and their needs and the working environment on the one hand, and the organizational structure, computers and the necessary work tasks on the other. Some readers may be surprised at this explicit statement of the analyst's values, and think that the analyst should be 'objective'. However, the authors argue that objectivity, which they define as non-involvement, is just as value laden a stance as

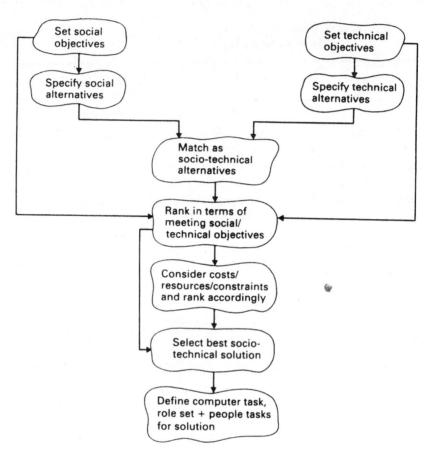

Fig. 6.30. Outline of socio-technical analysis and design to match and detect solution and role of set of objectives.

insistence on a democratic process.

An outline of this stage is shown in figure 6.30. The central concern is the identification of alternatives: alternative social arrangements to meet social objectives and alternative technical alternatives to meet technical objectives. All the social and technical alternatives are brought together to produce socio-technical alternatives. These are ranked, firstly in terms of their fulfilment of the above objectives, and secondly in terms of costs, resources and constraints — again both social and technical — associated with each objective. In this way, the best socio-technical solution can be selected and

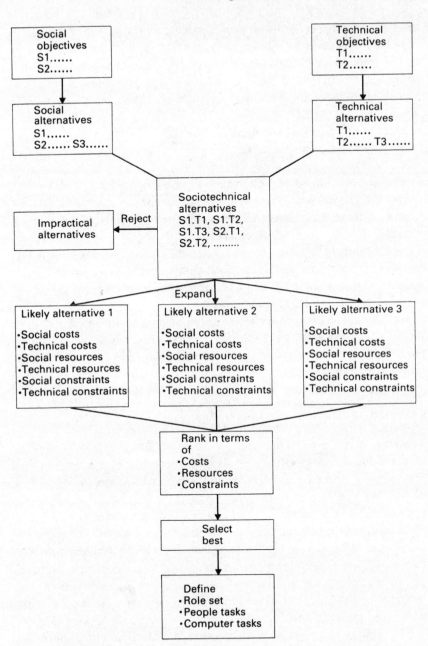

Fig. 6.31. Principles of socio - technical design.

the corresponding computer tasks, role sets and people tasks can be defined. A flowchart of the process is shown as figure 6.31.

The emphasis of this stage is therefore NOT on development, but on a statement of alternative systems and choice between the alternatives, according to important social and technical considerations. They include things like:

- Should every user have a terminal on their desk?
- Will there be retraining necessary?
- Will there be any redundancies caused?
- How urgent is the various information supplied?
- Will there be any new job responsibilities defined?
- Should there be a large central computer, or minicomputers, or a mainframe with a number of terminals?

There will then be a general recommendation of principle, that is no actual computers or packages will be specified at this stage. It is also clear that, in order to be successful in defining alternatives, the groundwork in the earlier stages of the methodology is necessary.

An important technique applicable to this stage is future analysis. This is described in Land (1982) and aids the analyst and user to predict the future environment so that they are better able to define and rank their socio-technical alternatives.

4 Design of Human—Computer Interface

This stage is concerned with the technical design of the human—computer interface and makes specific decisions on the technical system alternatives. For example, a decision will have been taken on whether to adopt batch or on-line facilities. Decisions must then be taken on the specific conversations and interactions that particular types of user will have with the computer and on the necessary inputs and outputs and related issues. Much will depend on the people using the system as to whether it will be command-driven, form-driven, menu-driven, near natural language, or an icon/mouse interface, or whether there will be some 'artificial intelligence' techniques used. For instance, by looking at previous records of a customer, the system could answer the question: 'Should Jones be given an extension in his credit limit?'

The authors suggest that very often the design will reflect the 'microcomputer revolution'. A package solution or prototype solution is suggested as more likely than a 'tailor made' solution, which is more traditional of mainframe systems. Wood-Harper *et al.* (1985) discusses problems of evaluating packages as there is no standard way of describing such software. But the Multiview analysis does provide a number of models of how the system should work in practice. The application described in Wood-Harper *et al.* used a prototype which 'became' the actual system when the users were happy with it. Application generators are available as prototyping tools. Prototyping is recommended by the authors who argue that it enables users and operators to see how the system will look and 'feel' and therefore helps the analysts to ensure that they are on the right lines before too much time and effort has been committed.

Once human—computer interfaces have been defined, the technical requirements to fulfil these can be designed. These technical requirements become the output of this stage and the input to stage 5, the design of technical sub-systems. The human—computer interface definition becomes a major output of the methodology.

5 Design of the Technical Sub-system

The inputs to this stage are the entity model from stage 2 and the technical requirements from stage 4. The former describes the entities and relationships for the whole area of concern, whereas the latter describes the specific technical requirements of the system to be designed.

After working through the first stages of Multiview, the technical requirements have been formulated with both social and technical objectives in mind and also after consideration of an appropriate human—computer interface. Thus, necessary human considerations are already both integrated and interfaced with the forthcoming technical sub-systems.

At this stage, therefore, a purely technical view can be taken so that the analyst can concentrate on efficient design and the production of a full systems specification. Many technical criteria are analysed and technical decisions made which will take into account all the previous analysis and design stages. The final major outputs of the methodology could include:

• The application sub-system which is concerned with performing the functions which have been computerized from the function chart.
• The information retrieval sub-system which is for responding to enquiries about data stored in the system.
• The database in which all the data are organized.
• The database maintenance sub-system which permits updates to the data

and provides the information necessary to check for data errors.
• The control sub-system which checks for user, program, operator and machine errors and alerts the system to their presence.
• The recovery sub-system which allows the system to be repaired after an error has been detected.
• The monitoring sub-system which keeps track of all system activities for management purposes.

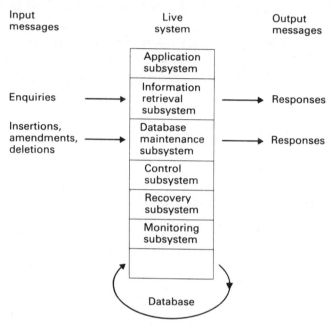

Fig. 6.32. Outline of the requirements for the technical specification.

Figure 6.32 shows a schematic of these requirements for the technical specification. These sub-systems cover all the things that have to be done by the computer system and the people operating it. These parts, or sub-systems, may be implemented in different ways and in different combinations. For example, the information retrieval sub-system may be just another aspect of the database management system and this may also include many of the necessary functions for control and recovery. The Multiview authors have separated them out because it is necessary to be sure that each one of them is catered for in the system.

Following full testing of all aspects of the system, there is a recognition that there will still be changes required and this should be regarded as 'the norm'. Information systems will develop and this requires an on-going relationship between users, analysts, and system creators or owners. The authors recommend that the Multiview framework be applied for these changes (at least with a 'token run') so as to ensure that the system is still meeting its real objectives.

The five stages incorporate five different views which are appropriate to the progressive development of an analysis and design project so as to form an application system which is complete in technical and human terms. To be complete in human as well as in technical terms, it must provide help in answering the following questions:

1 How is the computer system supposed to further the aims of the organization installing it?
2 How can it be fitted into the working lives of the people in the organization that are going to use it?
3 How can the individuals concerned best relate to the machine in terms of operating it and using the output from it?
4 What information system processing function is the system to perform?
5 What is the technical specification of a system that will come close enough to doing the things that have been written down in the answers to the other four questions?

Too often, the authors argue, methodologies and role players have addressed themselves to only a limited subset of these questions: for example, computer scientists to question 5, systems analysts to question 4, users to question 3, trade unions to question 2, and top management to question 1. Multiview attempts to address all these questions and to involve all the role players or stakeholders in answering all these questions. The emphasis in information systems, it is argued, must move away from 'technical systems which have behavioural and social problems' to 'social systems which rely to an increasing extent on information technology'.

Chapter 7
Methodologies: Issues and Frameworks

7.1 THE METHODOLOGY JUNGLE

The methodology area can justly be described as a jungle. Firstly there appears to exist many hundreds of system development methodologies. Longworth (1985) in a recent study identified over 300. If these are all different, then it is no wonder that there is so much confusion. Bubenko (1986) goes further and says that:

> 'It is a reasonable estimate that hundreds of more or less similar methodologies have been published. In practice, probably tens of thousands of more or less different approaches are being used. Most organizations have developed their own methodology and prescribed it in the organization's (data processing) handbook.'

It may of course be that, as Veryard (1985) suggests, the differences are often trivial and are made solely to differentiate methodologies in the market place.

In this chapter we hope to provide some help to understand this jungle. This will involve looking at many aspects of methodologies and providing a framework in order to evaluate them.

7.2 WHAT IS A METHODOLOGY?

Chapter 1 provided a working definition of the term methodology and although this has been adequate for our purposes, the question of what is a methodology now will be looked at in more depth. The term is not well defined either in the literature or by practitioners. There is very little agreement as to what it means other than at a very general level. The term is usually used very loosely and yet it is used very extensively.

This loose use of the term methodology does not of course mean that there are no definitions, simply that there are no universally agreed definitions. At the general level it is regarded as a recommended series of steps and procedures to be followed in the course of developing an information system. In a brief *ad hoc* survey this proves to be about the maximum that people will agree to, and of course such a definition raises many more questions than it answers.

For example:
- What is the difference between a methodology and a method?
- Does a methodology include a specification of the techniques and tools which are to be used?
- Does a collection of techniques and tools constitute a methodology?
- Should the use of a methodology produce the same results each time?

The questions that arise are fundamental as well as numerous. Unfortunately the problem will not be solved here, the most that can be achieved is that the issues will be aired. The information system community is in the process of debating the meaning of the term methodology in an information systems context, and it may one day have a universal definition. However, it may be more realistic to assume that this will never be achieved.

An information system methodology has been defined as a recommended collection of philosophies, phases, procedures, rules, techniques, tools, documentation, management and training for developers of information systems (Maddison 1983). According to this definition, a methodology has a number of components which specify:
- How a project is to be broken down into stages.
- What tasks are to be carried out at each stage.
- What outputs are to be produced.
- When they are to be carried out.
- What constraints are to be applied.
- What support tools may be utilized.

In addition, the methodology is supposed to specify how the project is to be managed and controlled, and support the training needs of the users of the methodology. This is all encompassed in a view or philosophy concerning the important and critical aspects of information system development.

Utilizing this interpretation of the term 'information systems methodology' makes it very much more than just a series of techniques and tools. This extended view of a methodology implies that a methodology needs to be closely and carefully described in order for it to be usable. This fits in with the practising world of commercial data processing, where a methodology is usually a product which is 'packaged' and might include:
- Manuals.
- Education and training.
- Consultancy support.
- Automated tools.
- Pro forma documents.
- Model building templates.

Colleagues from other disciplines argue that the term methodology is not apt in this context. They argue that the shorter more precise word 'method' is perfectly adequate to cover everything we mean by a methodology. However, this seems to substitute one ill-defined word for another. Checkland (1981) distinguishes between the two terms and says that a methodology:

> ' ...is a set of principles of method, which in any particular situation has to be reduced to a method uniquely suited to that particular situation' .

This is a somewhat different interpretation to that discussed earlier and in this text we use the term as defined in Maddison, above.

7.3 THE NEED FOR A METHODOLOGY

Chapter 2 took a historical view of the demand for methodologies, but it is worth stating more specifically what it is that people are looking for in a methodology. Obviously this varies substantially between individuals, but we can identify three main categories of perceived need: a better end product, a better development process, and a standardized process. We have not discussed the first aspect: it is important to discuss what we mean by a *better* end product that might be achieved by using the methodologies, techniques and tools described in this text.

1 A Better End Product

People may want a methodology to improve the end product of the development process, that is, they want better information systems. But this may mean different things to different people. It is difficult to assess the quality of information systems produced using any methodology. There does not seem to be any agreement within the information systems community on this issue (see, for example, IFIP-NGI 1986). In general, the value of an information system is tied up with the rather nebulous concept of 'usefulness'. The following represents an attempt to analyse the components of 'usefulness' of an information system:

Acceptability: whether the people who are using the system find the system satisfactory and whether it fulfils their information needs.

Availability: whether it is accessible, when and where required.

Cohesiveness: whether there is interaction between each component (sub-system) so that there is an overall integrated information system.

Compatibility: whether the sub-system fits with the rest of the integrated global system.

Documentation: whether there is good documentation to help communications between users, developers, managers and operators.

Easy to learn: whether the learning curve for new users is short.

Economy: whether the system is cost-effective and within resources and constraints.

Efficiency : whether the system utilizes resources to their best advantage.

Fast development rate: whether the time needed to develop the project was quick, relative to its size and complexity.

Feasibility: whether the system satisfies criteria relating to feasibility.

Flexibility: whether the system is easy to modify and whether it is easy to add or delete components.

Functionality: whether the system caters for the requirements.

Implementability: whether the change-over from the old to the new system is feasible.

Low coupling: whether the interaction between sub-systems is such that they can be modified without affecting the rest of the system.

Maintainability: whether it needs a lot of effort to keep the system running satisfactorily.

Portability: whether the information system can run on other equipment or in other departments.

Reliability: whether the error rate is minimized and outputs are consistent and correct.

Robustness: whether the system is fail-safe and fault tolerant.

Security: whether the information system is robust against misuse or correct use.

Simplicity: whether ambiguities and complexities are minimized.

Testability: whether the system can be tested thoroughly to minimize operational failure and user dissatisfaction.

Timeliness: whether the information system operates successfully under normal, peak and every condition, giving information when and where required.

Usability: ease of use, functionality, and so on, appropriate to the type (regular, casual), experience level, and so on, of user. (See Eason 1984.)

Visibility: whether it is possible for users to trace why certain actions occurred.

Of course optima in these criteria are not attainable, indeed some of these may work against each other. Ideally an information systems methodology can be 'tuned' so that emphasis can be given to those criteria which are particularly important in the problem situation

2 A Better Development Process

Under this heading comes the benefits that accrue from tightly controlling the development process and identifying the outputs (or deliverables) at each stage. This results in improved management and project control. It is usually argued that productivity is enhanced, that is, we can either build systems faster, given specific resources, or use fewer resources to achieve the same results. It is sometimes also argued that the use of a methodology reduces the level of skills required of the analysts, which improves the development process by reducing its cost.

3 A Standardized Process

The needs associated with this category relate to the benefits of having a common approach throughout an organization. This means that more integrated systems can result, that staff can easily change from project to project without retraining being necessary, and that a base of common experience and knowledge can be achieved. In short, all the normal benefits of standardization, including the specific benefit of easier maintenance of systems, can be achieved.

All the reasons contained in the above categories have been specified by the authors or vendors of methodologies as being benefits of adopting their particular methodologies. In contrast, a survey (Gray 1985) of benefits that purchasers look for in a methodology shows that the most important factors for them are:

1 Improved systems specifications, and

2 easier maintenance and enhancement.

Methodologies rarely actually address improvement of the maintenance task, although vendors often claim it as an indirect benefit, because by using the methodology the information system developed will require less maintenance.

7.4 THE LIMITATIONS OF A METHODOLOGY

The concerns of the systems developers who are thinking of adopting or purchasing a methodology are:

• What do they get, and

• are they guaranteed successful information systems as a result?

What do they get? To address the first question, they get what the vendor or methodology author gives them, and this differs greatly:

• A methodology can range from being a fully fledged product to being a vague philosophy outlined in a short pamphlet.

• A methodology can cover widely differing areas of the development process, from organizational problem-solving to the detail of implementing a small computer system.

• A methodology can cover conceptual issues or physical design procedures or the whole range of intermediate stages.

• A methodology can range from being designed to be applicable to specific types of problems in certain types of environments to a general purpose methodology.

• A methodology may be usable only by highly trained specialists or be usable by anybody.

• A methodology may require an army of people to perform all the specified tasks or it may not even have any specified tasks.

The list of variations are numerous.

Hopefully, it is clear that the adoptors of a methodology should be aware of what their needs are and choose their methodology accordingly. This does not always seem to have been the case. One organization that adopted a particular methodology found that they had to write detailed manuals themselves to specify what was required of their development staff. What they purchased was just a management overview without any detail.

Some methodologies are purchased as a product, others are available by purchasing a licence, others are obtained through a contract for consultancy work, and some by a combination of the above. The most expensive methodologies might cost up to half a million pounds sterling at 1988 prices.

Reproducibility: The answer to the second question posed above, 'are they guaranteed successful information systems as a result of using the methodology?', is clearly 'no'! However, this does raise the question of what a methodology is supposed to produce. If two teams of developers are using the same methodology on the same problem can the same results be expected, and if not why not?

Clearly the developers may interpret the demands of the methodology differently and thus end up with different results. The methodology may give a lot of leeway to the developers in terms of how they perform the specified tasks and so the results will be different. The developers may have varying skill levels, which will also produce differing results. However, it is sometimes argued that, given these variations, multiple uses of the same methodology in the same circumstances should yield roughly the same results. The tighter, more specific, the methodology, the more reproducible the results, particularly where the methodology specifies the exact techniques and tools to be employed under each circumstance.

This is a highly contentious area, but the implication is that if the results are reproducible, then we must be sure that the methodology specifies 'a best' way of producing information systems. We cannot say *the* best way, because there may be trade-offs between quality, quantity, the skill levels, reliability, generality, and so on. But we want a methodology that will produce good results. This implies that a methodology is not just a helpful set of guidelines that enables the developer to organize the development process more effectively and efficiently, but that it embodies a good way of developing systems. If it is reproducible then it leads to the development of particular solutions, and thus if we adopt a methodology, then this methodology must be, to our minds, a good way of doing things. If it is not, it will lead to problems, because the nature of the methodology will exclude other ways of doing things. For example, the adoption of a Data Flow Diagram-based methodology will, if it is rigidly followed, exclude the kind of analysis that Checkland's methodology recommends. There will, for example, be no analysis of conflict between various actors in the existing system.

White (1982) goes further and states that:

' ...the acid test of a methodology is its repeatability. Given the same access to people and facts about the organization, will different designers come up with essentially the same solution? If the answer is no, then the business is placing itself in the hands of its systems builders and gambling on their flair and judgement to come up with a satisfactory approach. This is a risk that many organizations are unwilling to take as they progress towards their goal of becoming "computerized companies". Instead, they are looking for an approach which can be treated as an engineering discipline and which will provide them with the means of verifying the completeness and correctness of any analysis and of the assumptions made at each stage in the development process. It is this type of approach that will give us a "repeatable" methodology'.

The question of reproducibility is not one that can be easily tested practically, it is impossible to create exactly the same environment in an organization for two sets of developers to practice on, and if we pitch them into the same environment then the fact that there are two sets of developers will influence the results. For example, the fact that one set will have talked to a user will influence the results when the second set of developers talks to that same user.

This lack of repeatability is often said to show that information systems is not an engineering discipline. However, engineering is also a creative profession. Will two engineers design the same bridge or two electronic engineers design the same circuit?

But the implication still holds that the methodology should embody a best way of developing systems. This is not always appreciated when methodologies are being selected. It may result in the development of inappropriate systems. The question of whether the methodology embodies a best way of developing systems is very rarely asked, the more usual questions are:

- Whether it fits in with the organization's way of working.
- Whether it specifies what deliverables (or outputs) are required at the end of each stage.
- Whether it enables better control and improved productivity.

As has been observed earlier, there exist probably hundreds of different methodologies. This implies that there are hundreds of 'best' ways of developing information systems. Many of them are probably quite similar when closely examined, but many of them do differ substantially on fundamentals.

7.5 BACKGROUND TO METHODOLOGIES

In understanding a methodology an important aspect is its background. Broadly speaking methodologies can be divided into two categories:
• Those developed from practice, and
• those developed from theory.
The methodologies in the first category have been evolved from usage and generally have been developed into commercial methodology products. The second category of methodologies have more usually been developed in universities or research institutions, and they are not usually produced as a commercial product, but are written up in books and journals.

Commercial Methodologies

The methodologies evolving from practice are probably the most widely known and some have quite a large number of users. The academic methodologies, on the other hand, are less well known and have relatively few users, although their influence may be greater than their actual user base. Some of the academic methodologies have been developed by individuals who have promoted their methodologies by means of consultancy to various organizations. Some of these have evolved into full commercial methodologies.

Early Development: The methodologies that have developed from practice each have a different history, but it was often the case that system developers found that some techniques were more useful than others, and they concentrated on improving their skills in using and improving these techniques. A common practice was for the people concerned to leave the organizations that they were working for, and either set up their own information system consultancy company or join an existing consultancy company where the opportunity to develop the techniques and methods was greater using their clients as 'guinea pigs'. At this stage it was not the methodology itself, but the consultancy work developing information systems that was sold to clients.

Most of the early methodologies relied on one technique, or on a series of closely related techniques, as the foundation stone of the methodology. Commonly, these techniques were either entity modelling or data flow diagramming but usually not both. It was only later that they began to include other techniques and to widen the scope of their methodologies. From time to time the development of the methodologies would go through periods of introspection where various aspects would be added and others dropped, and then the revised methodology would be put to the test again by usage.

Often consultants using the same methodology in a consultancy company would discover that they were doing things quite differently to their colleagues. They had their own styles and favourite aspects, and yet they were supposed to be applying the same methodology. It was at this stage that some of these consultancy companies realized that it was no longer good enough to rely on some *ad hoc* processes called a methodology and sell their own skills in its use to develop information systems for client organizations. The methodology itself had to be the product. In one organization this realization came when it was discovered that no one person had responsibility for the methodology and its content. People in the organization could just add things to it as they thought fit. The main reason for this was the nature of the consultancy business itself. Nobody was responsible for the methodology because it was not something that was sold, it was simply a feature of consultancy. The consultants made a living by charging for their time on client projects, there was no mechanism for spending a lot of time developing a product, it was not cost effective in the short term view that most consultancies took.

Obviously this had to change. Most consultancy organizations eventually realized that the methodology was one of their most saleable assets, and that the methodology had to be:
- Produced as a product.
- Made consistent.
- Marketed.
- Maintained.
- Developed continually.

The consultancy houses finally invested in their methodologies. As a result of this investment, a number of things have happened.

Filling the gaps: It was realized that most of the methodologies had quite a few gaps in them, or, if not complete gaps, they had areas that were treated much less thoroughly than others. This was usually as a direct result of their background of development — they had concentrated on a single development technique in their early days. These gaps needed to be filled because the clients of the methodologies assumed that the methodologies covered the whole spectrum of things necessary to successfully develop an information system to completion. It was often quite a surprise for users to find that this was not the case. For example, a methodology based on entity modelling techniques might have been very powerful for data analysis and database design, but not so comprehensive when it came to specifying the functions and designing the applications, and might not help at all in, for example, its support for dialogue design. Almost all information system methodologies went through a process — to a greater or lesser extent — of filling the gaps and making the methodology more comprehensive.

Expanding the scope: Another process was that of expanding the scope of methodologies. This occurred because the methodologies did not address the whole of the life-cycle of systems development. Frequently the implementation phase was not included, some did not include design, others did not address analysis. So decisions were taken to expand the scope of the methodologies.

One of the most important aspects of this expansion of scope was to take the methodologies into the area of strategy and planning. The traditional life-cycle of systems development usually started with a stage termed project selection, or problem identification, or some such name. This stage was characterized by the identification of some problem that needed solving, or some area of the business that needed computerizing, or some application that needed building. The development process was viewed as a one-off, *ad hoc*, solution to the identified problem, and whilst this may have been a reasonable approach in the early days of systems development, it was now no longer valid. Organizations had had many such 'identified problems' solved in this one-off manner and found that although the individual problem may have been solved to some extent, the existence of a variety of different one-off systems in a business did not lead to harmony.

Further, it was realized that these individual problems were not so 'individual', and that almost all areas of the business needed to interact and integrate in some way. In particular, the requirements of tactical and strategic levels of management needed integration across traditional functional boundaries.

A series of systems developed as individual solutions, at different times and without reference to each other, is unlikely to be the ideal starting point for such integration. Yet, for many organizations, this is just what existed, and methodologies needed to address themselves to this problem if they were to provide more than improved implementations of one-off systems.

In order to achieve this, some methodologies turned themselves to the topic of information systems strategy. This involved the recognition that:

1 Information systems are a fundamental part of the organization, and that they contribute significantly to the success of the enterprise.

2 Information should be viewed by the organization as a resource in the same way as the more traditional resources of land, labour and capital.

Such a resource has to be controlled, co-ordinated and planned. These resources are not free. Further, the controlling and planning must take place at the highest level in an organization in order for these resources to contribute effectively to fulfilling its needs. Thus, the starting point for effective information system development methodologies can be seen to be a strategic plan for the organization and a specification of the way in which information systems can contribute to the achievement of that plan.

In practice it was found that although most organizations, but by no means all, had some kind of strategic or corporate plan, this plan did not usually address the role of the information systems. For this reason some methodologies incorporated the required strategy plan into their scope. This not only helped to ensure that the information systems met the high level needs of the organization, but effectively pushed the information system function up the hierarchy of importance in the organization.

A competitive advantage: Another reason for addressing information systems strategy at a high level in an organization is that not only can the information system make the running of the business easier and more efficient, but that it is perceived that information systems and information technology can change the nature of the business. It can change the product or the service that the organization offers quite fundamentally. Further, it is often argued that it can give the organization a competitive advantage in the market place.

The banking industry provides examples of this. The National Girobank in the United Kingdom was able to establish itself in competition with established banks by using technology to centralize its operation and eliminate the need for the local branch manager. The Bank of Scotland has a customer base in the South-East of England without a traditional branch network there. The bank has achieved this by offering home banking, using modern technology. It is only a few years ago that the established way of competing was through an extensive branch network. Thus, instead of reacting to the moves of competitors, the decision-makers can make the first move using the information provided by the system and gain 'competitive advantage' (Porter and Millar 1985 develop these ideas).

Theoretical Methodologies

The development of theoretical or academic methodologies has been somewhat different. As already indicated, they started life as research projects in universities or research institutions. Here the researchers took a more theoretical viewpoint, they identified a problem area, which was the specification and development of information systems. This was certainly a relevant problem area in that, in practice, it was proving very difficult to develop effective systems.

What intrigued the academic researcher in particular was that there did not seem to be any standard techniques or approaches based upon sound theoretical concepts. This was clearly a challenge. The challenge was taken up by a number of people from a number of different background disciplines. It was often felt that methods were already available and successfully being used in other disciplines and that these only needed a small amount of adaptation to be useful in the area of information system development. Mathematicians, psychologists, linguists, social scientists, engineers, sociologists, and many people from cross disciplines turned their attention to the challenge.

This did not of course happen all at the same time nor in numerical terms did many people actually get involved, but some of the approaches proved interesting and useful. Some were published in some form or another, some were simply theoretical statements, yet others were applied.

In some other areas, the development of techniques and methods by academics was very influential on practice, particularly in the areas of data base design and software engineering. But in the case of information systems development methodologies, at least initially, they were almost completely ignored. In the longer term there is evidence that some of the ideas are beginning to permeate the practice.

The reasons for this slow take-up are debatable. Some would argue that the research-based methods were not good enough or not practical or that they were no better than the new methods that the practitioners were already developing themselves. Some of the academic methods involved relatively revolutionary changes to current practice and thought, and could not be introduced on an evolutionary basis. Others argued that they were interesting but as yet unproven. This was in general undoubtedly true as the academics could not easily try out their methods in the same practical environments as the practitioners and consultancies. As Bubenko (1986) argues, when referring to academic methodologies:

'A very small fraction of these...(have) been applied to practical cases of a realistic size and complexity. The acceptance of "academic" methods in practice is low and, in general, the rate of transfer of research results and "know-how" from scientific research to industry is embarrassingly slow.'

Some sought to overcome this problem by persuading organizations to try their methods under the control and guiding hand of the academics themselves. This is the practice known as action research, and as this process evolved and the methods became more practical, the academics often charged for their services and in effect were operating as consultancies. Some set up small consultancy offshoots to further develop and propound their methods. Although this helped publicize the methods, in general the consultancies remained very small.

A variety of themes addressed by academic researchers were discussed in section 3.9.

Blended Methodologies

As outlined earlier, the commercial methodology vendors sought to fill the gaps in their product, but at roughly the same time a number of other organizations entered the fray with new methodology products. These were only new in the sense that they sought to blend together what was seen as strong features of a variety of existing methodologies, in particular the combination of entity modelling techniques with data flow diagraming techniques. A typical example is SSADM. Some of these blended methodologies have proved successful in the market place.

Other methodologies blended in a somewhat different way, in that they sought to blend not just the data and process techniques of entity modelling and data flow diagramming, but to blend the benefits of problem solving/system type methodologies with more traditional information system based methodologies. An example of this is provided by Multiview.

7.6 ISSUES IN METHODOLOGY COMPARISONS

There are two main reasons for comparing methodologies:
1 *An academic reason*. To better understand the nature of methodologies (their features, objectives, philosophies, and so on) in order to perform classifications and to improve future methodologies.

2   *A practical reason.* To choose a methodology, part of one, or a number of
     methodologies for a particular application, a group of applications, or as a
     standard for an organization.

The two reasons are not totally separate, and it is hoped that the academic
studies will help in the practical choices and that the practical reasons will
influence the criteria applied in the academic studies. This synergy is a basis
for some present-day action research. We will look at a number of issues
relating to methodology comparisons in this section.

An important attempt to examine methodologies in general has been the
series of conferences known as CRIS (Comparative Review of Information
Systems Design Methodologies). These conferences have been organized by
the IFIP (International Federation of Information Processing) WG (Working
Group) 8.1. The first conference in 1982 invited authors of methodologies to
describe their methodologies and apply them to a case study. The chosen case
study was the organization of an IFIP conference (see Olle *et al.* 1982).

The second conference in 1983 consisted of a series of papers which
analysed and compared the features of various methodologies (see Olle *et al.*
1983) and the third conference in 1986 addressed the issue of improving the
practice of using methodologies (see Olle *et al.* 1986).

There is a 1988 conference, CRIS88, which had not yet taken place at the
time of writing. This looks at ways in which computers can be used during
the construction of information systems, and the proceedings are likely to be
a useful addition to the discussions found here in Chapter 5.

Although the CRIS conferences have undoubtedly contributed significantly
to the field, they have also been criticized for a number of reasons. The first
two criticisms below relate to the 1982 Conference, and the third and fourth
points address the 1983 Conference:

- Firstly, many of the methodologies addressed have been purely theoretical
  ones without any, or very few, practical users.
- Secondly, the original case study consisted of a specification of the user
  requirements and therefore no analysis was required. This obviously
  restricted many of the methodologies.
- Thirdly, the feature analysis comparison sometimes created more problems
  than it solved. Some of the methodology authors have argued that those
  performing the feature analysis had not understood, nor correctly
  interpreted, their methodology (a problem that may be evident in Chapter 6
  of *this* text).
- Fourthly, the feature analysis took no account of the practicalities of
  applying the methodology in a commercial environment, nor did it

evaluate the likely success of particular features. They were simply listed as existing.

Any comparison of methodologies is open to similar criticisms and it must be recognized that there are inherent problems in attempting the task. Checkland (1987) argues that it is impossible to *prove* if success or failure of an information system can be attributed to the methodology used. He asks developers of systems perceived to be successful to prove that another methodology would not have been better, and of course they cannot. He asks the developers of systems, where there have been problems, to *prove* it was not their incompetence that led to the problems rather than the methodology, and once again they cannot. This dilemma occurs because of the problems, discussed in section 7.4, of not being able to repeat the experiment or use a control, as in a scientific experiment.

Another problem inherent in the comparison of methodologies is the fact that methodologies are not stable, but are in fact moving targets. There are a number of reasons for this, but the two main influences are: firstly, that the discipline of information systems is relatively new and has not established a consensus of views, and secondly, that the continuing catalogue of technical developments cause methodologies to change.

These result in particular problems when comparing methodologies. Firstly, the documentation of methodologies is frequently changing. Therefore there exists a version problem and it is often difficult to know which version of a methodology is being applied in a particular situation or which is the latest version. Secondly, for commercial reasons the documentation is not always published or readily available to people or organizations not purchasing the methodology. Thirdly, the practice of a methodology is sometimes significantly different to that prescribed by the documentation. Fourthly, individual consultants or developers using the methodology often interpret it in quite different ways from their colleagues.

A further, well recognized problem, concerns terminology. Any new discipline is likely to be full of different terms for the same phenomena and similar terms that actually refer to different phenomena. Information systems appears to exhibit rather more than its fair share of this. It is unhealthy, as it not only leads to confusion and poor communication, but to a restriction of development, due to the inability to enhance and expand upon earlier research work. Progress in most successful disciplines is usually a process of evolutionary development, for, 'out of the blue', quantum leaps are rare. Any restriction in evolution is therefore very serious. Bubenko (1986), for example, states that terminological confusion makes: '...it extremely difficult to reject 'new methods' which, essentially, do not contribute anything new and which do not advance the state of the art'.

The most well known approaches to methodology comparisons attempt to identify a set of idealized 'features', followed by a check to see whether different methodologies possess these features or not. The implication being that those that do possess them or at least score highly on a features rating are 'good' and that those that do not, are 'less good'. The set of features must be chosen by somebody and are thus subjective, although often purported to be objective. The most obvious indication of this is the kind of comparison conducted by particular methodology vendors in which their methodology scores highly and the competition poorly. The comparison has been designed to give this result. We are more familiar with this kind of comparison in relation to automobiles or soap powders.

The problems of this kind of comparison led Maddison (1983) and his colleagues to abandon an attempt to determine how well a methodology met a particular criterion through the notion of scoring. Although Maddison still identifies a relevant set of features, and then considers which methodologies support these features and in what ways, they abandoned the idea of scoring and left the readers to set their own scores and weightings if they wished. In this way, the feature analysis could be matched with the assessor's own particular situation. This was useful but still subjective, in that the original choice of features determines what is compared. Maddison defined a list of over 100 features. These have been condensed under the following major headings:

(a) Does the methodology cover all aspects of the systems analysis and design process from planning to implementation?
(b) Are the steps well defined?
(c) Is the methodology data or process orientated?
(d) How are the results at each stage expressed?
(e) To what types of applications is it suited?
(f) Does it aim to be scientific or behavioural?
(g) Is a computer solution assumed? What are the other assumptions made?
(h) Who plays the major role — the analyst or the user?
(i) What built-in controls are there to evaluate the success of each stage?
(j) Is the methodology simply an attempt to link a number of techniques and tools or does it have its own philosophical base?

One of the contributions of the Maddison comparison was the identification of the importance of the philosophy to a good understanding of the methodology. The features of a methodology were very much dependent upon that philosophy. Without this understanding, the methodology was difficult to explain. However, many methodologies did not actually state their underlying philosophy, it had to be searched for, and this made analysis difficult.

Some commentators took this argument somewhat further, and identified a much wider ranges of issues which were relevant for comparing methodologies. In general, these studies suggest the criteria but do not actually perform the comparison task! This is nevertheless useful. Bjorn-Anderson (1984), for example, identifies a checklist of areas of concern that he believes methodologies should deal with:

1 What research paradigms/perspective forms the foundation for the methodology?
2 What are the underlying value systems?
3 What is the context where a methodology is useful?
4 To what extent is modification enhanced or even possible?
5 Does communication and documentation operate in the users dialect, either expert or not?
6 Does transferability exist?
7 Is the societal environment dealt with, including the possible conflicts?
8 Is user participation 'really' encouraged or supported?

Catchpole (1987) makes a useful contribution by summarizing the views of a number of authors concerning the important areas of concern when comparing methodologies, and suggests the following set of requirements for the design of a methodology:

Rules. Tozer (1985) identifies the need for formal guidelines in a methodology to cover phases, tasks and deliverables; techniques and tools; documentation and development aids; and guidelines for estimating time and resource requirements. These rules ought not to be too restrictive, but provide guidelines.

Total coverage. A methodology should cover the entire systems development process from strategy to cut-over and maintenance.

Understanding the information resource. Macdonald (1983) suggests that a methodology should ensure effective utilization of the corporate information resource, in terms of the data available and the processes which need to make use of the data.

Documentation standards. All output, using the methodology, should be easily understandable by both users and analysts.

Separation of logical and physical designs. There should be a separation of logical descriptions and requirements (for example, what an application does, what the interactions are, and what data is involved), that is *what the system is*, from any specific technical or physical design solutions (for example, hardware, software, communication channels and documents), that is *how it is done.*

Validity of design. A means is required to check for inconsistencies, inaccuracies and incompleteness.

Early change. Any changes to a system design should be identifiable as early as possible in the development process because costs associated with changes tend to increase as the development work progresses.

Inter-stage communication. The full extent of work carried out must be communicable to other stages. Yao (1985) argues that each stage has to be consistent, complete and usable.

Effective problem analysis. Problem analysis should be supported by a suitable means for expressing and documenting the problems and objectives of an organization.

Planning and control. Careful monitoring of an information system is required and a methodology must support development in a planned and controlled manner to contain costs and time scales. It should be possible to incorporate a project control technique, though this need not necessarily be part of the methodology.

Performance evaluation. The methodology should support a means of evaluating the performance of operational applications developed using it (Wasserman and Freeman 1976).

Increased productivity. This is a frequent justification for a methodology, sold to management in financial terms (Bantleman 1984).

Improved quality. A methodology should improve the quality of analysis, design and programming products and hence the overall quality of the information system.

Visibility of the product. A methodology should maintain the visibility of the emerging and evolving information system as it develops (Wasserman and Freeman 1976).

Teachable. Users as well as technologists should appreciate the various techniques in a methodology in order that they can verify analysis and design work.

Information systems boundary. A methodology should allow definition of the areas of the organization to be covered by the information system. These may not all be areas for computerization.

Designing for change. The logical and physical designs should be easily modified.

Effective communication. The methodology should provide an effective communication medium between analysts and users.

Simplicity. The methodology should be simple to use, for 'if a methodology is misunderstood, then it will be misapplied' (Tozer 1985).

Ongoing relevance. A methodology should be capable of being extended so that new techniques and tools can be incorporated as they are developed, but still maintain overall consistency and framework.

Automated development aids. Where possible, automated aids such as data dictionaries and modelling tools should be used since they can enhance productivity.

Consideration of user goals and objectives. The goals and objectives of potential users of a system should be noted so that when an information system is designed, it can be made to satisfy these users and assist them in meeting goals and objectives (Land 1976).

Participation. The methodology should encourage participation by such attributes as simplicity, the ability to facilitate good communications, and so on.

Relevance to practitioner. The methodology has to be appropriate to the practitioner using it, in terms of level of technical knowledge, experience with computers, and social and communications skills. Episkopou and Wood-Harper (1986) describe a framework for selecting an appropriate information systems design strategy based on assessing the characteristics of the problem solver and problem owner.

Relevance to application. The methodology must be appropriate to the type of system being developed, which might be scientific, commercial, real-time or distributed (Macdonald 1983, Tozer 1985).

In discussions of Catchpole's thesis, Land suggested that to this list should be added:

A systematic way of looking into the future. This should enable possible future changes in requirements to be predicted and the system to be designed in such a way that the future change can be easily accommodated. This is known as *futures analysis* and is described in Land (1982).

The integration of the technical and the non-technical systems. The methodology should not only address the technical and non-technical aspects of a system but should make provision for their integration.

Scan for opportunity. The methodology should enable the system to be thought about in new ways. Rather than being viewed as simply a solution to existing problems it should be seen as an opportunity to address new areas and challenges. The scan should identify factors that inhibit this and find ways of overcoming them.

We would also add to Catchpole's list:

Separation of analysis and design: This separation ensures that the analysis of the existing system and the user requirements are not influenced by design considerations.

Bubenko (1986) identifies three alternatives to feature analyses . These are as follows:
1 Theoretical investigations of concepts, languages, and so on.
2 Experiences of actually applying the methodology to realistic cases.
3 Cognitive—psychological investigations.
The first approach is argued to reduce the problems of subjectivity inherent in feature analyses by carrying out studies on well-defined, narrow, subject areas within specific terms of reference. Bubenko quotes Kung (1983) as an example of such a study. This concerns a comparison of the expressive power of various specification languages, and although the narrow focus makes the likelihood of objectivity greater, it seems that the same problems still apply. For example, Kung states that a conceptual model needs to be understandable, and he tests for various elements, one of which is unambiguity. However, we have already seen that the more unambiguous a specification, the more formal it needs to be. Unambiguity is therefore a constraint on informality, and this implies that natural language is not suitable. Thus, despite the study's narrow and carefully controlled domain, it is still highly subjective.

Comparisons of the second type are very difficult and resource consuming, but can be useful. These are often known as case study approaches or action learning. The objectives of the study need to be fully explicit and adhered to in the performance of the study. It is extremely difficult to account for environmental factors such as an analyst's competence in such studies, and we run again into Checkland's 'proof' dilemma. It is also difficult to make a number of such studies comparable. A further problem is that many such studies are closely linked with consultancy activities, and it is not always the 'experiment' which is of prime importance. However, consultancy work might be the only way to gain real-world access.

Bubenko admits that his third comparison approach is virtually non-explored. He is thinking of areas such as software psychology and human factors in human—computer interaction, although he is aware of the difficulties that these kind of studies present. He suggests some issues that might be addressed in this way. One is the question of whether graphical techniques give better 'understanding' than formal language approaches, often epitomized by the statement 'a picture is worth a thousand words'. He also adds the question of 'What is understanding?', so it is clear that he has not underestimated the difficulties of this approach!

A number of other commentators have suggested alternative approaches to an overall feature analysis when selecting methodologies. They adopt a more pragmatic approach and suggest that there is no benefit to be gained from finding, in isolation, a 'best' methodology, because the approaches are not necessarily mutually exclusive. One or more approaches may be suitable, depending on the circumstances. Thus there should be a search for an appropriate methodology in the context of the problems being addressed, the applications, and the organization and its culture. Davis (1982) has advocated the *contingency approach* (see also Benyon and Skidmore 1987 and Avison *et al.* 1988). He offers guidelines for the selection of an appropriate approach to the determination of requirements, rather than to the selection of a methodology itself (although the same principles may well apply). Davis suggests measuring the level of uncertainty in a system, This will help ascertain the appropriate methodology. There are four measures:

1 System complexity or ill-structuredness.
2 The state of flux of the system.
3 The user component of the system, for example, the number of people affected and their skill level.
4 The level of skill and experience of the analysts.

Once the level of uncertainty has been ascertained, the appropriate approach to determining the requirements can be made. For low uncertainty, the traditional method of interviewing users would be appropriate. For high levels of uncertainty, a prototype or an evolutionary approach would be better. For intermediate levels of uncertainty a process of synthesizing from the characteristics of the existing system might be appropriate. Variations of this contingency approach have been suggested by a number of authors.

Episkopou and Wood-Harper (1986) argue: ...'that a suitable approach should be determined by examining variables within and around the problem situation'. They identify three areas of concern:

- *The problem content system.* This is the system that contains the problem and its environment, including the problem owner.
- *The problem solving system.* This is the system which makes use of a methodology or approach, it includes the problem solver.
- *The approach choosing and matching system.* This involves an examination of the ideology of each approach, the associated tools, the inquiry system, and the costs.

The interesting aspect of this approach is the importance it gives to the problem solving system as part of the problem, whereas the Davis approach only involves the problem content system.

Another comparison framework based on the ideas of systems thinking is NIMSAD (Normative Information Model-based Systems Analysis and Design) (Jayaratna 1986). This proposes eight stages of interest:

1 *Introduction to the real world.* This looks at how methodologies depict and perceive reality, that is, the segment of the real world in which problems are perceived.

2 *Understanding the situation of concern, the concepts, models and theory.* This identifies the ability of the analysts to gain a rich understanding of the situation of concern, it includes the effects of their own values, models, relationships, and so on.

3 *Diagnosis (where are we 'now').* This is the capture of a static representation of the situation of concern. It is not the 'real world' but an expression or model of it.

4 *Prognosis outline (where do we want to be and why).* This is the definition of expectations involving a critical evaluation of those expectations.

5 *Systems analysis.* This is the conceptual mapping of the prognosis (desired state) on the diagnosis (current state), sometimes called *inter-gap analysis.* This includes an analysis of why and what prevents achievement, and also the identification of a relevant notional system.

6 *Logical design.* This identifies the elements necessary to support the above

notional system.

7 *Physical design.* The analysis of the 'ways and means' of achieving the logical design.

8 *Implementation.*

Despite all the difficulties described in the above discussion, which may imply failure from the outset, comparisons continue to be made, because it is becoming increasingly important in a world where large numbers of widely differing methodologies claim the same promises of universal applicability and overall usefulness. According to Floyd (1986), we must '...view methods themselves as objects of study. In so doing we must develop methods for the investigation of methods, concepts for the description and comparison of methods, and criteria for their evaluation and assessment'. We therefore present a sample comparison (in section 7.8) based on our framework (of section 7.7), in the spirit of this demand that Floyd identifies, but in the sure knowledge of the problems inherent in the task.

7.7 A FRAMEWORK FOR COMPARING METHODOLOGIES

The reader should now be aware that comparing methodologies is a very difficult task and the results of any such work likely to be criticized on many counts. There are as many views as there are writers on methodologies. The views of analysts do not necessarily coincide with users, and these views are often at variance with those of the methodology authors. Thus the following is simply another set of views and is unlikely to satisfy all the players in the methodologies game.

The framework suggested for comparative analysis reflects the concepts and features discussed above, and builds upon the earlier work of Wood-Harper and Fitzgerald (1982) and Fitzgerald *et al.* (1985). In this work six major approaches to systems analysis were identified: (i) General Systems Theory Approach; (ii) Human Activity Systems Approach; (iii) Participative (Socio-Technical) Approach; (iv) Traditional (NCC) Approach; (v) Data Analysis Approach; and (vi) Structured Systems (Functional) Approach. With the exception of the General Systems Theory Approach, they were all methodologies used in practice. General Systems Theory was included because of its important influence on systems analysis and systems thinking in general.

In this text, General Systems Theory has been examined in section 3.1, Human Activity Systems in section 6.7, Participative Approaches in section

3.3, The Traditional Approach in section 2.2, the Data Analysis Approach in section 3.8, and the Structured Systems Approach in section 3.7.

The Wood-Harper and Fitzgerald analysis seeks to contradict the notion that these approaches are simple alternatives and that it does not really matter which one is selected as a systems development standard. The analysis tries to show that there exist fundamental differences between the approaches and the analysis contributes to the selection of an appropriate methodology for the particular requirements. Further, the paper argues, different approaches might in fact be complimentary and usefully exist side by side. The analysis is based on a discussion of the approaches in terms of three criteria: paradigm, model and objective.

This analysis is now extended in the following framework to include a variety of other criteria that it is hoped make the framework both an academic as well as practical help for comparing methodologies.

There are seven basic elements to the framework as follows, some elements are broken down into a number of sub-elements:
1   Philosophy
    • Paradigm
    • Objectives
    • Domain
    • Target
2   Model
3   Techniques and tools
4   Scope
5   Outputs
6   Practice
    • Background
    • User base
    • Players
7   Product

The framework is not supposed to be fully comprehensive and one could envisage a number of additional features that might usefully be compared for particular purposes, for example:
• the speed at which systems can be developed,
• the size of the specifications produced, or
• the potential for modification by users to suit their own environment.

Indeed, Rzevski (1985) has argued that it is meaningless to compare methodologies without stating the purpose of the comparison in advance, but in this book it is necessary to provide a generalized framework. This gives a set of features that proves to be a reasonable guide when examining an individual methodology and when used as a basis for comparing methodologies.

The headings are not mutually exclusive and there are obviously inter-relationships between them. For example, some aspects of philosophy are reflected in the scope of the methodology.

Each of the above listed elements in the framework will be briefly described and then a sample application of the framework is made to the methodologies of Chapter 6. The reader is also invited to apply the framework to the methodologies of their own choice.

Philosophy

The question of philosophy is an important aspect of a methodology because it underscores all other aspects. It distinguishes, more than any other criterion, a 'methodology' from a 'method'. The choice of the areas covered by the methodology, the systems, data or people orientation, the bias or otherwise towards computerization, and other aspects, are made on the basis of the philosophy of the methodology. This philosophy may be explicit but in most methodologies the philosophy is implicit. Indeed, many feature analyses have neglected this aspect completely, partly because methodology authors seldom stress their philosophy. However, it is important as it is a crucial key to understanding many aspects of a methodology and it is the aspect of the framework which we shall discuss most in this section.

In this context we regard 'philosophy' as a principle, or set of principles, that underly the methodology. It is sometimes argued that all methodologies are based on a common philosophy that suggests that they wish to improve the world of information systems development. Whilst this is true to some extent, this is not what is meant here by philosophy.

As a guide to philosophy the four factors of paradigm, objectives, domains, and applications are highlighted.

Paradigm: Wood-Harper and Fitzgerald (1982), in their taxonomy of current approaches to systems analysis, identify two paradigms of relevance. The first is the science paradigm, which has characterized most of the hard scientific developments that we see in the latter part of the twentieth century, and the second is the systems paradigm, which is characterized by a holistic approach.

The term paradigm is defined here in the sense that Kuhn (1962) uses it — a specific way of thinking about problems encompassing a set of achievements which are acknowledged as the foundation of further practice. A paradigm is usually regarded as subject free, in that it may apply to a number of problems regardless of their specific content.

As Checkland (1981) summarizes it, the science paradigm consists of reductionism, repeatability, and refutation.

> 'We may reduce the complexity of the variety of the real world in experiments whose results are validated by their repeatability, and we may build knowledge by the refutation of hypotheses'.

The science paradigm has a long and successful history and is responsible for much of our current world. The systems paradigm has a much shorter and less successful history but was evolved as a reaction to the reductionism of science and its perceived inability to cope with living systems and those categorized as human activity systems.

Science copes with complexity through reductionism, breaking things down into smaller and smaller parts for examination and explanation. This implies that the breakdown does not disrupt the system of which it is a part. Checkland argues that human activity systems are systems which do not display such characteristics, they have *emergent properties* (that is, that the whole is greater than the sum of the parts) and perform differently as a whole or as part of a system than when broken down to their individual components.

This led directly to the development of the systems paradigm which is characterized by its concern for the whole picture, the emergent properties, and the inter-relationships between parts of the whole. The science and systems paradigms are closely related to concepts of hard and soft thinking discussed in section 6.7.

Hirschheim (1985a) argues that the science paradigm embraces the ontological position of realism. Ontology is concerned with the essence of things, that is, the nature of the world. Burrell and Morgan (1979) identify two basic ontological positions: realism and nominalism. Realism accepts that the universe is composed of objectively given, immutable objects and structures. These exist as empirical entities, on their own, independent of the observer's appreciation of them. This means that there exists *out there* a reality which is discoverable and definable. It may be difficult to discover and define, but because it exists it is possible. Correct definitions of reality may be obtained, or if we make a poor attempt at the process of defining it, less accurate definitions may result.

From an information systems point of view we refer to the slice of reality that we are concerned with as the *universe of discourse* (UoD). In the case of the realism ontological assumption, it means that our information system models can depict that reality, either more or less accurately. Better models will be more accurate and therefore it is worth searching for the better models. Hirschheim (1985a) defines the entity based data models used in information systems methodologies as objectivist, that is, they embody the realism position, and Wood-Harper and Fitzgerald (1982) argue that Data Flow Diagrams also embody this assumption.

The alternative ontological assumption is nominalism. This asserts that the UoD is not definable as a reality, but only exists subjectively. Different people or different groups will perceive reality differently and that different perceptions are not wrong, but reflections of different viewpoints, cultures, or societies. Thus reality does not exist as proposed in the realism position, but is perceived in a variety of different ways and is influenced by a wide variety of phenomena which, in general, are not well understood. These include language, symbols, names and culture. This makes the search for an accurate reflection of reality immaterial. What is needed is a methodology that can handle a variety of different perceptions of a subjective reality.

There are many implications in an information systems context if we adopt a nominalist position. We need a methodology that does not make a realism assumption. Further, the kind of techniques and tools used must also reflect this philosophy. The data that is collected should not be thought of as 'facts', but more as perceptions from a particular point of view. Thus, sales targets are not necessarily a set of facts, but perhaps part of a political process which negotiates between sales personnel, management, and directors. This negotiation may have far reaching implications, relating to people's lives, their remuneration, job satisfaction, self esteem, and so on.

It is difficult to find examples of techniques which do not adopt the realism position, although Klein and Hirschheim (1987) identify rule-based approaches such as LEGOL (LEGally Oriented Language) (Stamper 1978, Cook and Stamper 1980) as having a subjectivist perspective. This is because LEGOL focuses on the meaning of the language of the law which is socially determined. The law is a good example, for there is no universally agreed reality of 'what the law is'. It is a series of interpretations, and any modelling of the law must recognize this. It is interesting to note that most people are relatively happy with this nominalist view of the law, but are not prepared to recognize the validity of the concept elsewhere. It would also appear that more recent attempts to build expert systems relating to the law have run into problems because their authors have adopted an objectivist position.

It might be argued that it is not, in practice, necessary to accept or reject either ontological position. The slice of reality with which information systems are concerned does not usually involve other languages or cultures, and there is a good enough consensus of reality amongst the players for it not to be a problem. The view of reality is a management and organizational view, and information systems are usually developed to support the most powerful people in such an environment. In this case there is no debate about what is a 'fact' or what a process or action is for. A date-of-birth in a personnel system is a fact about an employee's age. It might be used to evaluate seniority, pension contributions, retirement dates, or, in general, operate a company's ageist policy. In which case, if this is true, this slice of reality is objective for the purposes of building an information system for the client, which happens to be a particular brand of management. The fact that this reality may or may not be subjective is immaterial.

Objectives: One fairly obvious clue to the methodology philosophy is the stated objective or objectives. Some methodologies state that the objective is to develop a computerized information system. Others, for example, ISAC, have as an objective to discover if there really is a need for an information system. So there exists a difference in that some methodologies are interested only in aspects that are 'computerizable' and others take a wider view. Other kinds of systems improvement including manual or organizational change is possible. This is an important difference because it determines the boundaries of the area of concern.

The problem with concentrating only on aspects to be automated, is that this is an artificial boundary in terms of the logic of the business. There is no reason why the solution to a particular problem should reside only in the area that can be automated. More likely the problem needs to be examined in a wider context.

It has often been found that 'computerization' *per se* is not the answer. What is required is a thorough analysis and redesign of the whole problem area. It may be viewed as 'putting the cart before the horse' to decide that computerization is the solution to a particular problem. Clearly a methodology that concerns itself solely with analysing the need for a computer solution is quite a different methodology from one that does not. In choosing and understanding a methodology, it might be a good idea to ask the question:

'could the use of this methodology lead to the implementation of a purely organizational or manual solution?'

If the answer is 'no' then the methodology is not addressing the same problems as one to which the answer is 'yes'. It is interesting to note that many of the most widely used methodologies would seem to answer 'no' to this question.

Domain: The third factor relating to philosophy is the domain of situations that methodologies address. This has also been discussed above and is closely associated with the objective. Early methodologies, such as the conventional approach discussed in Chapter 2, saw their task as overcoming a particular and sometimes narrow problem. Obviously the solving of the problem, often through the introduction of a computer system of some kind, might be beneficial to the organization. However, the solution of a number of these kinds of problems on an *ad hoc* basis at a variety of different points in time can lead to a mish-mash of different physical systems being in operation at the same time.

Even if the developments of solutions to the different problems have been well co-ordinated, and the later systems have been designed with the earlier systems in mind, it is often found that the systems and problems inter-relate and the solution to a number of inter-related problems is different to the sum of the solutions to the individual problems viewed in isolation.

This has led to a number of methodologies adopting a different development philosophy. They take a much wider view of their starting point and are not looking to solve, at least in the first instance, particular problems. The argument is a basis of the systems and planning approaches described in sections 3.1 and 3.2. In other words, it is argued that in order to solve individual problems, it is necessary to analyse the organization as a whole, devise an overall information systems strategy, sort out the data and resources of the organization, and identify the overlapping areas and the areas that need to be integrated. In essence, it is necessary to perform a top-down analysis of the organization, sort out the strategic requirements of the business, and in this way ensure that the information systems are designed to support these fundamental requirements.

Target: The last aspect of philosophy is the applicability of the methodology. Some methodologies are specifically targeted at particular types of problem, environment, or type or size of organization, whilst others are said to be general purpose.

Model

The second element of the framework concerns an analysis of the model that
the methodology adheres to. The model is the basis of the methodology's
view of reality, it is an abstraction, and a representation of the important
factors of the information system or the organization.

The model works at a number of levels: firstly, it is a means of
communication; secondly, it is a way of capturing the essence of a problem
or a design, such that it can be translated or mapped to another form (for
example, implementation) without loss of detail; and thirdly, the model
provides a representation which provides insight into the problem or area of
concern.

Models have been categorized into four distinct types (Shubik 1979):
1 verbal,
2 analytic or mathematical,
3 iconic, pictorial or schematic, and
4 simulation.

The models of concern in the field of information systems methodologies
are almost exclusively of the third type, although there are methodologies,
not examined in this book, for example ACM/PCM (Brodie and Silva 1982)
and those mentioned in the formal methods discussions of section 3.6, that
have models of the second type. The reason for the current dominance of
iconic, pictorial or schematic models is because of the perceived importance
of using the models as a means of communication, particularly from user to
analyst. A further important aspect of the models in information systems
methodologies is whether they represent ways of viewing data, processes, or
both.

It has been stated that a model is a form of abstraction. An abstraction is
usually viewed as the process of stripping an idea or a system of its concrete
accompaniments. Abstraction can be viewed as any simplification of systems
and objects at any level, for example the physical to the logical.

A benefit of abstraction is the easier development of complex applications.
It provides a way of viewing the important aspects of the system at various
levels, so that high levels have the 'essence' of the system and low levels
introduce detail that does not compromise that 'essence'. Abstraction looses
information and so a model should only loose that information which is not
part of the 'essence' of the system.

Abstraction is closely related to hierarchical decomposition and as Olive
(1983) states:

'Each level of the decomposition provides an abstract view of the lower levels purely in the sense that details are subordinated to the lower levels. For this to be effective, each level in the decomposition must be understandable as a unit, without requiring either knowledge of lower levels of detail, or how it participates in the system as viewed from a higher level'.

The selection of the levels by which a system is defined depends on the purpose of the investigation and design, but it is suggested that there are some 'natural' or 'inherent' levels, and traditionally these are the conceptual level, the logical level, and the physical level (see figure 7.1). The conceptual level is a high level description of the Universe of Discourse (UoD) or the object system from a particular perspective, in our case this perspective is one of information systems or information processing. The description may be a static or a dynamic one, or a combination of both. Olive (1983) views a conceptual model as:

'...the definition of the problem structure of an information system, like a map defines the problem structure of a transport system. It can also be seen as the "setting up of the equations" of an application. This set of "equations" constitutes a basis for the various processing solutions'. Olive adds that 'there is no direct correspondence between the state of the object system and the contents of the database of the future information system, nor between derivation rules and its processes.'

Thus a conceptual model does not imply any particular database content nor processing activities. Conceptual models cause great confusion, and Olive suggests that the role and purpose of the level should be given a great deal more attention and clarification by the authors of methodologies. One confusion is that the language of conceptual modelling is sometimes the same as for logical modelling. An entity model is often described as a conceptual model and it can be so, but it should be remembered that under these definitions it describes the UoD and is not necessarily going to be part of the information system.

The logical level is a description of the information system without any reference to the technology that could be used to implement it. Its scope is the information system itself and it is not concerned with the UoD. Olive describes the main purpose of the logical model as providing the requirements specification of the information system. The physical level is a description of

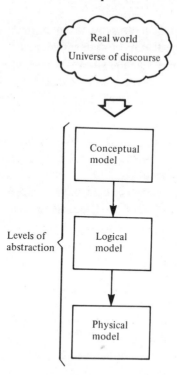

Fig. 7.1. The three level modelling schema.

the information system including the technology of the particular implementation.

There are other forms of abstraction than those for defining information systems in general. A well known model for developing database applications is the Semantic Hierarchy Model. This identifies three forms of abstraction: classification, aggregation and generalization (Smith and Smith 1977), and Brodie and Silva (1982) identifies a fourth form of abstraction which is called Association. These four forms of abstraction allow the integration of both data and process modelling, in that they allow integrity constraints to be defined at the same time as the data.

Techniques and Tools

A key element of the framework is the identification of the techniques and tools used in a methodology, but as these have been extensively discussed in Chapters 4 and 5 they will not be further elaborated here.

Scope

The scope of a methodology is the next element in the framework. Scope is an indication of the stages of the life-cycle of systems development which the methodology covers (see section 2.2). Further, an analysis of the level of detail at which each stage is addressed is useful. The problem with using the stages of the life-cycle as a basis for the examination of scope, is that there is no real agreement on what are, or should be, the stages of the cycle. This is perhaps a problem that can be overcome because most life-cycle variations can be mapped onto one another.

A more serious problem is that some notable figures in the information system field have described the life-cycle as unsuitable to the needs of systems developers in the 1980s (McCracken and Jackson 1982). They argue that the development of rapid development tools (prototyping) has changed the traditional picture and that to apply the life-cycle restricts development to a rigid pattern and perpetuates the failure of the industry to build an effective bridge between user and analyst.

They are really saying two things:
- Firstly, that the process of development is much speeded up and that the users' perceptions of what is possible and desirable changes during development. Requirements analysis should not terminate early in the development of an information systems project but should permeate through the whole process.
- Secondly, that the end result of prototyping might be the design of the desired system and that it might then be specified for development in a conventional programming language. In this case design comes before specification, quite the reverse to the normal life-cycle view.

As a counterbalance to this view of the 'life-cycle as harmful', Dearnley and Mayhew (1983) have suggested ways that prototyping could be adopted into the systems life-cycle approach.

Whilst this is an interesting discussion, it need not invalidate the element of scope in the comparison framework , as it would be possible to include the ability to prototype as a feature of scope.

Outputs

The next element in the framework concerns the outputs from the methodology. It is important to know what the methodology is producing in terms of deliverables. For example, is it an analysis specification or a working implementation of the system?

Practice

The next element of the framework is termed the Practice and is measured according to: the methodology background (section 7.5); the user base (which is an indication of the number of times it has been used); the participants in the methodology (for example, is it to be undertaken by users themselves or analysts); and what skill levels are required.

Product

The last element of the framework is the product of the methodology, that is, what purchasers actually get for their money. This may consist of software, written documentation, an agreed number of hours training, a telephone help service, and so on.

7.8   THE COMPARISON

Originally we constructed a series of tables giving a comparison of methodologies against each element of the framework. On balance, we decided to abandon this approach, because it was felt that a tabular representation gave too definitive an impression about how methodologies meet certain criteria, which we did not want to imply. Instead, we offer a discussion of some aspects of the methodologies in the context of the framework described in section 7.7. This discussion is selective and intended to be a basis for stimulating debate rather than to be regarded as a statement of 'facts' about methodologies. It represents only one subjective view of the methodologies.

The methodology Multiview, discussed in section 6.8, being a hybrid methodology and combining elements of many of the other methodologies, is not specifically included in the following application of the framework.

Element 1 of the framework concerns the philosophy of the methodology. There are a number of sub-elements to philosophy, the first of which is that of paradigm. In this context we discuss the science paradigm and the systems paradigm. It is argued that SSM and ETHICS belong to the systems paradigm and that STRADIS (Gane and Sarson), IE, SSADM, JSD and ISAC belong to the science paradigm. It is clear that SSM adopts the systems paradigm, indeed it is explicitly stated to do so by the methodology author. This is one of the few cases where the issue is addressed as part of the methodology itself. But even if we were not so told, it is clear that the methodology uses many of the systems concepts and does not adopt a reductionist approach.

In ETHICS it is the belief in the interaction of the social and the technical sub-systems (the socio-technical approach) that leads to an advocation of the participative design philosophy. The work system is analysed for variances or weaknesses which prevent the system's objectives being realized. These variances are often discovered at sub-systems boundaries, particularly where the social and technical sub-systems meet. The ideas of job enrichment and participative design are particular solutions to the more common variances which are encountered. In addition, ETHICS makes no attempt to break down the system into its constituent parts for the purpose of understanding the problems. Thus, the underlying paradigm for ETHICS, it is argued, is also the systems paradigm.

In the analysis of the paradigm, ISAC presented the greatest problem and generated the most discussion. ISAC is often regarded as a participative methodology. For example, Maddison (1983), in describing its philosophy, states that:

'...ISAC is based on the importance of people in an organization. This includes all people, for example end users, public users, funders. The activities that people have to perform need to be improved in order to overcome various problems and the best people to do this are the users themselves. The methodology helps people achieve this.'

Whilst it is clear that ISAC is firmly in the participative tradition, we believe that this does not mean it automatically incorporates the systems paradigm. The ETHICS methodology is also highly participative, but it is more the socio-technical aspects which lead us to classify that as being of the systems paradigm. ISAC adopts a highly reductionist approach to the understanding of systems. Its authors state that:

'...the only way to solve complex problems is to divide them into sub-problems until they become manageable. A requirement for this to work is that the solution to the sub-problems gives the solution for the problem as a whole, that is, that the division in sub-problems is coherent.'

This would appear to be a categorical endorsement of the science paradigm and a rejection of the concept of emergent properties. On the other hand, there are a number of areas where ISAC adopts some system's notions, such as the hierarchy of systems. It recognizes the need to understand wider problems and implications than that specified by the scope of the system. There is other support for the systems paradigm. Iivari and Kerola (1983), for example, suggest that ISAC 'is socio-technical in spirit'. However, for our classification, we believe that the features of the methodology must be the determining factor, not what might be the spirit of the authors. We therefore classify ISAC as of the science paradigm.

One of the interesting aspects of this dilemma is not so much whether the classification is right, but the discussion and debate generated. The debate proves insightful and causes many questions to be asked of the methodologies which are very difficult to answer. It may be suggested that the solution is to turn to the methodology authors themselves, but this would not necessarily result in definitive 'right or wrong' answers to such questions. It may be that the methodology can be, and is, used in ways that the methodology authors had not intended or envisaged. Lundberg (1983), one of the authors of ISAC, complains that the methodology is often judged on its descriptive techniques which concern documentation, rather than the work methods. He characterizes this as 'doing things right' versus 'doing right things' respectively. He maintains that the work methods, that is, 'doing right things', is the more important of the two. Yet it is probable that users of the methodology (using it without his guidance) put their effort into 'doing things right'. This again emphasizes the benefit of applying this kind of framework which will help highlight these issues.

The second sub-element of philosophy concerns the objectives of the methodology. There are many objectives that could be discussed, but for the purposes of this framework it is of prime importance whether the objective is to build a computerized information system or whether wider improvements and more general problem solving are involved. Some of our methodologies indicate their position more clearly than others. ISAC, for example, decides on systems development as the suitable development measure only if the change analysis indicates that there are problems and needs in the information systems area. In other situations other development measures are chosen, for example: (i) development of the direct business activities, such as production development, product development, or a development of distribution systems; (ii) organizational development; or (iii) development of personal relations (communication training). We therefore see that ISAC is very much more than the development of computerized systems, as self evidently are SSM and ETHICS.

On the other hand we classify JSD, SSADM, STRADIS and IE, not as general problem solving methodologies, but as having a clear objective to develop computerized information systems. There are sometimes claims made that the methodologies are applicable whether the system is going to be automated or not, for example in STRADIS, but we can find no evidence that this is ever put into practice and was, perhaps, never an original objective.

Closely related to the above objectives is the sub-element of domain. This separates methodologies which deal with the overall planning of information systems in the organization with those concerned with the solving of specific problems within the organization and the building of information systems to overcome those specific problems. This does not imply that planning methodologies do not also consider the building of specific information systems, but that the domain they address is wider than that of overcoming a specific problem. IE (and BSP, which was discussed in outline in section 3.2) are identified as being of the planning type and the rest as the problem solving type. IE has as its first stage information strategy planning. Here an overview is taken of the organization in terms of its business objectives and related information needs and an overall information systems plan is devised for the organization. This clearly implies that it is a planning approach adopting the philosophy that an organization needs such a plan in order to function effectively, and that success is related to well planned information systems. There might also be attempts to extend methodologies to include a business analysis phase, such as that in Avison (1985), or combining methodologies such as SSM and SSADM, but the 'brand-name' methodologies discussed, with the exception of IE, do not have this planning element to any extent.

The final sub-element of philosophy in the framework is concerned with the target system to be developed, that is, whether the methodology is aimed at particular types of application, types of problem, size of system, environment, and so on. This is a difficult area, because almost all methodologies claim to be general purpose, though this might simply be a marketing ploy. This claim is clearly made within certain assumptions. In the majority of cases, a large organization with an in-house data processing department is assumed. Further, it is usually assumed that bespoke (tailor-made) systems are going to be developed, rather than using a collection of inter-related packages. STRADIS is a case in point. It is stated to be applicable to the development of any information system, irrespective of size. However the main technique of STRADIS is data flow diagramming which, it is argued later (in section 7.9), is not suitable for the development of management information systems. The claims of the vendors have to be tempered by an examination of the methodology itself.

If we consider database applications, for instance, IE and SSADM have been designed for this type of application, whereas JSD has been found most suitable for real-time processing applications. Floyd (1986) describes her user experiences with JSD and concludes that it can only be applied to problems that are inherently sequential, which would seem to exclude database applications. The vendors of JSD deny this but are changing the methodology phasing to overcome this kind of criticism. They are also expected to extend their methodology to include a 'project management view' which will make it more relevant to data processing type applications.

The size of organizations that the methodologies address is also an important aspect of target. Multiview has been designed to be applicable in relatively small organizations (perhaps using microcomputers), whereas IE, STRADIS, JSD and SSADM have all been designed for use in large organizations. There is, however, a version of SSADM, called Micro SSADM, which is intended to help develop information systems on microcomputers.

The second element of the framework deals with the model or models that the methodology uses. Section 7.7, in discussing the framework, indicates the rich variety of models that can be investigated — the type of model, the levels of abstraction of the model, and the orientation of the model in terms of data or process. In this section we look only at the process orientated models that are used in the methodologies.

The primary model of STRADIS is the data flow diagram. The DFD also appears in SSADM and ISAC as an important model, although not the only one. It is also used in Wilson's (1984) description of SSM (but not in Checkland's version), referred to as 'a "Gane and Sarson" type diagram'! It features also in IE, though in a slightly different form and it plays a much less significant role. The DFD is predominently a process model, data is only modelled as a by-product of the processes. A DFD models the flow of data and where data is stored from the viewpoint of the processes that are performed.

The models in JSD, ETHICS, and SSM (Checkland), are also, in their various ways, process orientated, but they do not use DFDs. The structure diagram, which depicts the structure of processes, is the primary model of JSD. In SSM, the rich picture, which is a model of the problem situation, is a model of processes and structures and their relationships. ETHICS uses a socio-technical model which involves the interaction of technology and people and the processes performed. It is interesting to note that of the identified model types this is not a pictorial model type but a 'verbal' or narrative model.

The third element of the framework is that of the techniques and tools that a methodology employs. These have been examined in Chapters 4 and 5, and those recommended are usually made explicit by the vendors of the methodologies. The tools that are recommended in a methodology sometimes change quite rapidly as new tools become available or present ones are adapted. It is useful to see if new techniques and tools can be easily accommodated in a methodology. It is also instructive to take a view of a methodology stripped of its techniques and tools and see what is left.

The fourth element of the framework is scope. We look at methodologies in terms of what stages of a traditional life-cycle they address. This is difficult and, more importantly, may misrepresent methodologies that do not adhere to the traditional structure of feasibility study, analysis, design, implementation and maintenance. In addition, a phase of strategy has been added to this structure. A methodology based on prototyping might not fit comfortably into this analysis and therefore an alternative view of scope might be necessary. In our analysis, ETHICS and SSM, and to some extent JSD, do not fit well into this traditional life-cycle, and therefore it is important that this aspect should not be viewed in isolation from the rest of the framework, and that our warnings about this exercise are heeded.

In our analysis of scope, *strategy* is used to indicate whether the methodology addresses any aspects which relate to an organization-wide context, and that deals with overall information systems strategy and planning, rather than just that of the particular area under consideration. IE is identified as addressing this in some detail. SSM also deals with the wider context, as a result of systems thinking philosophy, although there is no strategic planning stage as such. We define *feasibility* in financial or economic terms (that is, in terms of a cost-benefit analysis). Of course this is a narrow view of feasibility, as it is usually defined to include social, technical and user feasibility. ISAC and STRADIS include economic feasibility in their methodologies, although ISAC does not identify a specific feasibility phase, (it is contained in some of the analysis steps). The *analysis* stage, which includes user requirements analysis, is covered in detail in a wide variety of different ways by all the methodologies. JSD, however, does not specifically address user requirements analysis. The methodology starts with an assumption that the statement of the user requirements is given, and provides no procedures for determining what these might be. The *design and implementation* stages are covered by all the methodologies, in varying levels of detail, with the exception of SSM. Some provide only a few guidelines whilst others are more explicit. ISAC suggests the use of JSP in the data systems design phase and therefore we have represented the design stage for ISAC only with an open box. *Maintenance* is defined as being covered by a methodology only if it is specifically addressed in terms of tasks. The fact that maintenance may in general be improved by the use of the methodology in earlier stages is not regarded as coverage of maintenance.

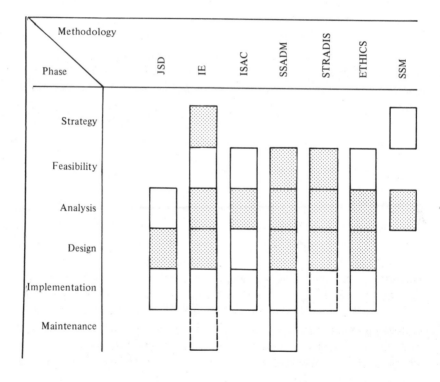

Fig. 7.2. Scope of methodologies.

Figure 7.2 summarizes this analysis of scope. The shaded area indicates that the methodology covers the stage in some detail and provides techniques and tools of support, an unshaded area means that the methodology addresses the area, but in less detail. In this case there is less guidance from the methodology and more for the developers to do themselves. The broken lines indicate areas that are briefly addressed or mentioned, but no procedures, techniques or rules are provided.

The fifth element of the framework is concerned with outputs. This is an investigation of what is actually produced in terms of deliverables at the end of each stage of the methodology. The outputs of methodologies differ quite substantially, not only in terms of what should be produced but also in the level of detail that the methodology specifies. This is closely related to the degree that the methodology is seen as a blueprint for action, that is, how detailed are the rules about how to proceed and how much is left to the discretion of the analyst.

A related issue concerns how, and to what extent, the analysts know that they are proceeding correctly. As an example, ISAC specifies in some detail the outputs of the change analysis stage (A-graphs), but the process of generating change alternatives are not described in any detail. This is regarded as the creative part of the methodology and not amenable to specification. The identification of such areas in a methodology is regarded as an important contribution to an understanding of that methodology.

The penultimate element of the framework is the practice or use of the methodology. It contains the sub-elements of background, user base, applications, and players. The background of the methodology broadly identifies its origins in terms of academic or commercial. IE, SSADM, and STRADIS lie in the commercial sphere, whereas ISAC, JSD, ETHICS and SSM have academic backgrounds, though this does not mean that they are not now commercial methodologies.

The user base, perhaps surprisingly, is often difficult to discover and is possibly less widespread than vendors would have us believe. Wasserman *et al.* (1983) produced a survey of 24 methodologies and found that nearly half had been used on 10 or fewer projects. Many organizations are still using traditional approaches or their own variations of approaches to suit themselves. The methodologies that are generally regarded as having significant numbers of users, say about 100 and above, are STRADIS, SSADM, IE, JSD and ISAC. Although ETHICS and SSM have a smaller user base, the ideas expressed in them have been influential.

The last sub-element of practice requires an analysis of the players involved. This requires answers to the questions 'who is supposed to use the methodology?' and 'what roles do they perform?'. It also attempts to identify the skill levels required. The traditional view of information systems development is that a specialist team of professional systems analysts and designers perform the analysis and design aspects and professional programmers design the programs and write the code. The system is then implemented by the analysts and programmers. This general view is still taken by SSADM, JSD, STRADIS and IE

SSM, ISAC and, in particular, ETHICS, take a different view, and users have a much more pro-active role. In ETHICS, the users perform the analysis and design themselves and the data processing professionals are used as consultants as and when required. In addition, ETHICS incorporates a facilitator role, whose task is to guide the users in the use of the methodology. Facilitators do not actually perform the tasks themselves, but smooth the path and ensure that the methodology is followed correctly. The facilitator should be expert and experienced in the use of the methodology.

The levels of skill required by the players varies considerably. In almost all methodologies considerable training and experience is necessary for at least some of the players. Further, many make significant demands on the users, in which case the methodology would be expected to include training aspects. This may significantly increase the time taken to develop a project. ETHICS, which makes heavy demands on the users, recognizes and addresses this problem. Even where methodologies adopt the more traditional roles, professional analysts and designers can find them quite difficult to learn at first (and some complain laborious as well), with new vocabularies, techniques and tools to work with.

The final element of the framework is that of product. This describes what is supplied when purchasing a methodology and at what cost. Most methodologies have a range of products and services available, which can be taken or not, although there is likely to be a minimum set. The product is also likely to be changing rapidly, mainly due to the increasing numbers of software support tools available. For this reason we do not analyse methodologies in terms of product here, though it is obviously an important factor when choosing a methodology.

This discussion of methodologies using the framework is by no means comprehensive, but is intended to be illustrative of the issues that the framework raises. It is likely to be contentious, it is meant to stimulate debate, to open discussions rather than be taken as a statement of facts. The framework is in practice most effective when methodologies are assessed for a specific purpose.

7.9 THE FUTURE

So where does all this leave the concept of information systems development methodologies? The first thing to be said is that it is still very early in the historical perspective. This means that methodologies are likely to develop quite fundamentally and possibly in directions that we cannot as yet foresee.

One direction is to refine existing information systems methodologies, improving the tools and techniques incorporated into present methodologies and extending methodologies to incorporate successful aspects of other methodologies. It is sometimes argued that in the future all the various methodologies will develop and evolve in scope and techniques in this continual improvement strategy, until ultimately they become very similar and that one day there will be in effect one single methodology. Our view is that this is a highly unlikely proposition, at least in the short term, if only because of competitive marketing. More fundamentally, a methodology which includes all the 'best' features of other methodologies and where the scope has been expanded to cover the whole breadth of information systems development may lack a coherent philosophical base. For one thing, the various parts may not fit together as an organized whole. Further, if the philosophies and objectives of the methodologies are examined, then it becomes clear that they are attempting to do fundamentally different things. Compare, for example, STRADIS and SSM.

Another possibility that is sometimes propounded is the contingency approach, as is attempted by Multiview. This enables choice of aspects of the methodology to be made according to the dictates and requirements of each situation. This is certainly a flexible approach to take, but it might lose many of the practical benefits that a methodology is supposed to provide, such as common methods and improved control.

The automation of information systems development, which seemed to have been an ambitious but unrealistic goal in the 1960s and 1970s, is becoming more plausible in the 1980s. The development of automated tools to help the systems development process such as documentation aids, analyst workbenches and fourth generation systems, are becoming a most important aspect of the continuing development of information systems methodologies. This influence is particularly to be seen in the commercial market-place.

Indeed it is sometimes argued that the presence and quality of automated tools are currently the main consideration that influences the purchasers of methodologies. As a result, almost all the major methodology vendors are in the process of developing and refining automated tools to support their products. These tools originally had very simple objectives of providing automated support to some previously manual tasks, such as documentation, but it is becoming clear that they are having a more fundamental effect. They are beginning to simplify the methodologies, making the various activities more consistent, and in some instances shortening the process itself. Macdonald (1987) has shown a number of examples where the use of the Information Engineering Facility (IEF) has in places changed the Information Engineering methodology itself. Apart from speeding up the manual processes, some of the steps have become redundant and fewer manual iterations and cross-checks are required. In one example, Macdonald shows that the drawing of some data flow diagrams and procedure decomposition diagrams have become unnecessary, because they were really used only to document some intermediate design decisions and provide a check on the consistency of the design. This is now all ensured by the software, from other information sources, so cutting out some steps in the methodology itself.

Further fundamental changes as a result of the automation process are also likely. The goal of a number of automated tools is to automate the production of programming code based on the specification developed by the methodology. This process is far enough advanced to indicate that this is a practical and not too distant prospect. Firstly the specification is unlikely to be as we traditionally think of it. It is not necessarily a document at all but might be a prototype, that is, the specification may be the software itself or it might be the integrated combination of various formalized data dictionary elements. The implication being that the specification of a system will not have to be communicated to a set of programmers, but will be input to code generators and so needs to be expressed in quite different terms to those that currently exist. There is no need for user validation and the signing off of the systems specification at this stage, as this will all have been agreed at an earlier stage of the analysis process in terms more acceptable to the user.

Apart from these points concerning the specification, a perhaps more interesting effect on methodologies is that there will be no need for them to address the programming side of the development. Currently most methodologies that are at all comprehensive devote much effort towards the design and production of code. Indeed some methodologies, for example Jackson System Development, have evolved directly from principles of programming design. This is not to say that these principles are no longer valid, it is that these aspects will be absorbed into the automated part of the methodology.

What about the developments that have taken place in the packages market? In the last few years, partly due to the influence of the microcomputer, package solutions have been heavily advocated as a cost-effective way of developing information systems. However, most methodologies still assume that systems will be developed in-house and that they will be tailor-made. Surely systems development methodologies cannot ignore the benefits that packages can provide for very much longer. They must address the problems of package evaluation and selection. They must develop tools and techniques that help to decide when a package solution is appropriate in an organization and when a tailor-made solution will be more relevant and effective. In addition, the packages must be integrated into the organization's existing systems: methodologies cannot assume that systems in organizations will be simply one thing or the other, they will be a mixture of packages and tailor-made systems. For example, the information collected as part of a package solution must still be part of, and integrated into, the organization's data dictionary. Currently, packages are often treated as something separate and outside of the corporate information view. It is not that all methodologies ignore packages completely, it is the fact that they have not provided the tools and techniques to handle them.

Closely related to the pressure on methodologies to address packages are the forces exerted by microcomputers (see Avison 1986). In particular, the fall in cost of computer power has brought many more organizations into the frame as potential users of computers. Even the smallest business can afford quite sophisticated information systems. Current methodologies, however, are still almost exclusively geared towards large businesses. They make assumptions that all users of information systems are large organizations with in-house data processing departments and large budgets. It is probably now the case that these larger organizations are in the minority, at least in straight numerical terms, and therefore there is going to be growing demands for methodologies that address smaller businesses without all the back-up and support of an established data processing culture.

The demand of managers for computer support is certainly a force for change. Managers have seen the successful application of computing to the operational requirements of the business and are requiring similar support for the activities that they perform. The development of the spreadsheet as a decision-making tool is an indication of this requirement. But spreadsheets are only a very small aspect of their needs. Far more powerful and flexible systems are required. Research indicates that managers, particularly at the tactical and strategic levels, have requirements that are totally different to those at the operations level. The tools and techniques for analysing strategic needs are likely to be quite different from the current tools. Characteristics of this strategic level are typically irregular, *ad hoc* and variable activities, based on information gathered, much of which is external to the manager's own organization. The operational level, on the other hand, is typified by regular, repetitive, rule-based activities using internal information. There is obviously a continuum between the two extremes. It is clear that current methodologies address almost exclusively the operational needs. The tools and techniques for analysing the strategic needs will have to be quite different. There is no point in analysing a strategic activity and constructing detailed data flow diagrams and logic representations if it is a rare and somewhat *ad hoc* activity unlikely ever to be repeated in exactly the same way. Thus approaches suitable for analysing operational systems such as invoicing or production control are likely to be totally unsuitable for analysing strategic decisions such as locating a new factory or identifying and bringing to market a new product. Future methodologies will increasingly need to address these kinds of requirement.

A related management aspect is that increasingly information systems and information technology are being viewed by organizations, not just as ways of replacing and improving deficiencies of their existing administrative systems, but as ways of offering new and improved services and products and of gaining a competitive advantage in the market place. This implies that information systems must be treated as part of the overall strategic elements of the business. The banks, for example, have adopted this view and see themselves as marketing services via information technology. In this kind of business it is inconceivable to think of information systems and information technology as detached from the overall planning and strategy, and yet this is what most methodologies still tend to do.

Expert systems are just beginning to emerge in the commercial market place targeted at business applications rather than the traditional AI scientific and medical arena. There are particular problems in developing expert systems which do not exist in exactly the same way in the development of information systems. The identification of rules is one, and the allocation of probabilities is another. Indeed the expert systems community is already beginning to realize that the real problem is not so much the technical ones but rather the knowledge acquisition and knowledge representation processes.

Any systems analyst could have told them this years ago! It seems that expert systems are going through the same historical development pangs as information systems. This has led some to see whether the solutions developed in the information systems field might be applicable. It seems unlikely that information systems will have nothing to offer to the development of expert systems. Feldman and Fitzgerald (1985) have shown how the information systems technique of action modelling, which is a diagramming technique for modelling the detail of processes, can readily be used to model the objects required for expert systems. It is probable therefore that some methodologies will adapt themselves to handle both expert systems and information systems development in the near future.

A common perception is that we are at the end of a series of radical changes in systems development and that we are beginning to reach some kind of steady state. Clearly some of the identified themes of Chapter 3 will continue to be relevant, and they will be important aspects of methodologies of the future. However, there are a number of forces for change that mean that we cannot look forward to a calm and relatively stable period of consolidation in the information systems development arena and that, on the contrary, we may be at the beginning of a new set of changes to the current methodologies. These forces of change are identified as the continued automation of many significant aspects of the development process, the influence of packages and the microcomputer market, the increase in the number of customers without a data processing culture, the demand by managers (particularly at strategic levels) for real management information and decision support, and the development of expert systems in the industrial and business world. None of these forces for change are particularly new, but we argue that current methodologies do not adequately address the implications of these demands and that they will need to continue to change and develop in the future at least as much as they have done in the past.

(A fuller discussion of the topics in this section is found in Avison and Fitzgerald, 1988).

Bibliography

Ackoff, R.L. (1971) Towards a system of system concepts, *Management Science*, **17**.

d'Agapeyeff, A. and Hawkins, C.J. (1987) *Report to the Alvey Directorate on the Second Short Survey of Expert Systems in UK Business*, IEEE/Alvey Directorate, London.

Avison, D.E . (1981) Techniques of Data Analysis, *Computer Bulletin Series II*, **29**, September, 1981.

Avison, D.E. (1985) *Information Systems Development: A Database Approach*, Blackwell Scientific Publications, Oxford.

Avison, D.E. (1986) Information Systems Development Methodologies for Microcomputer Applications, *Management Forum*, September 1986.

Avison, D.E. (1987) *Mastering Business Microcomputing*, Macmillan, Basingstoke.

Avison, D.E. and Catchpole, C.P. (1988) Information systems for the community health services, *Medical Informatics*, June 1988.

Avison, D.E. and Fitzgerald, G. (1988) Information systems development: current themes and future directions, *Information and Software Technology*, October 1988.

Avison, D.E. and Wood-Harper, A.T. (1986) Multiview - An exploration in information systems development, *Australian Computer Journal*, **18**, 4.

Avison, D.E., Fitzgerald, G. and Wood-Harper, A.T. (1988) Information systems development: a tool kit is not enough, *Computer Journal*, 31, 4.

Bantleman, J.P. (1984) A feature analysis of the LBMS system development method, in *Structured Methods State of the Art Report*, **12**, 1, Pergamon Infotech, Maidenhead.

Beer, S. (1985) *Diagnosing the System for Organizations*, John Wiley, Maidenhead.

Bemelmans, T.M.A. (Ed) (1984) *Beyond Productivity: Information Systems Development for Organizational Effectiveness*, North Holland, Amsterdam.

Benyon, D. and Skidmore, S. (1987) Towards a tool kit for the systems analyst, *Computer Journal*, **30**, 1.

Bertalanffy, L. von (1968) *General Systems Theory*, Braziller, New York.

Bjorn-Anderson, N. (1984) Challenge to Certainty, in *Bemelmans*. (1984).

Bjorner, D. and Jones, C. (1982) *Formal Specifications and Software Development*, Prentice-Hall, Englewood Cliffs, New Jersey.

Blokdijk. (1980) A participative approach to systems design, in Lucas *et al.* (1980).

Boland, R.J. and Hirschheim, R.A. (Eds) (1987) *Critical Issues in Information Systems Research*, John Wiley, Maidenhead.

British Computer Society (1977) Data Dictionary Systems Working Party Report, ACM SIGMOD Record, 9, 4, Dec. 1977.

Brodie, M.L. and Silva, E. (1982) Active and Passive Component Modelling, in Olle *et al.* (1982).

Bubenko, J.A, Jr. (1986) Information System Methodologies — A Research View, in Olle *et al.* (1986).

Buckingham, R.A., Hirschheim, R.A, Land, F.F. and Tully, C.J (Eds) (1987a) *Information Systems Education: Recommendations and Implementation*, CUP, Cambridge.

Buckingham, R.A., Hirschheim, R.A, Land, F.F. and Tully, C.J. (1987b) Information systems curriculum: a basis for course design, in Buckingham *et al.* (1987a).

Bullen, C.V. and Rockart, J.F. (1984) A Primer on Critical Success Factors, CISR Working Paper 69, Sloan Management School, MIT, June 1984.

Burnstine, D.C. (1986) *BIAIT: An Emerging Management Engineering Discipline*, BIAIT International, Petersburg, New York.

Burrell, G. and Morgan, G. (1979) *Sociological Paradigms and Organisational Analysis*, Heinemann, London.

Cardenas, A.F. (1985) *Data Base Management Systems*, 2nd edn., Allyn and Bacon, Boston.

Carlson, W.M. (1979) Business Information Analysis and Integration Technique (BIAIT), *The New Horizon, Data Base*, 10, 4, Spring (1979).

Catchpole, C.P. (1987) *Information Systems Design for the Community Health Services*, PhD Thesis, Aston University, Birmingham.

Chang, C -L. and Lee, R.C.T. (1973) *Symbolic Logic and Mechanical Theorem Proving*, Academic Press, New York.

Checkland, P.B. (1981) *Systems Thinking, Systems Practice*, John Wiley, Chichester.

Checkland, P. (1987) Systems Thinking and Computer Systems Analysis: Time to Unite, DEC Seminar Series in Information Systems, presentation given at the London School of Economics, 5th November 1987.

Chen, P.P.S. (1976) The entity-relationship model — toward a unified view of data, *ACM Transactions on Database Systems*, 1.

Churchman, C.W. (1979) *The Systems Approach and Its Enemies*, Basic Books, New York.

Codd, E.F. (1970) A relational model of data for large shared data banks, *Communications of the ACM*, 13.

Codd, E.F. (1971) A Data Base Sublanguage founded on the Relational Calculus, *Proc. 1971 ACM SIGFIDET Workshop on Data Description, Access and Control* (November, 1971).

Codd, E.F. (1974) Seven steps to rendezvous with the casual user, in Klimbie and Kofferman (1974).

Connor, D. (1985) *Information System Specification and Design Road Map*, Prentice Hall, Englewood Cliffs.

Cook, S. and Stamper, R. (1980), LEGOL as a tool for the study of bureaucracy, in Lucas *et al.* (1980).

Cougar, J.D. and Knapp R.W. (1974) *Systems Analysis Techniques*, John Wiley, New York.

Cougar, J.D, Colter, M.A. and Knapp, R.W. (1982) *Advanced Systems Development / Feasibility Techniques*, John Wiley, New York.

Crowe, T. and Avison, D.E. (1980) *Management Information from Data Bases*, Macmillan, Basingstoke.

Curtice, R. M. and Dieckmann, E.M. (1981) A Survey of Data Dictionaries, *Datamation*, March 1981.

Daniels A. and Yeats D.A. (1971) *Basic Training in Systems Analysis*, 2nd edn., Pitman, London.

Date, C.J. (1984) *A Guide to DB2*, Addison Wesley, Reading, Mass.

Date, C.J. (1986) *An Introduction to Database Systems*, **1**, Addison Wesley, Cambridge, Mass., 4th edition .

Davis, G.B. (1982) Strategies for information requirements determination, IBM Systems Journal, **21**, 1.

Davis G.B. and Olsen M.H. (1984) *Management Information Systems: Conceptual Foundations, Structure and Development*, 2nd edn., McGraw-Hill, New York.

Davis, L.E. (1972) *The Design of Jobs*, Penguin, Harmondsworth, Middlesex.

Davis, W.S. (1983) *Systems Analysis and Design: A Structured Approach*, Addison Wesley, Reading, Mass.

Dearnley, P.A. and Mayhew, P.J. (1983) In favour of system prototypes and their integration into the systems development cycle *Computer Journal*, **26**, 1.

DeMarco, T. (1979) *Structured Analysis: Systems Specifications*, Prentice-Hall, New York.

Dertouzos, M.L. and Moses, J. (1979) *The Computer Age: A Twenty Year View*, MIT Press.

Downs, E., Clare, P. and Coe, I. (1988) *Structured Systems Analysis and Design Method: Application and Context*, Prentice Hall, Hemel Hempstead, Herts.

Dumdum, U.R. and Klein, H.K. (1986) The need for organizational requirements analysis, in Nissen and Sandström (1986).

Eosys Limited (1986) *Top Executives and Information Technology — Disappointed Expectations*, Eosys.

Eason, K.D. (1984) Towards the experimental study of usability, *Behaviour and Information Technology*, 2, 2.

Episkopou, D.M. and Wood-Harper, A.T. (1986) Towards a framework to choose appropriate information system approaches, *Computer Journal*, **29**, 3.

Feldman, P. and Fitzgerald, G. (1985) Representing rules through modelling entity behaviour, *Proceedings of the Fourth International Conference on the Entity-relationship Approach, IEEE*, Computer Society Press, pp 189-98.

Feldman, P. and Miller, D. (1986) Entity model clustering: structuring a data model by abstraction, *Computer Journal*, **29**, 3.

Fitzgerald, G., Stokes, N. and Wood, J.R.G. (1985) Feature analysis of contemporary information systems methodologies, *Computer Journal*, **28**, 3.

Floyd, C. (1986) A Comparative Evaluation of System Development Methods, in Olle *et al.* (1986).

Galliers, R. (1986) *Information Systems Planning*, London School of Economics.

Gane, C. and Sarson T. (1979) *Structured Systems Analysis: Tools and Techniques*, Prentice-Hall, New York.

Gradwell, D.J.L. (1983) *ICLs DDS, DD Update*, British Computer Society, London, April 1983.

Gray, E.M. (1985) An Empirical Study of the Evaluation of Some Information Systems Development Methods, Unpublished paper, presented at 1985 conference of the Information Systems Association, Sunningdale Park, Reading.

Grindley, C.B.B. (1966) SYSTEMATICS - A nonprogramming language for designing and specifying commercial systems for computers, *Computer Journal*, August 1966, in Cougar and Knapp (1974).

Grindley, C.B.B. (1968) The use of decision tables within systematics, *Computer Journal*, August 1968, in Cougar and Knapp (1974).

Grindley, C.B.B. (Ed) (1987) *Information Technology Review 1987/88*, Price Waterhouse, London.

Grundén, K. (1986) Some critical observations on the traditional design of administrative information systems and some proposed guidelines for human-oriented system evolution, in Nissen and Sandström (1986).

Hekmatpour, S. and Ince, D. (1986) *Rapid Software Prototyping*, Open University, Technical Report, 86/4.

Herzberg, F. (1966) *Work and the Nature of Man*, Staple Press.

Hirschheim, R. (1985a) Information Systems Epistemology: An Historical Perspective, in Mumford *et al.* (1985).

Hirschheim, R. (1985b) *Office Automation: A Social and Organizational Perspective*, John Wiley, Maidenhead.

Holloway, S. (Ed) (1985) *Proceedings of Conference on Data Analysis in Practice*, BCS, London.

Horowitz, E. (1985) *A Survey of Application Generators, IEEE Software*, January 1985

Howe, D.R. (1983) *Data Analysis for Data Base Design*, Arnold, London.

Huuskonen, P., Nikkinen, N. and Savolainen, V. (1986) Knowledge based approach to the information systems development contingency theory, in Nissen and Sandström (1986).

IBM (1971) The Time Automated Grid System (TAG), in Cougar and Knapp (1974).

IBM (1975) Business Systems Planning, in Cougar, Colter and Knapp (1982).

IFIP-NGI (1986) Information Systems Assessment, IFIP 8.2 Conference at Leeuwenhorst, Netherlands.

Iivari, J. and Kerola, P. (1983) A sociocybernetic framework for the feature analysis of information systems design methodologies, in Olle *et al.* (1983).

Jackson, M.A. (1975) *Principles of Program Design.*, Academic Press, New York.

Jackson, M.A.. (1983) *Systems Development*, Prentice-Hall, New Jersey.

Jayaratna, N. (1986) Normative information model-based systems analysis and design (NIMSAD): A framework for understanding and evaluating methodologies, *Journal of Applied Systems Analysis*, **13**.

Keen, P.G.W. (1987) MIS Research: current status, trends and needs, in Buckingham *et al.* (1987a).

Kent, W. A. (1978) *Data and Reality*, North Holland, Amsterdam.

Kent, W.A. (1983) Simple guide to five normal forms in relational theory, *Communications of the ACM*, **26**, 2.

Klein, H.K. and Hirschheim, R.A, A comparative framework of data modelling paradigms and approaches, *Computer Journal*, **30**, 1.

Klimbie, J.W. and Kofferman, K.L (Eds) (1974) *Proc. of the IFIP Conference on Data Base Management*, North Holland, Amsterdam.

Kuhn, T.S. (1962) *The Structure of Scientific Revolutions*, University of Chicago Press, 2nd edn., Chicago.

Kung, C.H. (1983) An analysis of three conceptual models with time perspective, in Olle *et al.* (1983).

Land, F. (1982) Adapting to changing user requirements, *Information and Management*, **5**, 59-75.

Land, F. and Hirschheim, R. (1983) Participative systems design: rationale, tools and techniques, *Journal of Applied Systems Analysis*, **10**.

Land, F. (1976) Evaluation of systems goals in determining a design strategy for a computer based information system, *Computer Journal*, **19**, pp 290-94.

Lee, B. (1979) *Introducing Systems Analysis and Design*, Vols **1** and **2**, NCC, Manchester.

Lobell, R. F. (1983) *Application Program Generators, A State of the Art Survey*, NCC, Manchester.

Longworth, G. (1985) *Designing Systems for Change*, NCC, Manchester.

Lucas, H.C., Land, F., Lincoln, T.J. and Supper, K. (Eds) (1980) *The Information Systems Environment*, North Holland, Amsterdam.

Lundberg, M. (1982) The ISAC approach to specification in information systems and its application to the organization of an IFIP working conference, in Olle *et al.* (1982).

Lundberg, M. (1983) Some Comments on the ISAC Approach in Connection with the CRIS-2 Papers, unpublished paper, The Institute for Development of Activities in Organisations, Stureplan 6 4 tr, S-114 35, Stockholm, Sweden.

Lundberg, M., Goldkuhl, G. and Nilsson, A. (1979a), A systematic approach to information systems development — I, Introduction, *Information Systems*, **4**.

Lundberg, M., Goldkuhl, G. and Nilsson, A. (1979b), A systematic approach to information systems development — II, Problem and data oriented methodology, *Information Systems*, **4**.

Lundberg, M., Goldkuhl, G. and Nilsson, A. (1982), *Information Systems Development — A Systematic Approach*, Prentice-Hall, Englewood Cliffs, New Jersey.

Lyytinen, K. (1987) A Taxonomic Perspective of Information Systems Development: Theoretical Constructs and Recommendations, in Boland and Hirschheim (1987).

McCracken, D.D. and Jackson, M.A. (1982) Life Cycle Concept Considered Harmful, ACM SIGSOFT, Software Engineering Notes, **17**, 2, April 1982.

MacDonald, I.G. (1983) System Development in a Shared Environment — The Information Engineering Methodology, *Proc. of the BCS Conference on Data Analysis Methodologies*, at Thames Polytechnic, April 1982.

MacDonald, I.G. (1987) Automating Information Engineering, unpublished paper, JMA, London.

MacDonald, I.G. and Palmer, I. (1982) System development in a shared data environment, the D2S2 methodology, in Olle *et al.* (1982).

McGettrick, A.D. (1980) *The Definition of Programming Languages*, CUP. Cambridge.

Maddison, R.N (Ed.) (1983) *Information System Methodologies*, Wiley Heyden.

Maddison, R.N (Ed.) (1984) *Information System Development: A Flexible Framework*, British Computer Society, London.

Madsen, K.H. (1987) *Breakthrough by Breakdown: Metaphors and Structured Domains*, presented at the IFIP WG8.2 conference on Information Systems Development for Human Progress in Organizations, in Atlanta, Georgia, May 29-31 1987.

Martin, J. (1980) *Strategic Data Planning Methodologies*, Savant Institute, Carnforth, Lancashire, Nov. 1980.

Martin, J. (1982a) *Application Development without Programmers*, Prentice-Hall, Englewood-Cliffs, New Jersey.

Martin, J. (1982b) *Fourth Generation Languages*, **1**, Prentice-Hall, Englewood Cliffs, New Jersey.

Martin, J. (1983) *Fourth Generation Languages*, **2**, Prentice-Hall, Englewood Cliffs, New Jersey.

Martin, J. and Finkelstein, C. (1981) *Information Engineering*, Vols **1** and **2**, Prentice-Hall, Englewood Cliffs, New Jersey.

Martin, J. and McClure, C. (1983) *Structured Techniques for Computing*, Volume **1** and **2**, Savant Institute, Carnforth, Lancashire.

Martin, J. and McClure, C. (1985) *Action Diagrams: Clearly Structured and Program Design*, Prentice-Hall, Englewood-Cliffs, New Jersey.

Mayhew, P.J. and Dearnley, P.A. (1987) An alternative prototyping classification, *Computer Journal*, **30**, 6.

Mitchell, W. (1985) Information Engineering, in Holloway (1985).

Mumford, E. (1983a) *Designing Human Systems*, Manchester Business School.

Mumford, E. (1983b) *Designing Participatively*, Manchester Business School.

Mumford, E. (1983c) *Designing Secretaries*, Manchester Business School.

Mumford, E. (1986) *Using Computers for Business*, Manchester Business School.

Mumford, E, Hirschheim, R.A, Fitzgerald, G. and Wood-Harper, A.T (Eds) (1985) *Research Methods in Information Systems*, North-Holland, Amsterdam.

Mumford, E. and Weir, M. (1979) *Computer Systems in Work Design — The ETHICS Method*, Associated Business Press.

Myers, G. (1975) *Reliable Software Through Composite Design.* Petrocelli/Charter.

Myers, G. (1978) *Composite/Structured Design.* Van Nostrand Rinehold.

NCC (1986) *SSADM Manual*, National Computing Centre, Manchester.

Nelson, K. (1985) Technical requirements of a 4-GL, *Data Processing*, November 1985.

Nissen, H-E. (1986) *Investigation of Opinions on Good Information Systems Research*, IFIP WG8.2, 1986-08-15, available from Lund University, Sweden.

Nissen, H-E. and Sandström, G. (Eds) (1986) *Quality of Work versus Quality of Information Systems*, Lund University, Sweden.

Olive, A. (1983) Analysis of conceptual and logical models in information systems design methodologies, in Olle *et al.* (1983).

Olle, T.W, Sol, H.G. and Tully, C.J (Eds) (1983) *Information Systems Design Methodologies: A Feature Analysis*, North Holland, Amsterdam.

Olle, T.W, Sol, H.G. and Verrijn-Stuart, A.A (Eds) (1982) *Information Systems Design Methodologies: A Comparative Review*, North Holland, Amsterdam.

Olle, T.W, Sol, H.G. and Verrijn-Stuart, A.A. (Eds) (1986) *Information Systems Design Methodologies: Improving the Practice*, North Holland, Amsterdam.

Page-Jones, M. (1980) *The Practical Guide to Structured System Design*, Yourdon, New York.

Palmer, I. and Rock-Evans, R. (1981) *Data Analysis*, IPC Publications, Surrey.

Parsons, T. and Shils, E. (1951) *Towards a General Theory of Action*, Harvard University Press, Mass.

Pergamon (1987) *Analyst Workbenches: State of the Art Report*, **15**, 1, Pergamon-Infotech, Maidenhead.

Porter, M.E. and Millar, V.E. (1985) How information gives you competitive advantage, *Harvard Business Review*, July-August 1985.

Rasmussen, K. (1986) What is wrong (and what is right) with entity modelling, *Database Bulletin*, March 1986, BCS, London.

Ratcliff, B. (1988) *Software Engineering: Principles and Methods*, Blackwell Scientific Publications, Oxford.

Rockart, J.F. (1979) Chief executives define their own data needs, *Harvard Business Review*, March-April 1979.

Rosenquist, C.J. (1982) Entity life cycle models and their applicability to information systems development life cycles, *Computer Journal*, **25**, 3.

Rzevski, G. (1985) *On the Comparison of Design Methodologies*, working paper, School of Computer Science, Kingston Polytechnic, Surrey.

Shneiderman, B. (Ed) (1978) *Improving Database Usability and Responsiveness*, Academic Press, New York.

Shubik, M. (1979) Computers and modelling, in Dertouzos and Moses. (1979).

Smith, J.M. and Smith, D.C.P. (1977) Database abstraction: aggregation and generalization, *ACM Transactions on Database Systems*, **2**, 2.

Smyth, D.S. and Checkland, P.B. (1976) Using a systems approach: the structure of root definitions, *Journal of Applied Systems Analysis*, **5**, 1.

Sommerville, I. (1985) *Software Engineering*, Addison Wesley, 2nd ed.

Stamper, R. (1978) Aspects of data semantics: names, species and complex Physical objects, in Bracchi and Lockemann (1978).

Stamper, R. (1987) Semantics, in Boland and Hirschheim (1987).

Stevens, W.P, Myers, G.J. and Constantine, L.L. (1974) Structured design, *IBM System Journal*, **13**, 2 pp 115-139.

Taylor, F.W. (1947) *Scientific Management*, Harper and Row.

Teichroew, D. and Hershey, E.A. (1977) PSL/PSA: A computer-aided technique for structured documentation and analysis of information processing systems, *IEEE Transactions on Software Engineering*, **SE-3**, 1, in Cougar *et al.* (1982).

Teichroew, D, Hershey, EA. and Yamamoto, Y. (1979) The PSL/PSA approach to computer-aided analysis and documentation in Cougar *et al.* (1982).

Tozer, E. (Ed) (1984) *Applications Development Tools — A State of the Art Report*, Pergamon-Infotech.

Tozer, E. (1985) A review of current data analysis techniques, *Proc. of the BCS Conference on Data Analysis in Practice*, Huddersfield Polytechnic.

Utterback, J. M. and Abernathy, W.J. (1975) A dynamic model of process and product innovation, *Omega*, **3**, 6.

Vainio-Larsson (1986) Metaphors as communicators of conceptual ideas, in Nissen and Sandström (1986).

Veryard, R. (1985) What are methodologies good for?, *Data Processing*, **27**, 6, July/August, 1985.

Veryard, R. (1986) The role of visibility in systems, *Human Systems Management*, **6**, pp 167-75.

Wasserman, A. I. and Freeman, P. (1976) *IEEE Tutorial on Software Design Techniques*, October 1976, IEEE Computer Society, New York.

Wasserman, A. I., Freeman, P. and Porchella, M. (1983) Characteristics of software development methodologies, in Olle *et al.* (1983).

Weinberg, V. (1978) *Structured Analysis*, Prentice-Hall, New Jersey.

Welke, R.J. (1987) *The New Architecture of PSL/PSA*, Ann Arbor, MI:MetaSystems.

Wetherbe, J.C. and Davis, G.B. (1983) Developing a long-range information architecture, *Proc. of the National Computer Conference*, Anaheim, Calif, May 1983.

White, P. (1982) Towards a repeatable methodology, *Perspective*, **1**, 2, April 1982.

Wilson, B. (1984) *Systems: Concepts, Methodologies, and Applications*, Wiley, Maidenhead.

Wirth, N. (1971) Program development by stepwise refinement, *Comm. ACM*, **14**, 4, pp 221-7.

Wood-Harper, A.T., Antill, L. and Avison, D.E. (1985) *Information Systems Definition: The Multiview Approach*, Blackwell Scientific Publications, Oxford.

Wood-Harper, A.T. and Fitzgerald, G. (1982) A taxonomy of current approaches to systems analysis, *Computer Journal*, **25**, 1.

Yao, S. B. (1985) *Principles of Data Base Design: Logical Organization*, **1**, Prentice Hall, Englewood Cliffs.

Yourdon, E. (1975) *Techniques of Program Structure and Design*, Prentice-Hall, New Jersey.

Yourdon, E.N. (Ed) (1979) *Classics in Software Engineering*, Yourdon, New York.

Yourdon, E. and Constantine L.L. (1978) *Structured Design: Fundamentals of a Discipline of Computer Program and Systems Design*, 2nd edn., Yourdon, New York.

Zloof, M.M. (1978) Design aspects of the query by example data base management language, in Shneiderman (1978).

Index

Items in italic refer to names of cited authors (see also Bibliography); page numbers in bold indicate principal references.